Sukhoi Su-25

Frogfoot

CLOSE AIR SUPPORT AIRCRAFT

Sukhoi Su-25
Frogfoot
CLOSE AIR SUPPORT AIRCRAFT

Yefim Gordon and Alan Dawes

Airlife

First published in the UK in 2004 by
Airlife Publishing, an imprint of The Crowood Press Ltd
Ramsbury, Marlborough, Wiltshire SN8 2HR

www.crowood.com

British Library Cataloguing-in-Publication Data
A catalogue record for this book is available from the British Library

ISBN 1 84037 353 9

Typeset and designed by D & N Publishing
Hungerford, Berkshire.
Printed and bound in Great Britain by CPI Bath.

Contents

Introduction

IN early 1969, the question of air support for the Russian ground forces began to circulate within the Soviet Ministry of Defence, with concern focusing in particular on the ability to provide adequate air cover in the presence of heavy enemy anti-aircraft defences and small-arms fire. The idea of creating a specialised 'shturmovik' (*see* box) assault aircraft for direct air support of the ground forces in response to this requirement was formed after analysing the experience of using 'shturmovoi' aviation in World War Two and in local wars of the 1950s and 1960s. Defence ministry analysts also considered the capabilities of Soviet and foreign tactical aircraft designed for battlefield assault operations, as well as the orders of battle and performance of tanks and other armour used by the ground forces of potential adversaries, plus the organisation of their tactical anti-aircraft defences. Equally importantly, only a few months later, the defence ministry team also had the opportunity to study the American A-X programme. This had been set up in the spring of 1970 to create a battlefield close-air-support (CAS) aircraft for the protection of ground forces, which was then at the project definition stage. The AX System Program Office at Wright-Patterson AFB, Ohio, then issued a request for proposals (RFP) to twelve aircraft manufacturers on 8 May 1970, and on 18 December the Northrop and Fairchild Hiller entries were selected for prototype construction. The two aircraft were then destined to take part in a 'fly-before-buy' evaluation. On 1 March 1971 the Northrop A-X prototype was designated YA-9 and the Fairchild Hiller (later Fairchild Republic) prototype was designated YA-10, the latter being declared the winner of the A-X competition on 18 January 1973. Although clearly designed in mutual isolation, not to mention secrecy, with the first flight of the YA-9 trailing Sukhoi's early design work on the new 'shturmovik' by around four years, the YA-9 had a remarkably similar aerodynamic layout to the aircraft which eventually became the Su-25.

American aircraft such as the Douglas A-1 Skyraider, Douglas A-4 Skyhawk, Grumman A-6 Intruder, Cessna A-37 Dragonfly and North American OV-10A Bronco, plus the multi-role supersonic McDonnell Douglas F-4 and Republic F-105 Thunderchief tactical fighters suf-

---

'Shturmovik'

Although the word 'shturmovik' (pronounced *shtoor-moveek*) is translatable in the aviation context as 'assault' or attack aircraft (albeit literally 'stormer'), the 'shturmovik' concept remains peculiarly Russian and no translation is capable of conveying effectively the special significance which the word holds for Russian aviators, historians and aviation enthusiasts. Therefore, in order to preserve this intrinsic Russian quality, the word is used predominantly in transliteration throughout the book and only occasionally translated as 'assault' or attack aircraft where context requires it. The name 'shturmovik' was first applied in the aviation context to Sergei Ilyushin's legendary World War Two piston-engined Il-2 *Bark* and its successor, the Il-10 *Beast*, and gave rise to the creation of specialised 'shturmovoy' regiments to operate them. This in turn led to the creation of a separate specialised sub-branch of the Soviet Frontal (Tactical) Air Force, known as '*Shturmovaya Aviatsiya*' when the Su-25 entered service in 1981. ***Shturmovaya Aviatsiya***, comprising around 250 Su-25s organised into several regiments, remains an important component of the present-day Russian Air Force.

---

fered considerable losses during the long-drawn-out war in Vietnam primarily because of inadequate built-in protection and other negating factors. Among the latter, particular shortcomings were poor performance at low level and low *g*-tolerance levels, coupled with high flight speeds and their inability to use packed earth and grass strip airfields. It must be admitted that at the beginning of the 1960s the combat potential of tactical strike aircraft was highly exaggerated. Certainly, by reducing speed to 700–800 km/h (380–430 kt) the pilot obtained a specific advantage when attacking small targets on the ground, but at the same time his aircraft itself became a more convenient target for anti-aircraft artillery (AAA). Also in this period many armies had started to receive portable surface-to-air missiles (SAMs), designed to destroy low-flying aircraft. Consequently, a new and important attribute of the combat aircraft gradually started to assume special importance – the attribute of 'survivability' – that is, the ability to withstand punishing damage from SAMs and ground fire. In order to improve the survivability of its aircraft, the United States Air Force, for its part, adopted various emergency measures to upgrade and modernise its combat aircraft fleet for operations in field conditions, although these generally proved to be ineffective, with the exception of improvements to the 1950s-era Cessna A-37 Dragonfly. Partial armour plating of the cockpit, installation of

The originator of the airborne 'shturmovik' concept in the Soviet Air Force was the Ilyushin Il-2, later developed into the Il-10 shown here, which continued in service until the 1950s. Ruggedness, allied to simplicity of operation and handling, were the hallmark qualities of this quintessential utilitarian battlefield aircraft. These were also the qualities that Sukhoi wished to emulate in the Su-25. *(Yefim Gordon archive)*

protected rubber fuel tanks filled with polyurethane foam, fitting a simple sighting system and mounting weapons hardpoints under the wings enabled a small detachment of these diminutive and manoeuvrable aircraft to perform several thousand combat sorties over Vietnam without a single loss.

The Soviet fighters and fighter-bombers which were in service at this time and later, including the Su-7, Su-17, MiG-21, MiG-23 and MiG-27 also did not meet the requirements of aircraft intended for close air support of the army. This was because they did not have the essential armour plating in the cockpit to protect the pilot and vital equipment from ground fire and missile hits, plus their extremely high flight speeds, which led to the inability of the pilot to maintain visual contact with the target. Added to this was the difficulty of oper-

ating these aircraft from unprepared surfaces. The high flight speeds during bombing and air-to-ground gunnery operations left the pilot with little time to find, identify and attack the targets, and in addition it was necessary to break off from the attack earlier than was expedient, in order to avoid flying into the ground or through bomb and shell fragments. The use of helicopters for ground-support operations, if the enemy had strong air defence protection, was extremely undesirable because of their great vulnerability to AAA cannon fire, their low speed and their inadequate onboard weapons fit. As it turned out, subsonic MiG-17 fighters converted into fighter-bombers at the end of the 1950s proved to be more effective than most other aircraft in the role of close air support of ground forces. During realistic exercise scenarios, close-air-support

Originally intended as a follow-on to the highly successful MiG-15 in the interceptor role, the MiG-17 proved to be a particularly useful ground-attack fighter in the mould of the Hawker Hunter. Good low-speed handling and manoeuvrability made it an excellent weapons platform for the battlefield close-air-support role. *(Yefim Gordon archive)*

Although only just over a decade separated the operational philosophy of the Su-7B *Fitter-A* from its stable-mate the Su-25, the Su-7 was designed uncompromisingly in, and for, the 'supersonic era', when speed was the defining performance criterion for all Soviet fighter types. It is hard to imagine now that supersonic performance was ever deemed necessary for a ground-attack fighter! The carriage of the S-3K rocket armament of the Su-7 (here represented by the S-22-2/Su-7B second prototype) on big 'draggy' ladder-type APU-14U pylons, was unique to the *Fitter-A*. *(Sukhoi Design Bureau)*

versions of the MiG-17 consistently managed to identify and destroy targets on the first pass. Analysis of this experience carried out by Soviet military specialists convincingly proved the necessity of commencing work on designing and building a modern specialised battlefield assault aircraft, rather than relying on more dated designs, however effective they might be.

Being already *au fait* with these problems, a group of leading specialists in the design bureau led by Pavel Sukhoi discussed the idea of creating such an aircraft, and then submitted their thoughts to Sukhoi regarding the expediency of beginning preliminary design work, including:

- concept definition of the 'shturmovik';
- defining its position in the inventory of the Soviet Air Force;
- performance definition;
- selection of a navigation-attack system and weapons;
- study of alternative aerodynamic layouts of the aircraft;
- cost analysis;

- assessment of its suitability for series production and the time required to build a prototype.

Pavel Sukhoi approved the plan, and in a comparatively short period of time the preliminary design work was completed jointly with leading institutes of the Ministry of the Aviation Industry (MAP) and the Ministry of Defence. The Sukhoi Experimental Design Bureau (**Opytno-konstruktorskoye Byuro**, or **OKB**) submitted its proposal to the 'customer' (the traditional Russian euphemism for the Soviet, and later the Russian, Air Force) concerning the expediency of creating a new 'shturmovik', and this was accepted. In 1968, development of the specialised aircraft for close air support of the Soviet ground forces was initiated in the Sukhoi Design Bureau – the first step in the creation of the aircraft which was to become the Su-25. A particular feature of this aircraft was that it did not have any direct predecessors. Manufacture of the last series-production 'shturmovik' – the piston-engined Ilyushin Il-10M *Beast* developed from the Il-2 *Bark* – ceased in the early 1950s, and no further examples of this class of aircraft

With the advent of the 'jet age', Ilyushin had hoped to create a jet-powered successor to the Il-2 and Il-10 in the twin-jet Il-40 *Brawny*, giving 'second wind' to this uniquely Russian category of aircraft. Designed in two different configurations, the first of which, the Il-40-I, is shown here, it had a conventional appearance, albeit with a rather elongated nose, housing four 23 mm cannons. This layout was unsuccessful, leading to a revised configuration for the Il-40-II. *(Ilyushin Design Bureau)*

The Il-40-II retained the overall appearance of the original Il-40, but adopted an unusual air intake arrangement in order to avoid gas ingestion when firing the guns. To achieve this, the Il-40-II carried the four NR-23 cannon in a retractable pallet under the forward fuselage, suitably isolated from the intake face and capable of being fired almost vertically downwards. A pre-series batch of five aircraft was scrapped before completion at State Aviation Plant 168 at Rostov-on-Don because the Soviet leader, Nikita Khrushchev, believed the concept to be obsolete and the nation's future defences to be better served by missile forces. Had it not been for Khrushchev's characteristically arbitrary and dogmatic intervention in this and other military projects, along with Soviet industry's powerlessness to challenge his decisions, the shape of Russian military aviation would have been radically different from what it is today. *(Ilyushin Design Bureau)*

were built in the former USSR. However, in 1953, the Ilyushin Design Bureau had taken upon itself the task of designing a jet-powered battlefield 'shturmovik' designated the Il-40 *Brawny*. The aircraft was built in two distinctly different examples and successfully completed flight-tests, but as a consequence of the changing tactical operational requirements of the Soviet Air Force it did not go into series production. The prevailing view of the Soviet leadership at that time was that such an aircraft was not required.

Designed in that extravagant period of the Soviet era when the aviation industry was able to build a number of prototypes that differed substantially from eventual production versions, Sukhoi's delta-winged T-6-1 was later to undergo metamorphosis into the variable geometry Su-24 *Fencer*. The T-6 was one of the three specific lines of research pursued by Sukhoi when the Su-25 was being designed, and along with the swing-wing Su-17 family, developed from the Su-7, it resulted in a significant capability improvement for Soviet tactical air units. *(Sukhoi Design Bureau)*

Nevertheless, the word 'shturmovik' was to be heard again in the Soviet Union in the late 1960s in military aviation circles, being used to describe the newly proposed close-air-support aircraft. The first designers to undertake preliminary study of the new aircraft were, as stated above, from the Sukhoi Design Bureau, followed by a team from the Ilyushin Bureau. With this new project, the Soviet aircraft designers were attracted to the idea of using armour plating and the use of advanced concepts for the design of multiple redundant systems, to make an aircraft more resistant to combat damage. More particularly, the introduction of computer technology, initially using analogue techniques, then later digital methods, offered the potential of simplifying the handling of the aircraft at low level, removing from the pilot the stress associated with flying close to the ground in combat. Certain flight modes of the RSBN (*Radiosistema blizhney navigatsii*) short-range radio navigation system, which first appeared on tactical combat aircraft in the early 1960s, would allow the pilot to fly simply and accurately to and from the target area, albeit only within the operating range of the system's ground components. Some designers had initially attempted to resolve the problem of manoeuvring, and particularly take-off and landing performance, by using variable-geometry wings. Finally, it was also considered vital to increase the combat payload of the new aircraft – a parameter by which Soviet aircraft were traditionally considered inferior to those of their potential adversaries. Analysis of all of these trends in the design of a modern combat aircraft led the Sukhoi team to focus their attention on three main lines of study:

- modernisation of the Su-7B fighter-bomber by equipping it with a variable-geometry wing, a new navigation-attack system and the inclusion of air-to-surface missiles (ASM) in its arsenal of weapons. This line of approach led to the development of the Su-17/20/22 family of fighter bombers;
- the creation of the T-58M heavy 'shturmovik' (later redesignated T-6 and then subsequently the Su-24), and put into series production as a variable-geometry light frontal (tactical) bomber. This aircraft embodied all of the contemporary achievements of Soviet military aircraft design and was, effectively, the counterpart of the USAF F-111 tactical bomber;
- development of a heavily armoured, modern 'shturmovik', subsequently designated T-8 and eventually the Su-25 when it entered series production, distinguished from other Soviet (Russian) combat aircraft by its enhanced survivability.

What follows is an account of the development of this unique Russian combat aircraft which has been involved in combat operations throughout virtually all of its more than two decades of operational service.

1

The T-8 Project and its Competitors

I N March 1969, a competition was announced by the Soviet Air Force, the Ministry of Defence and the Ministry of the Aviation Industry of the Soviet Union, calling for designs for a new battlefield close-support aircraft. Participants in the competition were the Sukhoi Design Bureau and the Design Bureaux of A.S. Yakovlev, S.V. Ilyushin and A.I. Mikoyan. The competition placed great emphasis on the ability to provide the best possible combat effectiveness with a relatively cheap aircraft, which would be simple both to manufacture and to operate and have very high

survivability and reliability. Equally important was the fact that the aircraft had to be capable of being mass-produced in the shortest possible timescale. For this reason alone, most designers from the firms involved in the competition originally considered projects for a light close-support aircraft (**Lyogki Samolyot-Shturmovik**, or **LSSh**) based either on existing operational types, or on prototypes which had already been tested. Thus, the A.S. Yakovlev Design Bureau proposed its Yak-LSh (**Yak-Lyogki Shturmovik**), and the Ilyushin Bureau offered the Il-42 (later redesignated Il-102), based on the Il-40, two prototype examples of which had been built in the mid-1950s. The Mikoyan Design Bureau, for its part, put forward the MiG-21LSh, based on the highly successful MiG-21 *Fishbed* light tactical fighter, while the Sukhoi Design Bureau entered the fray with a version of the Su-15 *Flagon* interceptor. The latter was a surprise inclusion, resulting from the desire on the part of certain factions within the military hierarchy to have a close-support aircraft with supersonic capability. Consequently, among other designs projected by Sukhoi, the OKB developed the highly

The second of several Mikoyan concepts for an LSSh design, the '27Sh' embodied ideas from the MiG-21 and MiG-23 fighters, incorporating a new wing and pitot-type lateral air intakes. With the benefit of hindsight it is evident that the Su-25 was the more appropriate aircraft for the task, although the attraction of the '27Sh' for the MiG team was that it used as much proved technology as possible in what was intended to be a simple design. Unlike hybrids in the natural world, the '27Sh' did not turn out to be a successful synthesis of the better qualities of the MiG-21 and MiG-23. *(Yefim Gordon)*

modified version of the Su-15 under the designation Su-15Sh (Shturmovik). As became clear later, all of the above-mentioned aircraft failed, in various ways, to satisfy the requirements of the LSSh concept. Only a handful of designers actually considered the idea of creating an aircraft from a 'clean sheet of paper' which would fully meet the requirements of the Soviet Air Force.

The history of the aircraft, which was later to achieve fame as the Su-25, actually goes back one year earlier, to March 1968. This was when the senior lecturer in the Department of the Tactics of Combat Application at the Yuri Gagarin Air Force Academy, Ivan Savchenko, approached his friends in the Sukhoi Design Bureau with the suggestion of jointly developing a concept for a new close-air-support aircraft. Soon after, an action committee was formed, made up of members of the Design Bureau, which included Oleg Samoilovitch, a leading designer in the general projects team, Dmitriy Gorbachev, a leading engineer concerned with weapons effectiveness, plus V.M. Lebyedyev, Yu.V. Ivashechkin and A. Monakhov. It was decided, unofficially, to draft an outline proposal for the aircraft (which was given the preliminary designation of SPB (*Samolyot Polya Boya*), or simply Battlefield Aircraft), almost as a 'homework' task, or sideline, for the small group. Only when the aircraft's overall appearance had been established would they then offer the design for approval by General Designer Pavel Sukhoi himself.

Since up to this time the Soviet Air Force had not yet formulated its own operational requirements (*Taktiko-Tekhnicheskiye Trebovaniya*) for an aircraft of this type, the group's design work commenced by defining the basic concept for a close-support aircraft and its place in the operational systems doctrine of the Soviet Air Force. This involved definition of the required flight performance of the aircraft as well as the performance of the weapons system as a whole. Here, the designers eschewed the then fashionable idea of a multi-role aircraft, used both for strike operations and for air combat, a concept embodied in the design of the Su-17 and the MiG-23B, which were undergoing flight trials at that time. They concluded that the SPB should be a small, highly manoeuvrable aircraft, designed to operate at low level, powered by two well proved and reliable engines and offering the pilot excellent visibility from the cockpit.

The action committee examined several alternative aerodynamic configurations for their proposed design, including those employed on the North American OV-10A, SAAB 105, Douglas A-4 Skyhawk and the Fairchild Republic A-10. One of the group's first designs was for a twin-boom, twin-engined layout for the SPB. However, the preference in the end came down to a normal aerodynamic layout with a shoulder-mounted wing and lateral fixed-geometry air intakes feeding engines mounted in two separate nacelles on either side of the central fuselage area. A rugged tricycle undercarriage would facilitate operation from packed earth runways or grass strips.

It was planned to equip the original version of the SPB with two AI-25T bypass turbofans, each with a take-off thrust rating of 1,750 kgp (3,858 lb st), which were a modification of the Ivchenko AI-25 developed for the Czech-built Aero L-39 Albatros combat trainer. Apart from the installation of a built-in cannon, it was intended to arm the aircraft only with unguided weapons – principally bombs up to 500 kg (1,102 lb) calibre and rockets. The sighting system of the aircraft was planned to be as simple as possible and would consist of a fixed collimating gunsight and a laser rangefinder. The normal combat payload was to be 1,500 kg (3,307 lb) and up to 2,500 kg (5,511 lb) in overload configuration; normal take-off weight would be 8,200 kg (18,078 lb), while the maximum take-off weight was projected to be 10,000 kg (22,046 lb) and the aircraft was to be limited to a subsonic flight regime.

Oleg Samoilovitch and Yuri Ivashechkin presented the SPB project to General Designer Pavel Sukhoi for the first time on 29 May 1968. He readily approved the design, introduced a few minor changes and then ordered that work should commence on the development of the aircraft under the factory designation of T-8. At the same time, in conjunction with the Zhukovskiy Air Force Engineering Academy (*Voyenno-Vozdushnaya Inzhenernaya Akademiya/VVIA*), the first operational requirements were being formulated for a dedicated close-air-support aircraft. It was to become an organic component of the combat strength of the Soviet Air Force and was to have the following characteristics: it had to provide guaranteed protection for the pilot from shells of calibre up to 12.7 mm and shrapnel of weights up to 3 g. It had to be capable of operation from grass strips with a bearing strength of 2 kg/cm^2 (71.10 lb/in^2) and be simple enough to be flown by pilots of average ability and experience. It also had to be of technologically simple design, using readily available materials and to require minimal time for preparation for combat in normal operational conditions.

Even the original draft version of the operational requirements envisaged the creation of an aircraft capable of effective support for ground forces in conditions of heavy retaliatory activity by the enemy's tactical air defences. Fundamental principles were incorporated in the definition of the project, adherence to which would permit the design and creation of an aircraft with unique combat capabilities. In particular, the principle of total systems integration was embodied in the design process, placing special emphasis on the increased requirement for combat survivability. At every stage of the development of the T-8 project, design evaluations and reviews were undertaken which led to the creation of an effective 'combat survivable complex' (where 'complex' describes the aircraft and its essential systems as an integrated whole). In the Russian aviation context, the word 'complex' is widely used to mean a fully integrated system of interrelated elements. This would guarantee the ability of the aircraft to remain flyable even if it were to be hit by enemy anti-aircraft artillery (AAA) and portable surface-to-air missiles.

After the aerodynamicists had been brought into the development of the project, headed by Deputy Chief Designer I.E. Baslavski, the overall shape of the aircraft could be more precisely defined. Studies had shown that the greatest probability of survival of a battlefield ground-attack aircraft occurs within a speed range not exceeding 850 km/h (460 kt). A flight speed greater than 800–850 km/h (430–460 kt) is of little practical benefit over the battlefield, because of the lack of time available for visual acquisition and identification of the target. This parameter was the precondition for the design of a cheap, simple aircraft with a straight wing layout and mechanical controls. When selecting the type of engine for the new aircraft, operating economics and range performance requirements were taken into consideration, as well as take-off and landing performance. The powerplant was to consist of two engines located in the rear part of the fuselage, in nacelles separated by a supporting beam structure. The subsonic speed range chosen for the design would permit the use of simple fixed air inlets and exhaust nozzles.

A month after the start of work on the T-8 project, Pavel Sukhoi decided that it was sufficiently advanced to report progress to the 'official authorities'. In August 1968, a specific proposal was formulated, and a

A more serious competitor for the Su-25 was Ilyushin's anachronistic, but nevertheless 'successful', Il-102, a bold, if inelegant attempt to marry new technology and an old design. As with Mikoyan's '27Sh', the objective was to save time and money by using as much available and proved technology as possible, since the 1950s-era Il-40 which inspired it was a successful design, even if it did not go into production. Powered by two I-88 turbofan engines derived from the powerplant of the MiG-29 and built using more modern materials, the lineage of the Il-102 is very clear from this view of the sole prototype at Zhukovskiy. *(Ilyushin Design Bureau)*

Although the Il-102 prototype made a total of 367 flights, totalling almost 250 hours of tests, over a five-year period between 1982 and 1987, very few photographs have ever been published of the aircraft in flight. This underside view, in the best 'grainy' traditions of Soviet-era military aircraft photographs, nevertheless shows the aircraft's general layout to good effect, including the bulbous undercarriage housings.
(Yefim Gordon archive)

summary of the design project was drafted and sent to the Scientific Technical Committee of the General Staff of the Soviet Defence Ministry (***Nauchno-Tekhnicheski Komitet General'novo Shtaba Ministerstva Oborony – NTK MO***). The proposal was also submitted to the Headquarters of the Soviet Air Force, the Ministry of the Aviation Industry and the Headquarters of the Soviet Navy, plus TsAGI, the Central Aerohydrodynamics Institute at Zhukovskiy.

The first to respond, in September 1968, was the Scientific Technical Committee of the Ministry of Defence, with the conclusion that such an aircraft was not required. The leading scientific research institute of the Soviet Air Force sent a more cautious reply, suggesting that work on the T-8 project be continued. Other official bodies did not reply at all. Nevertheless, many highly placed military figures realised that inclusion in the inventory of the Soviet Air Force of a cheap and simple, mass-produced 'shturmovik-type' ground-attack aircraft would permit the renewal of the Frontal Aviation fleet in a comparatively short time. Equally importantly, it would enable the air force to reduce substantially the number of heavy tactical strike aircraft required for its front-line regiments. Taking this factor into consideration, the Minister of Defence, Marshall Andrei Grechko, sent a letter to the Minister of the Aviation Industry, Pyotr Dementiev, suggesting that a competition be held with the

objective of creating a new, light ground-attack aircraft. In turn, the Soviet Air Force had, by 19 March 1969 outlined its own preliminary operational requirements (***Taktiko-Tekhnicheskiye Trebovaniya***, or ***TTT***) for a light ground-attack aircraft (***LSSh***).

The Soviet Air Force's operational requirements specified a normal combat payload of 1,000 kg (2,205 lb), excluding ammunition for the built-in cannon, while the maximum load was to be 3,000 kg (6,614 lb). Range at sea level and a speed of 800 km/h (430 kt) was to be not less than 750 km (405 nm). The weapons payload was to include bombs of 100–500 kg (220–1,102 lb) calibre, unguided rockets (57–240 mm calibre), a rapid-fire cannon and short-range defensive air-to-air missiles. As already mentioned in the opening lines of this chapter, in that same month, the Minister of the Aviation Industry issued his request to the Sukhoi, Mikoyan, Ilyushin and Yakovlev Design Bureaux to begin work on the pilot project for a subsonic 'shturmovik' meeting the Soviet Air Force's operational requirements.

It was already clear at the start of the design definition stage of the LSSh that the concept put forward by the Sukhoi Design Bureau was the only one which satisfied the main criteria of the Soviet Air Force's operational requirements. The primary task of the LSSh was the destruction of group and small individual ground-based targets, acquired visually some 50 to 150 km (27–80 nm) behind the front line, but it was also required to destroy transport aircraft, helicopters and tactical fighters and bombers on enemy airfields. The selection of the optimum flight speed for these missions had a decisive significance in defining the overall layout of the aircraft.

In its aerodynamic layout, developed in line with the terms of the competition, the Sukhoi Design Bureau's T-8 LSSh project was a single-seat monoplane of normal configuration, with a shoulder-mounted straight wing. The wing was of trapezoidal shape in plan view, with a leading-edge sweep of 20°, and a thickness/chord ratio of 11%, constant along the entire span. The wing area was 19 m² (204.5 ft²), with an aspect ratio of 5:1, and it was equipped with leading-edge slats, double-slotted trailing-edge flaps, spoilers and simple ailerons. A single vertical fin and rudder assembly was mounted on the rear fuselage, and the horizontal stabiliser consisted of a tailplane, whose angle of incidence could be varied, fitted with separate elevators. The main undercarriage units were of the trailing link type and had a single braked wheel on each leg, fitted with 290 × 800 mm (11 × 31 in) tyres, while the steerable nose leg was also of trailing link design and had a single 180 × 620 mm (7 × 24 in) tyre.

Control of the aircraft, in all phases of flight, was designed from the outset to be manual, with actuation of all aerodynamic surfaces achieved by push rods. The pneumatic system was designed to provide retraction and extension of the undercarriage and opening and closing of the wheel doors, operation of the leading-edge slats, flaps, airbrakes and tailplane incidence adjustment, plus operation of the main wheel brakes. The system consisted of two independent supplies, the air reservoir being fed from compressors mounted on the engines.

The fuel tanks were divided into two groups, each of which had its own collector tank, feeding a single engine. Fire protection for the fuel tanks was provided by an inert gas system. The aircraft was also designed to have an oxygen system suitable for normal flight in an unpressurised cockpit. The pilot was to be provided with a Zvezda K-36 ejection seat, capable of saving the pilot in the event of an emergency at any stage of flight. Projected overall length of the aircraft was to be 12 m (39.37 ft), wingspan 9.75 m (32 ft) and height when parked in dispersal 3.9 m (12 ft 10 in).

Apart from the originally selected AI-25T engine for the T-8, various other non-afterburning engines which were then in development were considered. These included the Izotov TR7-117, the Lyul'ka AL-29 and the Tumanskiy R53B-300. All these engines offered similar take-off thrust ratings (in the region of 3,000–3,250 kgp [6,614–7,165 lb st]), and differed little in terms of weight and dimensions. The most economical of the

In spite of the indifferent quality of this photograph of the unpainted prototype on an early test flight, it is possible to appreciate the extensive wing and flap area of the Il-102 and the excellent rearward view for the tail gunner. Compared with its forerunner, the Il-40, the Il-102 had a low-set tailplane and a much shorter nose. Its greater overall size and larger wing made the Il-102 less manoeuvrable than the Su-25, and paradoxically it exhibited poorer combat survivability potential than the latter, two factors which were specifically required of the new 'shturmovik'. Failure to comply with these requirements effectively debarred the Ilyushin design from competing with the more nimble and better protected Su-25. *(Yefim Gordon archive)*

engines examined, in the particular flight regimes envisaged for the T-8, was the Tumanskiy R53B-300, although it would have required around five to seven years of development work to perfect and bring up to production status. Consequently, it was decided to power the new 'shturmovik' with an existing, series-produced engine: in this case, the RD-9B, with the afterburner section removed. This engine had been used on the MiG-19 fighter, and because it was not optimised for the T-8's planned role, the range of the new light 'shturmovik' was reduced by around 25–30%. The RD-9B had been suggested by the Minister for the Aviation Industry, Pyotr Dementiev, and had an afterburning thrust of 3,200 kgp (7,055 lb st), a maximum dry thrust of 2,500 kgp (5,511 lb st) and a 2,750 kgp (6,063 lb st) take-off thrust rating. In the end, the non-afterburning version of the RD-9B, with the subsequent designation R9-300 (or *Izdeliye 39* – Manufactured article 39) was accepted as the engine for the first stage of the pilot project for the T-8.

Modification of the engine, which included removal of the afterburner section and installation of a simple, fixed, exhaust nozzle, was carried out successfully at Plant No. 26 in Ufa, under the supervision of Chief Designer S. Gavrilov, where series production of the RD-9B was coming to an end at the time. The engine designation is often ascribed to the 'Gavrilov Design Bureau' for this reason. The take-off weight of the new aircraft with these engines was greater than originally calculated, resulting in the need for an increase in wing area and strengthening of the airframe. The second stage of the project envisaged the use of new engines. The design layout made it comparatively easy to change to a new type of engine (e.g. the R53B-300 or others) and, if necessary, to replace the engines of earlier aircraft equipped with the original R9-300. Engines selected for the second stage of the project would guarantee the performance characteristics defined in the Soviet Air Force's operational requirements. As stated above, the fact that the engines were mounted in individual nacelles would make it easy to replace the R9-300s, involving minimal modification, with any of the other engines selected for the second stage, dependent upon their level of development and production status.

Differing significantly from the eventual Su-25, this wooden mock-up of the T-8 LSSh displayed in Sukhoi's experimental factory hangar had a distinctly 'un-Russian' appearance, quite unlike any other contemporary Soviet designs. The advantage of the mock-up as a design tool with which to impress potential customers is evident here, the three triple-carriage pylons offering a somewhat improbable weapons-carrying capability for such a small aircraft. *(Sukhoi Design Bureau)*

It was planned to equip the T-8 in the first stage of development with a standard series-produced targeting and sighting system, as installed on later variants of the Su-7B and Su-17 fighter-bombers, and with a completely new system in the second stage. As previously mentioned, the Zvezda K-36 ejection seat was selected as the means of emergency egress for the pilot in all phases of flight. All external weapons were to be carried on six underwing hardpoints, while a seventh suspension point, on the fuselage centreline, was intended for the carriage of a pod for 'special equipment'. Internal armament was to consist of a built-in, twin-barrel cannon of 23 mm calibre, while two underwing PTB-600 (*Podvesnoy Toplivnyy Bak*) drop tanks, each of 600 litres (132 imp gal) capacity, were intended for ferry flights.

Particular attention was paid to the provision of an enhanced level of combat survivability for the new aircraft, compared with that provided on earlier types. Armour plating was used to protect virtually the entire cockpit area, while partial armour protection was applied to the engine nacelles and fuel system, offering protection in the most threatened parts of the airframe. Apart from this, the pilot was also to be provided with an armoured helmet and a hinged body shield worn on the chest. The engine layout was selected specifically with survivability in mind, using two widely spaced engines and duplicated engine controls, with two independent fuel systems. As mentioned above, each fuel supply system had its own collector tank, providing a fuel feed to each engine. The entire bottom and part of the sides of the fuel tanks were protected by a multi-layered sponge rubber lining, designed to prevent loss of fuel in the event of combat damage of the tanks' structure. Additionally, the fuel tank assembly was partially protected by elements of the retracted main gear, and the use of inert gas inside the tanks themselves reduced the likelihood of ignition and onset of fire if they were penetrated by shrapnel. Fire protection of the engines was provided by a duplicated extinguishing system in the nacelles. Increased combat survivability of the flight control system was obtained through the use of manually operated push rods, duplicated in the longitudinal axis. The elevators on each half of the tailplane had their own independent control system. The overall weight of all these enhanced survivability measures (armour plating, etc.) did not exceed 735 kg (1,620 lb), or around 9% of the empty weight of the aircraft. Radar cross section was to be reduced by the use of radio-absorbent coatings applied to the leading edges of the wings and tailplane and the lips of the engine air intakes.

The aerodynamic characteristics of the aircraft, originally embodied in the project, were rather ambitious. With the objective of achieving the defined performance levels, wide-ranging theoretical and aerodynamic studies were undertaken regarding the planform of the wing, its profile and aerodynamic twist and the type and performance parameters of its high-lift devices (*mekhanizatsiya*). The studies naturally also included definition of the overall shape of the aircraft. The T-8's resulting aerodynamic efficiency and excellent manoeuvrability would enable it to carry out the most difficult combat tasks in the limited airspace over the battlefield. Additionally, its excellent take-off and landing performance would provide increased flight safety when operating out of small unprepared airfields.

Alongside the single-seat combat variant of the T-8 LSSh, a twin-seat T-8UB (*Uchebno-Boyevoy*) combat trainer was also examined in the pilot project stage, with a tandem seating arrangement for the two pilots. It was also envisaged that this variant could be used for basic jet training. Only the forward part of the fuselage was changed, being lengthened by 1.25 m (4 ft 1 in) compared with the single-seater. The angle of view ahead and downwards for the pilot of the single-seat variant was 20°. The T-8 project was conceived from the outset as an aircraft which would be simple to build and maintain, capable of being used for rapid-reaction missions in support of the operational demands of the Soviet Army. It was designed to be flown by pilots with little operational experience and maintained by minimally trained ground servicing personnel. At the end of a three-month project study phase, a technical proposal concerning the T-8 LSSh was formulated by the Sukhoi Design Bureau, which was then sent to the Ministry of the Aviation Industry.

At this point, it is perhaps opportune to say a few words about the proposals put forward by the other design bureaux in the competition to select the new 'shturmovik'.

Approximately a year before the announcement of the competition, on 25 April 1968, a Commission of the Presidium of the Council of Ministers of the USSR, which assembled to discuss military-industrial questions, took the decision to start work on a jet 'shturmovik' developed by the Ilyushin Design Bureau. This aircraft was initially given the designation Il-42, although subsequently it was to be known as the Il-102. Sergei Ilyushin supported the idea of a subsonic 'shturmovik' from the very beginning. The main difference between Ilyushin's proposed Il-42 and the T-8 project developed by Sukhoi was the presence of a second cockpit in the Il-42 for a rear-facing gunner. This factor was to have a negative impact on the ultimate fate of the aircraft, since the Soviet Air Force requirement specifically called for a single-seat aircraft. The aerodynamic and design layout of the Il-42 did not differ substantially from the experimental jet-powered Il-40 'shturmovik' which was tested in the mid-1950s, although it was a completely new aircraft – a sort of 'retro' design in current parlance. Over the intervening period of 15–17 years since the appearance of the Il-40, many changes had taken place in the field of aircraft construction, with the availability of more economic engines, new materials, new manufacturing processes and new equipment. The Ilyushin team had not only managed to reduce the weight of their reinvented jet 'shturmovik', but had also expanded the range of combat tasks for which it could be used. Better and safer emergency escape systems were incorporated for the pilot and gunner of the Il-42, and a new wing design dispensed with the use of boundary layer fences on its upper surface, a dominant feature of the original Il-40.

The Mikoyan team developed several different variations on the LSSh theme. Mainly, these were variants of the MiG-21 modified to match the specific criteria of the operational requirements for the new aircraft. The simplest variant, with the code-name '*Izdeliye 7-23*' (Article 7-23) was a modification of the MiG-21PFM *Fishbed-F*, to which were added wing root extensions intended to improve the aircraft's low-speed manoeuvring performance. Under each wing there were three weapons pylons for the carriage of bombs or rockets, and the fuselage centreline pylon was retained for the carriage of a supplementary fuel tank. A second variant, known as '*27Sh*', was a hybrid of the MiG-21 and the MiG-23B, with a fixed swept wing and lateral air intakes. This aircraft also had three weapons pylons under each wing. However, the most advanced of the Mikoyan proposals was the '*27II*', better known as the MiG-21LSh, effectively a hybrid of the experimental MiG-21I '*Analog*' (originally built to test the wing shape and profile of the Tupolev Tu-144 *Charger* supersonic transport), and the MiG-23B *Flogger-F/H*. The MiG-21LSh was therefore of tailless delta configuration, with the ogival wing of the MiG-21I and the forward fuselage of the MiG-23B. The adoption of the large ogival wing enabled the designers to offer a greater number of underwing hardpoints for weapons carriage. It also had the fixed lateral intakes of the variable-geometry MiG-23B.

The Yakovlev OKB had developed its own Yak-LSh light 'shturmovik', details of which are, surprisingly, still classified, although from information published in the open press this appears to have been based on a highly modified version of the Yak-28 *Brewer* light supersonic tactical bomber. However, following its elimination in the pilot project stage of the competition, all further work on this particular design was terminated.

It is also worth noting that work on the development of an advanced light battlefield-support aircraft was conducted not only by these other aircraft design bureaux, but also by a number of leading Soviet scientific research institutes. Thus, for example, in 1967–8, a major study was undertaken by the State Scientific Research Institute for Aviation Systems (GosNIIAS), to determine the overall appearance and shape of an advanced tactical 'shturmovik'. Taking part in this study were a number of senior figures in the institute, including B.P. Toporov, G.K. Kolosov, G.A. Ryabik, O.S. Korotin and others. This work also involved the active participation of many of the institute's other specialists, in addition to those already mentioned above, particularly of those involved in the field of aircraft combat survivability, namely S.I. Bazazyants and A.F. Bukshin. This study resulted in establishing the need to create a new 'shturmovik' and setting out the main parameters for the aircraft's design and manufacture.

In this particular period, when the leadership of the Soviet Air Force was completely focused on the creation of a fleet of exclusively supersonic fighter-bombers, the results of the research conducted by GosNIIAS were, to some extent, sensational. It was met by the military with disbelief, and attempts to turn it into practical reality led to serious opposition from the Soviet Air Force. This opposition was so strong that the production line for any subsonic 'shturmovik' would have been shut down right from the start and would not have been reopened were it not for the decisive position adopted by the leadership of GosNIIAS. The latter (actively supported by Pavel Sukhoi and Sergei Ilyushin) had expressed their agreement with the conclusions of the institute's researchers and had stated their position in letters to the appropriate organs of State. The overwhelming conclusion was that there was a clear need for a subsonic battlefield close-air-support aircraft for the Soviet Air Force.

So, three months after the announcement of the competition, in June 1969, all four pilot projects for the new

LSSh submitted by the competing design teams were offered for scrutiny by the Scientific-Technical Commission of the Ministry of the Aviation Industry. In the end, preference was given to the designs submitted by Sukhoi and Mikoyan, who were both asked to continue working on their projects and build prototypes of their 'shturmovik' designs. For a number of reasons, the Mikoyan Design Bureau abandoned its participation in the competition, but development of the Sukhoi design was continued. Work on the Il-42 also continued in the Ilyushin Design Bureau, which had decided to develop the aircraft as a private initiative and build a prototype for flight-testing.

Presented in the table below are the main dimensional and performance characteristics of the winning contender in the pilot project stage of the competition.

Main specification of the LSSh submitted by the Sukhoi Design Bureau (for the pilot project stage)

1st Stage	
Engines	2 × Tumanski R9-300
Thrust	2 × 2,700 kgp (5,950 lb st)
2nd Stage	
Engines	2 × TR7-117 or 2 × AL-29 or 2 × R53B-300
Thrust	2 × 3,000 kgp (6,614 lb st)
Length (excl. pitot tube)	12.0 m (39 ft 4 in)
Height	3.9 m (12 ft 9 in)
Wingspan	9.75 m (32.0 ft)
Wing area	19.0 m² (204.5 ft²)
Wheel track	2.4 m (7 ft 10 in)
Wheel base	4.3 m (14 ft 1 in)
Take-off weight:	
Normal	8,200 kg (18,077 lb)
Maximum	10,570 kg (23,700 lb)
Maximum combat load	3,000 kg (6,614 lb)
Internal fuel	1,900 kg (4,188 lb)
Wing loading at normal take-off weight	432 kg/m² (88.5lb/ft²)
Thrust/weight ratio at normal take-off weight	0.73
Maximum speed at sea level	1,000 kph (540 kt)
Range at sea level with 1,200 kg (2,645 lb) combat load without drop tanks	750 km (405 nm)
Take-off run	390 m (1,280 ft)
Landing run	550 m (1,804 ft)

Towards the middle of 1970, working drawings had been prepared by the Sukhoi Design Bureau, and preparation for production and assembly of the nose section of the first prototype of the T-8 had commenced in Sukhoi's affiliated branch attached to the Novosibirsk aircraft manufacturing plant. However, before this, the Sukhoi OKB had commenced work on definition of the T-8's performance characteristics and the drafting of the 'tactical and technical task' (*Taktiko-tekhnicheskoye Zadaniye*, or *TTZ*) for the development of the preliminary design and associated documentation. Agreement on the precise definition of the aircraft's maximum speed proved to be particularly difficult. In August 1971, The Soviet Air Force announced its requirement for the maximum speed to be increased to 1,200 km/h (650 kt) at sea level, while carrying four B-8 rocket pods on the external pylons. In view of this radical change in the operational requirements by the Soviet Air Force, Pavel Sukhoi ordered that all work on the T-8 project should be suspended.

The military admitted that from the viewpoint of detecting and destroying small ground-based targets on the battlefield the optimum speed range was, indeed, in the subsonic region. Nevertheless, they still wanted a 'shturmovik' which had a maximum speed at sea level of not less than 1,200 km/h (650 kt), arguing that this was essential in order to defeat enemy air-defence systems. At this particular time, and largely in response to the above-mentioned high-speed performance requirement, the Sukhoi Design Bureau had started development work on a highly modified variant of the Su-15 *Flagon* (T-58) interceptor to fulfil the amended requirement. This work was undertaken on the instructions of Deputy Chief Designer Evgeny Ivanov. The assault version of the Su-15 was given the designation Su-15Sh, or T-58Sh (*Shturmovik*); its delta wing was replaced with a swept wing (or to be more precise, trapezoidal-shaped) of increased span, and the shape of the nose section of the fuselage up to Frame 10 was changed. The cockpit and engine compartments were to be protected by armour plating and the fuel tanks were also to be protected, while the original aircraft's systems and equipment would have been completely changed, along with the flight control and weapons systems. The maximum take-off weight of the Su-15Sh was projected to be 17,500 kg (38,580 lb) with a combat load of 4,000 kg (8,818 lb), while its internal fuel load was to be (9,920 lb). Projected maximum speed at sea level was 1,250 km/h (675 kt), and range at sea level, without auxiliary tanks and carrying a normal

The T-8 LSSh mock-up was eventually revised to show more heavily protected cockpit glazing than the one-piece panoramic windshield and hinged canopy of the original, the aircraft now looking a little more like the definitive Su-25. The aircraft's small size is also quite evident here, offering easy access to the weapons pylons and fuselage equipment bays, but the design was still far from perfect. *(Sukhoi Design Bureau)*

combat payload of 2,000 kg (4,409 lb), was calculated to be 600 km (324 nm).

At the same time, Sukhoi designers, who did not agree with the concept of a supersonic 'shturmovik', tried to show the military that an aircraft operating 30–50 km (16–27 nm) behind the front line would not escape detection by enemy air defences, but would actually remain permanently within his air defence protection zone. They therefore recommended that the maximum speed of the aircraft should be limited to 850 km/h (460 kt), or Mach 0.7 at sea level, thereby avoiding the unpleasant phenomenon of shock stall. In the end, the maximum speed at sea level, written into the TTZ tactical operating requirements, was 1,000 km/h (540 kt), or Mach 0.82. On the whole, however, the task for the new 'shturmovik' was agreed with the 'customer' (i.e. the Soviet Air Force) very quickly.

This was largely due to the influence of the Sukhoi Design Bureau's head of section dealing with matters of combat survivability, Zelika Yoffe, who used his old service connections with the Soviet Air Force to expedite the matter. In three days he was able to obtain agreement with the military over the tactical operational requirements drawn up by the Sukhoi OKB. It is of interest to note that before joining the Sukhoi OKB, Lieutenant-General Yoffe had been head of one of the Soviet Air Force's scientific research institutes and was initially opposed to the T-8 project.

At the end of November 1971, the Sukhoi Design Bureau received more precise operational requirements for the aircraft from the Soviet Air Force, the aircraft now also being referred to as the LVSSh (*Lyogkiy Voiskovoy Samolyot-Shturmovik*), or light army-support 'shturmovik' aircraft. These requirements were confirmed by the Deputy Commander-in-Chief of the Soviet Air Force, M.N. Mishuk, and agreed by Soviet Army HQ. According to the new requirements, the maximum combat load had risen to 4,000 kg (8,818 lb). The Air Force required that a new targeting and sighting system be installed on the aircraft, which led to a slight increase in weight, although this did not affect performance.

Work on the aircraft was only restarted in the Sukhoi OKB at the beginning of 1972, when Chief Designer Pavel Sukhoi himself confirmed its overall appearance and signed the order authorising the start of design definition. Mikhail Simonov was designated as project leader and the design team had to redraft all of the previously issued documentation. The broad aerodynamic concept of the aircraft was retained, but the overall contours of the 'shturmovik' and layout of systems and equipment were changed completely. The normal take-off weight of the LVSSh T-8 had increased to 10,530 kg

(23,214 lb), which in turn led to an increase in the overall dimensions of the aircraft. Fuselage length was increased from 12.54 m (41.14 ft) to 13.7 m (44.94 ft), while the wing area went up to 28.2 m² (303.55 ft²), albeit retaining the original shape and aspect ratio.

In order to meet the defined speed, manoeuvrability and take-off and landing performance requirements set by the Soviet Air Force, a total of 144 different wing variants were examined. A high wing loading was selected in order to achieve the required figure of 1,000 km/h (540 kt) and to permit reasonably comfortable flight in turbulent conditions at low level. Research was carried out to select the best combination of high-lift devices (*mekhanizatsiya kryla*) on the leading and trailing edges of the wing, in order to provide good take-off and landing performance. These studies showed that the most effective type of *mekhanizatsiya* was a combination of full-span leading-edge slats and

The Chief Designer of the T-8 project from August 1972 until October 1974, Oleg Samoilovitch, gives scale to the original wooden mock-up as he stands beside the aircraft outside the Sukhoi experimental factory. Compared with the Su-25 which evolved from this early T-8 project, the feature which is so obviously characterised by the mock-up is a certain delicacy of design which was at variance with the ruggedness required by the original Soviet Air Force specification for its new 'shturmovik'. *(Sukhoi Design Bureau)*

extending double-slotted trailing-edge flaps. An intermediate setting for the slats and flaps was incorporated, in order to improve turning performance while carrying out complex combat manoeuvring. This setting could be used at speeds up to 700 km/h (380 kt). The number of hardpoints under each wing was increased from three to five.

A radically new method of increasing the combat survivability of the engines was the use of a common accessories gearbox for the two engines. All power-generating sources and hydraulic pumps were housed in a common gearbox, located in the space between each engine. The gearbox was protected by armour plating and the armoured walls of the collector tank. (Later, this idea was used on the MiG-29.) Another feature of the complex of measures adopted to increase combat survivability was the use of polyurethane foam filling in the fuel tanks, instead of the more commonly used inert gas method. This was deemed to be more reliable. In the first stage of flight-testing, as decided earlier, it was anticipated that two R9-300 engines would be used, in spite of the fact that they were less economical and of insufficient thrust. In the second phase of testing the use of either the Izotov TR7-117 or the Tumanskiy R53B-300 was envisaged.

Two full-scale mock-ups of the LVSSh were built, in two different equipment configurations – one fully equipped and one with a simplified equipment fit. A 'mock-up commission' (*Maketnaya Komissiya*) studied the mock-up itself and the preliminary design documentation of the 'light army-support shturmovik' between 12 and 15 September 1972, the aircraft by this time having been given the military designation Su-25. The conclusion of the mock-up commission was that all of the operational requirements of the Soviet Air Force, in terms of performance using either the non-afterburning TR7-117 or R53B-300 bypass turbofans, had been achieved. (A mock-up commission is convened routinely to examine any new military aircraft project in Russia and is made up of representatives of the Defence Ministry, the Russian Air Force and the aviation industry.) From August of the same year, Oleg Samoilovitch assumed responsibility as Chief Designer of the T-8 project. On 25 December 1972 Yuri Ivashechkin was appointed Leading Designer in charge of the aircraft, and later (from 6 October 1974) he became project manager for the T-8.

2

Prototypes and Experimental Aircraft

The T8-1 (T8-1D) and T8-2 (T8-2D) prototypes

IN January 1972 work commenced on the design of the T-8 LVSSh, starting with preparation of the documentation for the construction of the first two prototypes, the T8-1 and T8-2, intended for flight-testing, plus an additional airframe, T8-0, for static fatigue testing. Pavel Sukhoi took this decision on his own, without the formal resolution of the Central Committee of the Soviet Communist Party and the USSR Council of Ministers, and even without an appropriate order from the Ministry for the Aviation Industry (MAP). Such a decision was extremely bold, since without the customary instructions from the highest authority no prototype aircraft could be built in the Soviet Union at that time. Preparation of

the design documentation was mainly carried out during 1973 and ran into 1974. Throughout 1973, work on the new assault aircraft was conducted unofficially in the Sukhoi Design Bureau, as a result of which the firm experienced great difficulties with the financing of the project. An example of this was when the working drawings of the first two prototypes were produced: more appropriate materials were unavailable, as steel plates were used to simulate the weight and dimensional characteristics of the cockpit armour.

The T8-1 was the first airframe to be assembled, completion of which, in the Soviet tradition of the day, was made just before one of the major national holidays – on 9 May 1974. A little before this, during one of his visits to the Sukhoi Design Bureau, the Minister for the Aviation Industry, Pyotr Dementiev, saw the assembled airframe of the new aircraft in the assembly shop and gave his approval for the preparation of a joint resolution relating to the building of prototypes of the 'shturmovik'. The joint resolution involved the Ministry for the Aviation Industry, the Ministry of the Defence Industries, the Ministry of Radio Industries and the Soviet Air Force. It cleared the way, in the absence of a special decree from the Communist Party and the Council of Ministers, for Sukhoi to receive all necessary components from relevant suppliers to build the first two prototypes.

Su-25 prototype T8-2D was used in the early trials of the R-95Sh engines selected to power the series-production Su-25, as well as in a number of other engine and flight systems tests, including the evaluation of 'side force control'. Some of the engine trials involved the selection of the best mounting angle to give a more neutral thrust line, in order to prevent pitch-up when full power was applied. *(Yefim Gordon archive)*

The so-called 'decision of the four ministers' was taken in May 1974 and determined the ultimate destiny of the aircraft, sealed on 6 May by the issue of an order from the Ministry for the Aviation Industry for the assembly of two prototypes of the T8. Aircraft T8-1, the first flying prototype (the yellow Bort No. 81 reflecting its prototype designation), was completed at Novosibirsk at the end of October 1974 (officially, just before the 7 November national holiday). This was followed by airframe vibration tests and adjustments to the engines and fuel system in the design bureau's facilities. Then, on the night of 23/24 November 1974, the aircraft was transported to the Sukhoi flight-test station at Zhukovskiy airfield to be prepared for its maiden flight. The Chief Test-Pilot of the Sukhoi Design Bureau, Hero of the Soviet Union Vladimir S. Ilyushin, son of the equally famous aircraft designer, was designated as leading pilot for the flight-test programme, along with V.P. Vasilyev as the leading flight-test engineer.

The jigs vacated by the T8-1 were immediately occupied by the first components of the T8-0, or so-called 'zero prototype', intended for static fatigue testing. The airframe of the T8-0 was completed on 12 September 1974, and fatigue testing of the structure commenced from the middle of that month. The full cycle of static tests was only completed in January 1976, although preliminary results had been obtained by the end of 1974, which gave Sukhoi sufficient data to plan

for the start of flight-tests. Preparation of the T8-1 for the commencement of the flight-test programme continued from the end of November to the end of December 1974, and included the installation of KZA (*Kontrol'no-Zapisyvayushchaya Apparatura*) parametric monitoring equipment and the carrying out of ground checks of all on-board systems, plus extensive engine runs. However, the first test flight was not achieved by the end of the year, as originally hoped for by the firm's senior designers and engineers, permission to do so only being granted on 9 January 1975. It was then planned to carry out the first flight on 13 January, this being preceded on 11 January by the customary high-speed taxi check down the main runway, raising only the nosewheel off the ground. After the high-speed taxi run, Vladimir Ilyushin reported the smell of smoke in the cockpit, although a full examination of the cockpit and a check of all systems revealed nothing untoward. V.P. Vasilyev, the T8 flight-test engineer, decided to conduct further engine tests, taking the engines up to the full take-off power setting.

The reason for the appearance of smoke in the cockpit only became apparent on 13 January, the day designated for T8-1's maiden flight, and in circumstances which could easily have had tragic consequences. The Deputy Chief Designer of the Sukhoi Design Bureau, Yevgeny I. Ivanov, was being pressed to achieve the first flight without further delays, and there had been no time to establish the reason for smoke in the cockpit

Representing a transitional standard somewhere between the T-8 LSSh mock-up and the definitive Su-25, prototype T8-1 (the designation reflected in Bort No. 81) is seen here on a flight-test in 1975. Particularly obvious in this view is the smaller fin size and absence of wingtip airbrakes, as well as the fairing for the under-fuselage gun pack, the mounting and location of which was changed on the production version. The engine nacelle and air intake profile, determined by the use of the Tumanskiy R9-300 engine, also differs from the definitive shape of production Su-25s. *(Sukhoi Design Bureau)*

before that date. Chief Test-Pilot Ilyushin also wanted to carry out the first short test flight as quickly as possible, and at the regular planning meeting arranged for that day Vasilyev agreed to the flight taking place, but only on condition that the engines should be run at full power again before take-off. During one of these test runs, a turbine blade in the starboard engine broke off, penetrating the engine casing and the lower starboard nacelle, causing a fire in the engine compartment. The technicians quickly managed to extinguish the fire and the aircraft itself was scarcely damaged, but the reason for the appearance of smoke in the cockpit on the first high-speed taxi run had been reliably established, comparatively safely, on the ground.

T8-1 was taken back to the Sukhoi hangar for repair, while the engine was sent back to the factory in Ufa in Bashkortostan for analysis of the blade failure. Specialists at the 'Soyuz' Engine Building Design Bureau in Ufa quickly established the cause of the problem, which required manufacturing changes to correct a design fault. In the middle of February, two modified engines were sent to Sukhoi's experimental plant in Moscow, and on 21 February Vladimir Ilyushin carried out another high-speed taxi check in T8-1. The postponed maiden flight of T8-1 was now set for Saturday 22 February 1975, and the aircraft was prepared with great attention to detail before finally taxiing out from Sukhoi's flight-test facilities at Zhukovskiy on that day. On this occasion, Vladimir Ilyushin did manage to achieve the aircraft's first flight, in the presence of the Deputy C-in-C of the Soviet Air Force, Marshal Aleksandr Nikolayevitch Yefimov, himself a noted wartime Il-2 'shturmovik' pilot with 222 combat missions in his logbook. Ahead now lay several years of tests and modifications before the T8 would be transformed into the now familiar Su-25 *Frogfoot*.

The first stage of flight-testing was carried out with T8-1 from February to November 1975, during which its basic performance was evaluated, its handling checked and engine performance monitored when launching or firing various categories of weapons. This stage of testing was mainly conducted by Vladimir Ilyushin. The wing profile adopted (modified SR-16) and the high-lift devices (*mekhanizatsiya*), comprising full-span leading-edge slats and extending double-slotted trailing-edge flaps, provide the aircraft with excellent aerodynamic qualities and a high maximum speed, plus good manoeuvrability, take-off and landing and spin characteristics. The designed-in combat survivability features were calculated to protect the pilot and major systems components from hits by anti-aircraft artillery shells up to 20 mm calibre. The T8-1 was also fitted with the navigation-attack system of the Su-17M2 *Fitter-D*, adapted for the new 'shturmovik' and enabling it to use a wide range of guided and unguided air-to-ground weapons. As already mentioned, the built-in cannon armament consisted of the VPU-22 (*Vstroyennaya Pushechnaya Ustanovka*), based on

This view of T8-1 reveals the shorter wingspan and narrower main wheels of the Su-25 prototype. *(Sukhoi Design Bureau)*

the podded SPPU-22-01 (*S'yomnaya Podvizhnaya Pushechnaya Ustanovka*) with paired, 23 mm GSh-2-23 cannon mounted under the forward fuselage, offset to starboard. This configuration required the nose undercarriage leg to be offset to port from the fuselage centreline by 50 mm (1.97 in). The maximum combat payload, on ten hardpoints, was 5,000 kg (11,023 lb) although later in the trials programme this was reduced to 4,000 kg (8,818 lb). The take-off weight of the T8-1 was 12,200 kg (26,896 lb), which considerably exceeded the 10,000 kg (22,046 lb) weight of the original specification. As a consequence, the aircraft's maximum permitted g-loading was limited to 6.5, whereas in the original operational requirements (TTT) this figure was required to be not less than 8 g.

On the initiative of Deputy General Designer Yevgeny Ivanov, the factory trials of the new 'shturmovik' led smoothly and seamlessly into joint trials with the 'customer' – i.e. the Soviet Air Force. Marshal Aleksandr Yefimov led the commission of representatives of the Soviet Air Force, while Lt.-Col. A.I. Marchenko headed the test team (*ispytatyelnaya brigada*) composed of specialists from the Red Banner State Scientific Test Institute of the Soviet Air Force (*Gosudarstvenny Nauchno-ispytatel'nyy Krasnoznamennyy Institut Voyenno-Vozdushnyye Sily – GNIKI VVS*) at Akhtubinsk in the Astrakhan region. Flights were conducted out of Zhukovskiy from February to the end of June 1975 with the objective of determining the T8-1's maximum speed, fuel consumption rates at various power settings and in different modes of flight, with varying weapons loads and with underwing fuel tanks. Particular attention was paid to the aircraft's stability and control, since the T8-1 incorporated unassisted flight controls (without hydraulic boosters), used for the first time on a modern jet aircraft after years of reliance on such systems on high-speed swept-wing designs. As anticipated, the absence of hydraulic boosters in the flying control circuits led to an increase in loads in the control column in the lateral and longitudinal axes. Large control forces, particularly when banking, and ineffective aileron response (noted by Vladimir Ilyushin on the first few flights) forced the designers to substantially modify the wing design. This involved increasing the aspect ratio, changing the shape of the ailerons and installing spring servo-compensators (trim tabs) in the longitudinal and lateral control axes.

During the first stage of flight trials it was decided to dispense with the planned use of tandem weapons pylons, so eight ordinary pylons were eventually mounted under the wings for the carriage of various types of weapons and auxiliary fuel tanks. The prototype T8-1 was flown to the Soviet Air Force Flight-Test Centre at Akhtubinsk to carry out a series of weapons-related flight trials from the beginning of July to the end of August 1975, involving air-to-ground gunnery and rocketry. These included firing the built-in VPU-22 cannon and podded SPPU-22-01 systems. Engine performance while firing different types of weapons was closely monitored, and salvo launches of 57 mm S-5, 80 mm S-8, 240 mm S-24 and 340 mm S-25 unguided rockets were also included. The tests established that it was possible to launch all of the above-named unguided rockets in salvoes, with the exception of the larger-calibre S-25. Simultaneous launching of several S-25s could, under certain circumstances, lead to flameout of the aircraft's engines. Nevertheless, modifications were incorporated later which did make it possible to launch S-25 rockets in this manner. Salvo firing of the 57 mm S-5 rocket from all eight UB-32 pods at the same time produced a dramatic effect, and during one such test firing the smoke and flames from the 256 rockets actually engulfed the aircraft. This led Soviet Air Force Flight-Test Institute pilot Oleg Tsoi, escorting the T-8 in a MiG-21U *Mongol* chase-plane, to think that the aircraft had exploded.

Another problem, which was also resolved successfully, was engine 'surge' caused by firing the VPU-22 cannon. The solution was to modify the gas ports (*lokalizatory*) in the barrels of the paired GSh-2-23 cannon to reduce the recoil force. In view of the fact that the aircraft's sighting system was not up to the planned operational standard for military service, guided weapons were not used in this stage of the trials. At the beginning of September 1975, T8-1 was ferried back to Sukhoi's flight-test station at Zhukovskiy and the first stage of the joint trials programme was completed by the end of November. Overall, it had been possible to confirm the anticipated performance characteristics of the T8-1, with the exception of range and a somewhat lengthier take-off run than calculated, from packed earth runway surfaces. Other deficiencies noted were the effects of the absence of airbrakes and a greater than anticipated time to prepare the aircraft for flight. In the concluding document issued by the joint trials commission it was stated that 'the Su-25 possesses broad capabilities in carrying out operations against ground and air targets in the tactical and "near operational depth" (*blizhnyaya operativnaya glubina*) of the enemy as a result of its flexibility of use, combined with simplicity of operation'. It was also stated that 'the aircraft is simple to fly and well within the competence of graduates of the Soviet Air Force's flying schools'. The commission also recommended improvements to the combat capabilities of the new 'shturmovik' by installing engines having a lower specific fuel consumption and a power rating in the 3,500–4,000 kgp (7,716–8,818 lb st) category. After completion of the first stage of flight-testing, it was decided in December 1975 to conduct a short programme of tests with T8-1 involving operations from the packed earth runways at Tretyakovo airfield, near Moscow. This programme actually commenced in January 1976 and the aircraft was flown by A.N. Isakov, one of the Sukhoi Design Bureau test-pilots.

As already noted, one of the shortcomings observed on the T8-1 by Air Force specialists was the absence of effective airbrakes. A search for the best location and geometrical shape of the brakes turned out to be a rather long-drawn-out process. When selecting the aerodynamic layout of the aircraft, around eight options for the location of airbrakes were studied, the most successful of which was to place them in the rear section of special wingtip fairings. The airbrakes selected for the T8-1 had an overall area of 1.2 m² (12.92 ft²) and were formed by the rear sections of the wingtip fairings, opening symmetrically, upwards and downwards into the airstream. They were to be used during manoeuvring flight throughout the entire flight envelope, and for landing. The efficiency of the layout was improved by around 60% by adding auxiliary surfaces of 0.6 m² (6.45 ft²) overall area, connected to the main airbrake surfaces by a kinematic linkage, the combined surface area and effectiveness of the brakes permitting steep dives at speeds less than 700 km/h (378 kt) without acceleration in the dive. The use of the particular layout for the airbrakes and their location at the wingtips increased the aspect ratio of the wing, its lift characteristics and the aerodynamic efficiency of the aircraft itself.

At the beginning of February 1976, the T8-1 prototype was modified to take the wingtip-mounted airbrakes in slightly enlarged fairings, but at the same time it was decided to abandon the idea of installing them on the engine nacelles, although they were tested in this location on T8-2. It was also decided to study the possibility of deploying the brakes asymmetrically, as side-force control surfaces, in order to allow the aircraft to be displaced laterally without changing its heading. As a result of additional flight-tests, the effectiveness of the new airbrakes was acknowledged to be perfectly satisfactory and they were recommended for installation on series-produced aircraft. In February and March 1976, flight trials were carried out with T8-1 to determine its performance with auxiliary fuel tanks of different shapes, including those of teardrop configuration. The objective of this was to establish whether they would avoid the strong sideways displacement ahead of the aircraft's aerodynamic centre of pressure, which had been observed when using the standard PTB-800 tanks. The aircraft was fitted with a yaw damper to improve longitudinal control, which involved a slight change to the design of the rudder. The area of the latter was reduced from 0.99 m² to 0.792 m² (10.66 to 8.52 ft²), removing around 30% of the upper rudder area. The upper section, with an area of 0.189 m² (2.03 ft²) was then used as a yaw damper, driven by an RM-130 motor installed in the base of the fin. The effectiveness of the cropped rudder turned out to be adequate to counteract the yawing moment caused by the loss of one of the engines. In the same year, the T8-1 was also involved in tests designed to eliminate vibrations in the longitudinal control axis in certain flight regimes, the shape of the tailplane leading edge was modified and trials were carried out with the podded SPPU-22 system firing in the rear hemisphere.

Towards the end of 1975, assembly of the second T8 prototype, T8-2, had been completed, and a number of minor design changes had been incorporated on the aircraft, which carried Bort No. 82 Blue. The modifications consisted of the following:

- the wing aspect ratio had been increased from 5 to 6.2, to improve lateral control;
- the design of the ailerons and flaps had been changed;
- airbrakes had been mounted on the sides of the engine nacelles;
- a built-in access ladder and folding footrest had been mounted on the side of the cockpit;
- the design of the opening part of the cockpit canopy had been changed and the Zvezda K-36L ejection seat had been installed.

Assembly of T8-2 had actually been completed in September of 1975, but because of the need to refine some of the systems and then take part in a ground display for leading figures of the Ministry of Defence at Sukhoi's production facility, the aircraft was only transferred to Zhukovskiy at the end of December. Sukhoi's Chief Test-Pilot, Vladimir Ilyushin, once again had the honour of taking yet another prototype of the new 'shturmovik' into the air, making its maiden flight on 26 December 1975. The leading engineer for the test programme for T8-2 was A.M. Sholosh.

An additional programme of flight-tests was carried out by T8-2 in the first half of 1976, which included:

- assessment of the structural strength of the wing;
- evaluation of the changes incorporated in the longitudinal control circuit;
- tests of various types of leading edge for the ailerons;
- evaluation of the effectiveness of the airbrakes mounted on the engine nacelles.

As a result of these trials, the optimum shape of the aileron leading-edges was established, along with the axial compensation required for these structures, while the engine nacelle location for the airbrakes was considered to be ineffective. In April 1976, T8-2 was ferried to Akhtubinsk to conduct a short programme to evaluate weapons effectiveness.

By the end of 1975, it had already become clear to the Sukhoi Design Bureau leadership and senior figures in the Ministry for the Aviation Industry that to continue work on the new 'shturmovik' at Sukhoi's experimental factory would soon become virtually impossible. The main reason for this was that a more important programme was getting under way, with greater priority over the subsonic 'shturmovik' – namely, the T-10 project, which was to mature into the now world-renowned Su-27 *Flanker*. It was necessary, therefore, to find another production base, where modifications could be incorporated on the two prototype T8s and preparation for series production could be set in train. Back in 1969, the first studies for the new 'shturmovik' and its possible future manufacturing requirements had been passed on to the Novosibirsk aircraft plant, but this facility was now very busy with the massive production programme involving the Su-24 *Fencer* tactical swing-wing bomber. Sukhoi had also conducted talks with the leadership of the Smolensk State Aviation Plant (Factory No. 475), Russia's oldest aircraft manufacturing factory, albeit to no avail. Unexpected 'manufacturing' proposals then suddenly emerged from the least likely quarter.

The creation of a new light assault aircraft in the USSR had not gone unnoticed by Russia's allies in the 'socialist brotherhood' of Eastern Europe. A little earlier, Romania had itself offered to design and develop a 'shturmovik' for the Warsaw Pact partner countries.

The second prototype, T8-2 (Blue 82), was completed in September 1975, but did not actually fly until December of that year. A number of modifications had been incorporated on this aircraft, including the installation of a wing of increased aspect ratio and airbrakes which were mounted at the rear of the engine nacelles. These were located part-laterally and part-ventrally on the nacelle, but they proved to be ineffective and were abandoned in favour of the wingtip installation eventually adopted. Unfortunately, they are not visible in this oblique view. *(Sukhoi Design Bureau)*

Then, the wish to participate in such a project was intimated by Poland, whose aircraft manufacturing plants at that time were not particularly over-burdened with work. In these particular circumstances, the Soviet Union was forced to make an official declaration that it was already working on the creation of such an aircraft, whose existence had already been discussed by representatives of the Soviet General Staff during regular meetings of Warsaw Pact members. At the beginning of 1976, the Polish government suggested that it would set up production of the new aircraft under the designation Su-25L (*Lisentzionnyy*, or licence-built) at the Polskie Zakłady Lotnicze (PZL) plant at Mielec. The engine for the new aircraft was to be a non-afterburning variant of the R13F-300 used in the MiG-21, and would be built at the PZL Rzeszów plant. This suggestion by the Poles made very sound economic sense, since the engine was in the inventories of all the Warsaw Pact countries at that time. In June 1976, the First Secretary of the Central Committee of the Polish United Workers Party, Edward Gierek, officially approached the General Secretary of the Central Committee of the Communist Party of the USSR, Leonid Brezhnev, with a request for the transfer of a licence to produce the Su-25 in Polish aircraft factories. The Polish aircraft industry was firmly set on establishing full-scale manufacture of the aircraft in the middle of the 1980s, although this did not come to fruition for a number of economic and political (mainly political!) reasons. Events then took quite a different turn.

The leadership of the Soviet Union had no intention of passing on to its 'friends', quite so precipitately, the new and secret aircraft and its associated new technologies. On 7 June 1976, a decree was issued by the Ministry for the Aviation Industry, in accordance with which production of the Sukhoi 'shturmovik' was to be transferred to the Soviet aircraft plant in Tbilisi, Georgia, which had just completed manufacture of the final batch of MiG-21 training variants. Three days before the issue of the decree, on 4 June, the second prototype, T8-2, was transferred to the Caucasus, to the Tbilisi plant named after Georgiy Dimitrov, for demonstration to the factory's management and workforce, as well as to the government of the Republic of Georgia. On 29 June 1976, by Decree No. 519-177SS of the Central Committee of the Communist Party of the Soviet Union, full-scale development of the Su-25 'shturmovik' and organisation of its series production was to commence in Tbilisi. So, this experience was a clear example of the fact that the Soviet defence industries did not always share production in a 'fraternal' manner with their so-called 'brothers-in-arms'.

Nevertheless, the Su-25 was later shown to the Soviet Union's socialist 'brothers', and on 29 June 1978 the aircraft was demonstrated to a Polish military delegation at Kubinka, led by the Polish Minister of Defence, Marshal (and future President) Wojciech Jaruzelski. It was flown by one of the Sukhoi Design Bureau's best test-pilots, Yevgeny Soloviev, who showed off the aircraft's excellent manoeuvrability in a display which was largely conducted at a height of around 50 m (165 ft). After the flight, the Polish leader presented the Russian pilot with Poland's highest military aviation award – the Silver Eagle – for his masterful demonstration of the 'shturmovik's' capabilities.

After completion of the first stage of joint flight-tests, it became obvious that the required flight performance could not be fully met by using the R9-300 engine, production of which had in any case ceased by this time. This had already been noted in the concluding statement of the results of the joint tests. A new engine with the required 3,500–4,000 kgp (7,716–8,818 lb st) thrust and low specific fuel consumption did not exist at that time, so the MAP leadership took the decision in the summer of 1976 to install a non-afterburning variant of the R-13F-300 in the T8 prototypes. As noted earlier, this engine was already widely used in numerous versions of the MiG-21 *Fishbed*, as well as the Su-15 *Flagon* air defence interceptor. In the second half of 1976, the Sukhoi Design Bureau started preparation of documentation concerning the modification of the first two T8 prototypes to take the new engine, which was given the designation R-95Sh (where 'Sh' indicates that this variant was intended for installation in the 'shturmovik').

It was decided to mount the new engines in the second prototype, T8-2, because flight-tests were continuing with T8-1 throughout 1976, aimed at eliminating various shortcomings which had been exposed during the course of the joint trials in the previous year. The increased dimensions of the new engines required a complete change of the design of the nacelles, air intakes and ducts and a number of ancillary engine systems. Airbrakes were installed in special fairings at the wingtips, this option having being tested earlier on the T8-1 prototype, and the entire complex of engineering modifications embodied in T8-2 was to be incorporated in the first prototype. After the modifications had been embodied and the new engines had been installed, the second prototype received the factory code designation T8-2D, where D stands for **Dorabotannyy**, or 'modified'. (This level of modification involves a series of improvements beyond the simple '**modifit-sirovannyy**', or 'modified' stage, usually involving substantial structural and/or systems changes. As with many Russian designations, however, this is not a hard and fast rule, and some substantially modified aircraft, such as the MiG-31M, improved *Foxhound*, were also described with an 'M' suffix.) The first flight of the upgraded T8-2 took place on 7 December 1976 in the hands of the Sukhoi Chief Test-Pilot, Vladimir Ilyushin. In the closing weeks of 1976, T8-1 was also relocated to the Sukhoi Design Bureau facility, where it was planned to undergo modification to the T8-1D standard, also destined to be the pattern aircraft for series production.

As already mentioned above, Decree No. 519-177SS of the Central Committee of the Soviet Communist Party had been issued on 29 June 1976, which defined the long-term programme for the new Su-25 'shturmovik'. According to the Decree, whose principal objective was acceleration of the pace of work on the new aircraft, the Soviet Air Force had to deliver the technical operational requirements (TTT) for the aircraft to the Sukhoi Design Bureau in the first quarter of 1977. The Sukhoi Design Bureau in turn had to present the new aircraft for State trials in the second quarter of 1978, with these having to be completed by the fourth quarter of 1980. A corresponding order was issued on 20 July by the Ministry for the Aviation Industry (MAP), in accordance with which the Tbilisi Aircraft Manufacturing Plant (Factory No. 31) was to build a further two prototypes (T8-3 and T8-4), which were in effect to become the first two series-production Su-25s. The Tbilisi plant, along with the Sukhoi Design Bureau, was therefore required to hand these aircraft over for State trials in the second quarter of 1978, and the MAP order also established the time for completion of the initial tests as being the end of 1980.

By this time, production of engineering documentation to facilitate modification of the T8-1 prototype into the T8-1D had been completed, this aircraft then being able to serve as the template for series production. At the end of 1976 T8-1D was transferred to Tbilisi, where preparation for series production had already been set in train from the beginning of that year. At the beginning of 1977, tests of new ABVT-20 titanium armour had also been completed, based on VT-20 alloy. New operational requirements for the aircraft had been confirmed on 9 March 1977, and Sukhoi

duly submitted the preliminary design documentation of the modified aircraft to the Soviet Air Force ('the customer'). This included incorporation of the R-95Sh engines, a modified wing, an all-welded armoured cockpit, a new VPU-17 built-in cannon installation with GSh-2-30 (AO-17A) 30 mm twin-barrelled cannon and a more modern navigation-attack system taken from the Su-17M3 *Fitter-H*. This comprised the new KN-23 navigation suite, an ASP-17BTs-8 gunsight, the *Klyon-PS* (Maple) laser rangefinder, an RV-5M radio altimeter and a DISS-7 Doppler groundspeed and angle-of-drift indicator. The whole ensemble made it possible to employ the most up-to-date guided weapons, including laser-guided bombs, missiles and rockets. A mock-up commission was convened between 11 and 24 March, with the participation of the Soviet Air Force and associated institutes. At the same time, the Sukhoi design team fielded questions relating to the modified 'shturmovik' and its R-95Sh engines. (The latter procedure was similar to that of defending a thesis in a Russian university). Taking due account of the observations of the mock-up commission, the full set of working documents required for series manufacture of the aircraft was amended and then passed on to the production plant.

Modifications to T8-1 were somewhat protracted, and in the opinion of some key Sukhoi personnel, were simply not carried out at a pace appropriate to the type of programme which the aircraft represented. However, there were a number of sound reasons which were delaying the modification process. For example, it had been decided to equip the ailerons with spring-loaded servo compensators (trim tabs) to reduce the load on the control column, the design of which had been virtually copied directly from the Cessna A-37 Dragonfly. (An example of the American light attack aircraft had been supplied to the Soviet Union by Vietnam in 1977.) Because of their very narrow chord, the trim tabs required extremely high accuracy in their construction, and it took some time for the Tbilisi factory to achieve the required level of manufacturing quality. Although delayed, the first prototype was nevertheless modified to the T8-1D standard at the Tbilisi factory, differing from the original prototype in the following details:

- for the first time, the aircraft was equipped with a fully armoured all-welded cockpit, constructed from ABVT-20 titanium armour with a maximum thickness of 24 mm (0.94 in);

The prototype T8-1 was substantially rebuilt by Sukhoi to a standard closer to that of the definitive Su-25. Since the rebuild was so extensive, the prototype was redesignated T8-1D (***Dorabotannyy***) to reflect that this was more than just a simple modification. The R9-300 engines were replaced by the R-95Sh, which required revised nacelles and air intakes, a new longer-span wing was installed, with full-span leading-edge slats, and a new taller fin and rudder replaced the small assembly used on the original T8-1. *(Sokhoi Design Bureau)*

- a built-in access ladder was mounted on the forward fuselage under the cockpit;
- a new built-in VPU-17 gun installation, with a GSh-2-30 (AO-17) twin-barrelled cannon, was mounted on the left-hand side of the fuselage nose;
- a new wing was fitted, of 30.1 m² (324 ft²) area and with an aspect ratio of 6, differing from the original wing in having five-section leading-edge slats and not having spacers between the inner and outer sections of the trailing-edge flaps, while the ailerons were also of increased area and had fairings over the external operating jacks;
- the fuselage nose section was lengthened by 210 mm (8.27 in);
- the rear of the fuselage was lengthened by 240 mm (9.45 in);
- new air intakes were installed, with a 7° rearward angle of slope from the upper intake lip to the rear, when viewed from the side;
- new R-95Sh engines were installed in new, longer nacelles than those fitted to the original T8-1 prototype;
- the airbrakes were relocated from the sides of the engine nacelles and mounted inside flattened pods at the wingtips;
- the shape and size of the fairing between the wing and the fuselage was changed;
- a new vertical tail unit was installed, with area increased to 4.65 m² (50.05 ft²).

The design, shape and dimensions, and the corresponding volumes of the fuselage-mounted fuel tanks of the T8-1D differed from those of the future series-produced Su-25. The capacity of the internal fuel tanks of the T8-1D was 3,360 litres (739 imp gal), i.e. 300 litres (66 imp gal) less than that of the standard series-produced Su-25, although the useable fuel capacity of the wing tanks of the T8-1D and the future Su-25 was identical. The T8-1D prototype differed from the Su-25 in that it employed only gravity fuelling, whereas on production aircraft centralised fuelling was also incorporated, in order to improve turn-round times in operational use. The T8-1D also lacked armour protection around the oil tank of the starboard engine, the latex sponge protection system for the fuel collector tank, the fuel tank detonation suppression system using foam plastic and the fire protection system based on sheets of fibreglass filling the spaces between the walls of the fuselage fuel tanks and the engine air intake ducts. Moreover, the T8-1D was not equipped with many of the defensive systems of the production aircraft, including infra-red flare and chaff dispensers. Later, the shape of the rear fuselage of T8-1D was modified to accept built-in chaff and flare dispensers and a range of modifications was incorporated in virtually all the aircraft's systems.

The wingtip-mounted airbrake containers, having an aerodynamic cross-section in the longitudinal axis and an oval cross-section when viewed from the front, increased the aircraft's lift/drag ratio by a factor of one. Apart from this, the wingtip installation turned out to be the best and most efficient location for the airbrakes. This was particularly noteworthy in view of the fact that airbrakes of any kind had been excluded from the preliminary design of the T8. The airbrakes themselves, installed in the rear of the wingtip containers and employing a so-called 'crocodile jaws' method of operation, enabled drag to be increased by a factor of more than two without incurring the need to retrim the aircraft, or reducing the lift performance of the wing. Additional aerodynamic stabilising surfaces were studied, for mounting on the wingtip pods, but they were not adopted.

Equipping the 'shturmovik' with the new airbrakes permitted studies to be conducted to exploit the concept of using direct 'side-force control', a method of using an aircraft's aerodynamic surfaces to control its descending flight path without altering its heading.

Sukhoi studied the possibility of using simultaneous deflection of the rudder and extension of the airbrakes in such a way that they opposed the deflection of the rudder, balancing the nose-pointing action of the latter. However, the asymmetrical extension of the wingtip airbrakes exhibited a significant shortcoming – it produced a high lateral g-force, which in the words of test-pilot Vladimir Ilyushin caused him 'great discomfort'. It turned out that a lateral force of greater than 0.65 g was extremely uncomfortable for the pilot, which led to further experiments with 'side-force control' being abandoned. On the other hand, the experiments had proved that the fin, and the rudder in particular, were sufficiently effective to compensate for the yawing moment arising from asymmetric extension of the airbrakes.

As already noted, the modification programme for the first prototype had been fairly protracted and was only completed in April 1978. During this time, tests were being conducted quite intensively with the partially modified T8-2D prototype. After installation of new engines and incorporation of appropriate airframe changes (mentioned earlier), the aircraft was transported to Sukhoi's flight-test station at Zhukovskiy in November 1976, where it was test-flown on 7 December. A second test flight was performed on 17 December. A wider programme of factory flight-tests of T8-2D was conducted from January 1977, with the aim of

Prototype T8-1D seen during the early trials phase, just about to lift off for a routine test flight. This aircraft, along with T8-3, participated in the pre-service deployment trials in Operation *Rhombus* in Afghanistan from April to June 1980, the two aircraft completing around 100 sorties, of which just under half were assessed as combat sorties. This prototype was lost in an accident in January 1981 when test pilot Anatoliy Ivanov exceeded the maximum permitted diving speed and the aircraft went out of control, although Ivanov managed to eject safely. *(Sukhoi Design Bureau)*

The effectiveness of the cockpit armour was tested by firing at different panels from close range with various calibres of weapon and comparing results for differing thickness and armour quality. Combat survivability was one of the principal criteria set for the Su-25, and survival of the pilot in the cockpit was a priority area for protection.
(Sukhoi Design Bureau)

gathering performance data of the aircraft and its new engines. Unfortunately, after the first few test flights in December 1976, some new defects had been noted which had not been observed before. These were vibrations from the rear fuselage and a tendency to pitch up when engine power was increased. After carrying out a number of checks on the ground, the Sukhoi design team asked the engine makers to change the mounting axis of the R-95Sh, giving it a 2° downward deflection (according to other sources this figure was 3°). The angle of incidence of the tailplane was also changed from –5° to +5°.

The first test flights of T8-2D in February 1977, with the new tailplane angle and modified engine exhaust outlets, revealed that the problems had been cured, and the design team declared itself satisfied. In the same year, tests to establish the aircraft's stability and control were continued and an SBU-8 (*Sistema Bokovovo Upravlyeniya*) side-force control system was again tested to attempt to reduce lateral stick forces. Installation of the new wing, in concert with the modified control system, had substantially reduced the stick force from the ailerons. The new wing did, however, exhibit some unpleasant characteristics. At Mach 0.71, airflow around the ailerons began to separate, accompanied by vibration, reducing their effectiveness and causing 'tip stall'. It was later discovered that this critical speed could be increased to Mach 0.75, or 900 km/h (486 kt) at sea

level, by adopting a 'toothed' projection on the wing leading edge, in place of the more usual wing fence. However, the maximum permitted speed in normal operation was limited to 850 km/h (460 kt).

In October 1977, the aircraft took part in a special display of new aircraft and equipment held at Kubinka airfield, and by November of that year factory flight-tests of T8-2D had been completed successfully. Later, during the course of 1978–80, T8-2D was used in a number of flight-tests designed to improve the flight and engine control systems. Stability and control was established using spring-loaded servo compensators (trim tabs) on the ailerons and elevators, while engine performance was also checked during the firing of unguided rockets and other weapons. All modifications to T8-1 (T8-1D) were completed by the beginning of May 1978, and the aircraft was presented to the Soviet Air Force on 9 May for the first stage (Stage 'A') of Joint State Trials (***Gosudarstvennyye Sovmyestnyye Ispytaniya – GSI***) to be carried out. These were to be mainly concerned with aircraft stability and control.

(At this point, it is useful to explain that in the Soviet Union, between the 1970s and the 1990s, State trials of military aircraft consisted of two stages. In the first stage (Stage 'A'), the aircraft and its systems could be modified and improved, where necessary, while in the second stage (Stage 'B'), the aircraft was handed over to the GNIKI of the Soviet Air Force, and the manufacturer no longer had any rights to implement changes during the test programme. After successful completion of Stage 'B', an aircraft was usually delivered to the Air Force for operational trials in normal squadron conditions.)

The programme of State trials commenced in June 1978, the Sukhoi Design Bureau providing three test-pilots for the programme – Vladimir Ilyushin, A.N. Isakov and N.F. Sadovnikov, while the GNKII VVS provided A.A. Ivanov, V.V. Soloviev and V.N. Muzyka. The Soviet Air Force officially accepted the aircraft for tests on 26 June. At the beginning of July 1978, T8-1D and T8-2D were flown to Shchelkovo (alias Chkalovskaya) airfield outside Moscow, where they were supposed to take part in a display of new Soviet military combat aircraft, along with the Su-27 and MiG-29, for the benefit of the Soviet leadership. T8-1D was to be displayed in the static exhibition, while T8-2D was to be demonstrated in the air by Sukhoi OKB test-pilot Yevgeny S. Soloviev. In the event, the exhibition was cancelled, since the General Secretary of the Central Committee of the Soviet Communist Party, Leonid Brezhnev, had left the capital for his annual holiday.

T8-3 and T8-4 Prototypes and Operation '*Rhombus*'

After the cancelled display at Shchelkovo, the State trials continued. Stage 'A' of the trials revealed certain problems with the unboosted flying controls, the built-in cannon and various other systems. Apart from this, the tests were further complicated by the fact that there was only one fully modified aircraft available which conformed to the standard required by the Soviet Air Force. It had been assumed that the first two aircraft to be completed by the Tbilisi plant would have been available for the State trials by this time. The Decree of the Soviet Communist Party and the Council of Ministers, as well as the Ministry for the Aviation Industry's own order, had all been issued in the summer of 1976. However, work at the Tbilisi Aviation Plant was proceeding slowly and significantly behind the planned timetable. The third and fourth prototypes (T8-3, Bort No. 83 and T8-4, Bort No. 84 Red) were only completed and handed over for tests in 1979. T8-3 first flew on 18 June, piloted by Yuri A. Yegorov, while T8-4 made its first flight on 19 September 1979, in the hands of Vladimir Ilyushin.

All the main concepts which had been lodged in the design of the new 'shturmovik' were realised in prototype T8-3, and the design team had also managed to achieve some weight reductions in the construction of the aircraft. However, since fatigue tests had not been completed, the maximum operational *g*-loading of the airframe was limited to 5. The build quality of T8-3 and the manufacture of some of its major components was so low that after completion of flight-tests it was assigned to the firing range, where it was used to evaluate the aircraft's combat survivability when subjected to hits by various calibres of ammunition. The first Tbilisi-built example, T8-3, was assigned to State trials in August 1979 after it had been transferred to Sukhoi's flight-test station at Zhukovskiy and following installation of a KZA data recorder, plus the inclusion of certain minor modifications. The second aircraft, T8-4, was brought into the programme in December 1979. Thus, only three aircraft took part in the Joint State Trials in production configuration, instead of the four originally planned, and the second prototype, T8-2D, was only used as a test-bed for the development of particular systems. Responsibility for the Su-25 'shturmovik' was taken over on 15 February 1980 by Yuri Ivashechkin as Chief Designer of the programme. Stage 'A' of the State trials was officially completed on 30 May 1980. The document outlining the results of the trials observed that the tests and results achieved were sufficiently conclusive to permit the aircraft to proceed to Stage 'B'. Noteworthy positive achievements of the trials were the successful measures adopted to improve the aircraft's combat survivability, while on the negative side was the

The second production-standard Su-25, T8-4 (Red 84), is seen here outside the Tbilisi manufacturing plant where it was built, completing its maiden flight there on 19 September 1979 in the hands of Vladimir Ilyushin. In the summer of 1984, T8-4 was used in trials to assess the suitability of using the Su-25 for 'ski jump' launches from the simulated carrier deck at Saki airfield in the Crimea. Successful completion of these tests persuaded the Sukhoi designers of the viability of using the Su-25 as a carrier-capable trainer and led, eventually, to the design of the Su-25UTG. The decoration on the side of the nose is of a young boy wearing a leopard skin, attempting to strangle a lion – the image is probably taken from Russian folklore, but its actual provenance is unknown. *(Sukhoi Design Bureau)*

ineffective SBU-8 system, which had been installed with the objective of improving lateral control, albeit unsuccessfully.

Even before the completion of Stage 'A', in March 1980, a decision had been taken on the personal command of the Soviet Defence Minister, Marshall Dmitriy Ustinov, to undertake a series of special tests in real combat conditions in Afghanistan, using the Su-25 and the Yak-38 attack fighters. The decision to send the Soviet Navy's carrier-based Yak-38 *Forger* vertical take-off and landing (VTOL) light attack aircraft to Afghanistan was explained by the fact that it provided the opportunity to assess its combat potential in land-based operations from high-altitude airfields. In particular, it would provide the opportunity to assess its operation in conditions where there were no airfields with sufficiently long runways, or indeed, where there were no runways at all. The so-called Operation '**Romb**' ('*Rhombus*') was conducted separately from the main tests, from April to June 1980. The Commander-in-Chief of the Soviet Air Force, Marshal Pavel Kutakhov, promised that the results of Operation '*Rhombus*' would be taken into account and included in Stage 'B' of the State trials. After a short period of special preparations, the first and third prototypes of the Su-25 (T8-1D and T8-3), as well as six Yak-38 *Forgers* and their ground crews, were flown to Afghanistan between 16 and 18 April in Soviet Air Force transports. They were accompanied by Sukhoi Design Bureau personnel, led by Yuri Ivashechkin, a team from the Yakovlev Design Bureau and a group of test-pilots. The airfield selected as the base for the special operations was Shindand in western Afghanistan. The eight aircraft (two Su-25s and six Yak-38s) were formed into a separate trials squadron. The group was placed under the control of the Deputy Head for Scientific Affairs of GNKII VVS, Major-General V.V. Alferov. As a protective measure against possible combat damage, the internal fuel tanks of T8-1D and T8-3 were filled with polyurethane foam before departure for Shindand and the data recording systems were removed. The aircrafts' IFF (identification friend or foe) system was also changed, and the Yak-38 was similarly prepared for possible combat missions. There were four test-pilots in the Sukhoi group, N.F. Sadovnikov and A.A. Ivanov of the Sukhoi Design Bureau itself and V.V. Solov'iev and V.N. Muzyka from GNIKI VVS. Sorties were flown in pairs, with the Sukhoi duo led by Sadovnikov and the military duo led by Solov'iev. During their combat sorties, the Su-25s and Yak-38s were provided with air cover by Su-17s of the 217th Fighter-Bomber Regiment, commanded by Lt.-Col. Gorbenko and also based at Shindand.

The first week in Afghanistan was spent in gaining familiarity with the mountainous terrain and high-altitude airfield operations, followed by preliminary tests of the aircrafts' weapons systems. In the second week, the aircraft of the joint trials squadron were used for reconnaissance missions, using their weapons against moving targets. At the beginning of May 1980, the two prototype Su-25s took part in a large-scale combat operation near the town of Farah, with top cover provided by Su-17s, each aircraft carrying out three or four combat missions per day, armed with high-explosive and concrete-piercing bombs, as well as unguided rockets. The infantry groups on the ground were able to take their heavily fortified objectives with little effort under the cover of such effective air support. As far as the use of the VTOL Yak-38 in these high-altitude conditions was concerned, they turned out to be unsuited to combat operations, mainly as a result of the lack of engine power and their low combat payload. The combination of heat (summer temperatures up to 40°C) and rarefied air (Shindand is 1,150 m [3,773 ft] above sea level) meant that the Yak-38 could not perform vertical take-offs with a combat load of even only 500 kg (1,100 lb), or indeed with any warload at all. The Su-25, on the other hand, made light of take-offs with a 4-tonne (8,818 lb) weapons load in the same conditions. Thus, the Su-25 showed itself to be very useful in real combat conditions and confirmed its excellent combat performance in the course of Operation '*Rhombus*'. The ground forces liked it very much and it was able to perform combat sorties in Afghanistan where no other fixed-wing aircraft had been able to fly before.

Operation '*Rhombus*' ended on 6 June 1980, with a total of around 100 trials sorties flown by the first and third prototypes of the Su-25, 44 of which were categorised as 'combat' sorties. The document drawn up at the end of the trials noted the excellent take-off and landing performance of the aircraft, as well as its manoeuvrability, the wide range of weaponry that could be carried and the accuracy of target destruction. No special defects had been noted during the execution of Operation '*Rhombus*'. It was probably during this trial period in Afghanistan that some Soviet Air Force personnel started to refer to the Su-25 as the '*konyok-gorbunok*', or 'little hump-backed horse', the heroic character of a fairy story by the nineteenth-century Russian children's writer Pyotr Yershov. The nickname

Ironically, having survived live combat experience during Operation *Rhombus*, Afghan veteran T8-3 was also used for armour effectiveness trials on the ground, the cockpit section under test being defined by the white painted lines. Here the cockpit is being subjected to 23 mm cannon fire. *(Sukhoi Design Bureau)*

was appropriately descriptive, since the dumpy little aircraft performed a similar role for the Soviet Army as the eponymous hero did for his owner in the fairy tale, and it is in sharp contrast to the Fairchild A-10's less delicate sobriquet of 'Warthog'! It was some time later that pilots and groundcrew were to refer to the Su-25 as **Grach** (Rook) (*see* Chapter 7).

T8-5, T8-6, T8-9, T8-10, T8-11 and T8-12 Prototypes

In the first half of 1980, the Tbilisi Aircraft Manufacturing plant had rolled out two more prototypes, which were given the factory codes T8-5 (Bort No. 85) and T8-6 (Bort No. 86). (It should be noted at this point that factory codes T8-7, T8-8 and T8-13 were not issued.) The fifth prototype, i.e. the third Tbilisi-manufactured example, was to have been dedicated to spinning trials at the Flight-Test Institute (*Lyotno-Ispytatyel'nyy Institut – LII*) at Zhukovskiy. Spinning trials on all Soviet civil and military aircraft have traditionally always been performed by the LII at Zhukovskiy, where there are not only the appropriate test facilities, but also highly qualified personnel, including test-

pilots who specialise in this dangerous region of the flight envelope. Unfortunately, on 23 June 1980, T8-5 was destroyed during a test flight, killing Sukhoi test-pilot Yuri Yegorov. Even during early flight-tests severe vibration had been noted on this particular aircraft, but it had, nevertheless, still been planned to use the aircraft in spinning trials. It was discovered from the crash investigation studies and deciphering of the flight data recorder that the aircraft had broken up in mid-air as a result of inadvertently exceeding the g-limit, with a reading of 7.5 g being noted. This was ascribed to the generally poor build quality achieved by the Tbilisi factory. Subsequently, up to completion of flight-tests on prototype T8-11, the permitted operational g-loading of the Su-25 was limited to 5 units.

As a consequence of the aircraft's first combat experience, the Soviet Air Force set an additional performance requirement – the speed during a 30° dive should not exceed 700 km/h (378 kt). The airbrakes proved to be insufficiently effective to enable this criterion to be met, but the designers came up with a highly original method of resolving the problem: they fitted additional deflecting surfaces, which were mechanically (kinematically) linked to the main airbrake surfaces. This resulted in a 60% increase in the effectiveness of the brakes, without increasing the original surface area (*see* Chapter 4).

The second stage (Stage 'B') of the State trials of the Su-25 officially commenced on 18 June 1980, the main objective being to assess the aircraft's performance during weapons firing. Aircraft participating in this phase were the first (T8-1D), third (T8-3), fourth (T8-4) and sixth (T8-6) prototypes. Because of the accident involving the fifth prototype and the need to establish its cause, the flight-test phase of the Stage 'B' trials did not start until July, while the fourth Tbilisi-produced aircraft (T8-6) was only brought in to the programme in August 1980. The flight-tests of Stage 'B' involved test-pilot A.A. Ivanov of the Sukhoi Design Bureau and Oleg Tsoi from the GNKII VVS. Tsoi was a military test-pilot who later became a test-pilot with Sukhoi after leaving the Soviet Air Force. Two other test-pilots from GNKII VVS were also involved – V.V. Soloviev and V.N. Muzyka. The concluding flights of the trials were carried out with T8-4, operating out of Mariy airfield in Central Asia.

State trials of the Su-25 were completed at the end of 1980, on 30 December. As a consequence of the lack of aircraft for the trials programme, it had not been possible to conduct spinning trials, or fire the VPU-17 cannon. However, striving to get the new 'shturmovik' into service as quickly as possible, the Soviet Air Force leadership agreed to accept Stage 'B' without the flight-tests of the aircraft's spinning characteristics. In the document outlining the results of Stage 'B', signed in March 1981, it was noted that the performance of the aircraft corresponded, in the main, with the operational requirements of the Soviet Air Force and it was recommended that it be put into production. It was also recommended that it be accepted into Soviet Air Force service after the elimination of the noted defects. Before acceptance into service, it was decided to deliver series-produced examples to line squadrons and operate them

with certain specified performance limitations. (It is of interest to note that in the Soviet Air Force there was a difference between accepting an aircraft **for use**, when certain performance criteria were permitted to be at variance with established norms, and accepting an aircraft as **a full weapons system**, when all its performance characteristics had to meet the defined requirements.)

After completion of the State trials, several of the prototypes were subjected to further special tests. Thus, after analysis of the cause of the accident to the fifth prototype (T8-5), it was decided to equip the aircraft with a strengthened wing and to reinforce the rear fuselage. New, longer engine nacelle cowlings were fitted and the rear fuselage was lengthened, to incorporate ASO-2B (*Avtomat Sbrasyvaniya Otrazhateley*) chaff dispensers. Aircraft T8-9 (Bort No. 89) was transferred to the LII at Zhukovskiy to be used for the long-postponed spinning trials and for trials relating to stability and control, as well as structural strength. These flights were mainly conducted by the very experienced LII test-pilot, Alexander A. Shcherbakov, one of the Soviet Union's leading specialists in the spinning behaviour of modern jet fighters. The flying phases of these trials were supported by flight-test engineers A.I. Yevstratov (dealing with stability, controllability and spinning) and K.V. Goryachev (a specialist in aircraft structures). In the opinion of Shcherbakov, the Su-25 exhibited the safest and easiest to handle spin characteristics of all the aircraft he had ever flown. It would enter a spin only when the pilot himself wanted the aircraft to spin, and it would come out of a spin as soon as the pilot centralised the controls.

Aircraft T8-6 was employed in trials to determine the viability of using diesel fuel instead of aviation kerosene and was also involved in trials of an improved cannon. During one of the latter trials, the nosewheel undercarriage leg would not extend for landing, after the aircraft was subjected to severe vibration during the

Following the loss in June 1980 of prototype T8-5, which had been designated as the airframe to be used for spinning trials, this vitally important part of the test programme was eventually resumed using T8-9 (Blue Bort No. 89). The spinning trials were carried out by Alexander Shcherbakov, a Zhukovskiy Flight Test Institute test-pilot considered at that time to be the most experienced Soviet pilot in this critical flight regime. (*Yefim Gordon archive*)

firing of the cannon. Test-pilot Oleg Tsoi landed the aircraft with the nosewheel leg in the retracted position on the grass alongside the main runway and the aircraft was returned to flight status after some simple repair work. In parallel with the trials of T8-9, T8-10 (Bort No. 10 Blue) was used in a series of test flights involving the use of the airbrakes on only one side of the aircraft, under the guidance of flight-test engineer V.L. Zaitsev. In 1982, test-pilot A.A. Ivanov had to make a forced landing beyond the airfield perimeter with the undercarriage retracted, immediately after taking off from Tbilisi. After repairs, this aircraft was also returned to airworthiness and both of these incidents were later used in defining the methodology for Soviet Air Force pilots when faced with the need to carry out forced landings with the undercarriage retracted. The prototypes were also used to study the possibility of carrying out gunfire and rocket launches aimed to the rear. The rationale for this was that it was thought that using rearward-firing guns and rockets would make it possible not only to destroy the main target in one single pass, but also to destroy its defensive positions as the 'shturmovik' pulled away from the attack. Experiments were carried out with T8-10 equipped with B-8 rearward-firing rocket pods and SPPU-22-01 gun pods mounted 'back to front', the twin barrels of which could be deflected downwards by 23°. However, these weapons options were not actually recommended for operational use by the Soviet Air Force. In 1982, Kh-25ML (AS-10 *Karen*) and Kh-29L (AS-14 *Kedge*) laser-guided air-to-surface missiles were tested on the Su-25 for the first time.

There were other losses of prototypes in the flight-test programme, and in January 1981 the first prototype, T8-1D, was destroyed during a weapons release trial when test-pilot A.A. Ivanov exceeded the permitted diving speed. After reaching Mach 0.86 the aircraft started to experience tip stall and did not respond to aileron inputs. Test-pilot Ivanov ejected from the aircraft at a height of around 1,200 m (3,940 ft). It was decided in 1982 to install hydraulic boosters in the aileron control circuit to resolve the problem of insufficient aileron effectiveness at high speeds. A full set of documents relating to the modification of the aircraft's control system was sent to Tbilisi, and the aircraft's Chief Designer, Yuri Ivashechkin, visited the factory in January 1983. The Su-25's wing was fitted with hydraulic boosters which were supplied from two separate hydraulic systems, the main and a reserve system. In an emergency it was envisaged that manual

reversion would be possible. In the first half of 1983, after installation of BU-45A hydraulic boosters in the aileron circuit of T8-11 (Bort No. 66), along with new airbrakes, a short programme of factory flight-tests was undertaken. As a result of the successful embodiment of the improvements it was recommended to introduce these changes in future production aircraft. The addition of the aileron boosters permitted the maximum operating speed to be increased to 1,000 km/h (540 kt).

The modified T8-11 was also fitted with anti-glare shields for the taxiing/landing lamps. For some considerable time, flights in poor weather had not been carried out on the new 'shturmovik', but during one particular night-time landing Sukhoi's Chief Pilot, Vladimir Ilyushin, switched on the landing lights, which were mounted just below the forward part of the airbrake housing, and was immediately 'blinded' by the glare. Attempts to adjust the angle of the beam projected by the lights had not produced any worthwhile results, but the problem was eventually resolved by the simple expedient of mounting small vertical plates on the airbrake housing to protect the pilot from the glare. These had the form of a broad chord delta 'winglet' with a squared-off tip, mounted under the wing at the junction of the airbrake housing and the wing, with the 'trailing edge' of the 'winglet' facing the direction of flight. The shape and location of the vertical plates was sufficient to prevent the intense beam of the lights from affecting the pilot's night vision.

Prototype T8-11 was also used to develop the use of the KMG-U (**Konteiner Malogabaritnykh Gruzov-Unifitsirovannyy**) weapons dispenser, literally a 'universal container for small loads'. It was 'universal' in the sense that it was designed for use on several types of fixed-wing fighters, as well as the Mi-24 *Hind* combat helicopter, the 'small loads' being different types of bomblet munitions. The aircraft was also used for equally important trials to determine the viability of using automobile diesel as a fuel in place of normal aviation kerosene. Earlier, the aircraft had been used in structural integrity trials, the results of which had enabled the operational *g*-loading to be increased to 6.5. Additionally, T8-11 took part in trials involving the application of a special graphite compound on parts of the airframe, designed to reduce susceptibility to detection by ground radars, these trials coming under the overall project name of 'Astra'. Later, T8-12 (Bort No. 12 Red) was used for similar 'stealth' trials, where the aircraft was given a special coating to absorb radio waves and a special camouflage paint scheme to reduce its detectability in the

Su-25 prototype T8-11 (Bort No. 66) was used to test the BU-45A hydraulic aileron boosters and modified airbrakes in early 1983. This aircraft was also involved in proving the effectiveness of the landing-light anti-glare shields, mounted at the inboard edge of the wingtip airbrakes. Although equipped here with a full complement of eight B-8M1 80 mm rocket pods and self-protective AA-8 *Aphid* air-to-air missiles, T8-11 was also used to evaluate the use of the KMG-U weapons dispenser on the Su-25. *(Yefim Gordon)*

visible spectrum. The aircraft was also used for the development of a new podded electronic jamming system known by the designation L-203.

It should be mentioned at this point that Yuri V. Ivashechkin was nominated Chief Designer of the new Sukhoi ground-attack aircraft at the end of January 1983. Previously, work had been led by Vladimir Petrovitch Babak, who had worked for the Ministry for the Aviation Industry until 1980, and had then transferred to the Sukhoi Design Bureau as Deputy Chief Designer.

T8-14 and T8-15 Prototypes

In 1987, the Tbilisi plant began to produce the Su-25 with the R-195 engine, which was an improved development of the R-95Sh, with reduced infra-red signature, but offering increased thrust of 4,500 kgp (9,920 lb st) in an emergency power setting. These engines, however, had been installed in a further development of the aircraft, the T8M-1, built in 1984 at the Ulan-Ude Aviation Plant as a prototype of a dedicated anti-tank variant of the Su-25. Later, it was decided to install the R-195 in the basic Su-25 as well. The first

'shturmovik' to be built by the Tbilisi plant with the R-195 engine was T8-14. Externally, this aircraft differed from the earlier models by the installation of an additional air intake to cool the engine exhaust efflux, plus a conical fairing aft of the final turbine stage, which partially screened the hot efflux from the turbines. In addition to flight-tests of the engines in this airframe, it was also used for trials involving the firing of infra-red decoy flares. In 1988, T8-14 was destroyed in a crash which was attributed to a faulty fuel system, although the pilot, E. Lepilin, was able to eject safely. The cause of the accident was later determined to be an erroneous fuel flow indicator, which showed that 600 litres (132 imp gal) remained when the tanks were, in fact, empty. After this setback, development of the R-195 continued throughout 1989 and 1990, using prototype T8-15 (Bort No. 15 Blue), the engine's State trials being carried out in this airframe, which was also used later as the prototype of the Su-25BM (***Buksirovshchik Misheney***) target-towing variant. The aircraft was displayed at the Paris Air Show at Le Bourget in June 1989, with a new Bort Number 301. Since the R-195 engines were still secret at the time, they were replaced with the old R-95Sh versions before the aircraft was flown to France, although the engine nacelles retained the modifications designed for the R-195, i.e. the additional air intakes and the diffuser cone. Eventually, T8-15 was handed over to the aviation museum at Khodynka, near Moscow, where it is still on display as Blue 301.

Altogether, during the design, manufacture and testing of the Su-25, more than forty research and trials programmes were carried out, the most interesting of these probably being the trial involving the carriage of the IAB-500, a simulated version of the RN-61 tactical nuclear bomb.

A Few Words about the Competitors

As already mentioned in the first chapter, the Ilyushin Design Bureau had decided to go ahead with the development of its own Il-42 project after its failure to be selected in the LSSh competition. Ilyushin built and flew a single example of this anachronistic design as a 'private initiative' project. The aircraft was given the new designation Il-102 and strongly resembled the 1950s Il-40, which was itself a rather clumsy attempt at creating a 'latter-day' jet-powered Il-2/10 Shturmovik. The Il-102 retained the layout of these designs,

with a rearward-facing gunner, plus a rear gun turret, which increased the take-off weight of the Il-102 by 700–800 kg (1,543–1,764 lb). By way of compensation for this shortcoming, the thick twin-spar wing permitted internal carriage of some of the aircraft's weapons, which reduced its drag characteristics. The design of the main undercarriage units was changed on the Il-102, compared with the earlier Il-40, allowing them to retract forward into fairings under the wings. This created space for additional external weapons carriage. The total number of hardpoints for weapons and fuel was sixteen. The Il-102 was powered by two Tumanski I-88 engines, which were based on the RD-33 of the MiG-29, but without the afterburner section. Later, the engine was given the designation RD-33I (i.e. 'I' for Ilyushin). This engine enabled the maximum combat load to be increased to 7,200 kg (15,873 lb) and take-off weight to go up to 22,000 kg (48,500 lb). A twin-barrelled GSh-30 30 mm cannon was installed in an NU-102-1 trainable turret under the fuselage, which was able to turn through up to 15° and had a 500-round magazine. A single-barrelled cannon of 45 mm calibre was also proposed. Machine-guns and cannon of 12.7 mm, 23 mm and 30 mm could also be carried in podded installations under the wings. A rear gun turret equipped with a GSh-23 twin-barrelled

Prototype T8-15 was used as an engine test-bed for the R-195 engine, identified in this view from the additional cooling air intakes above the rear of the nacelle and the protruding tip of the exhaust gas cooling cone fitted to this powerplant. Although intended as an alternative powerplant for the standard Su-25, the R-195 was eventually to be used mainly in the Su-25BM target tug and the later uprated Su-25T and Su-25TM variants. *(Sukhoi Design Bureau)*

ABOVE: This forward underside view of T8-15 shows the eventual location of the ten under-wing pylons, the GSh-30-2 cannon and the slightly offset nosewheel. The square dielectric panel covers the antenna of the DISS-7 Doppler navigation system, and the downward-deflected window of the Klyon-PS laser rangefinder is visible in the nose cone. *(Sukhoi Design Bureau)*

BELOW: The R-195 engine trials airframe, T8-15, which originally wore Blue Bort No. 15, was displayed at the 1989 Paris Air Show with new Bort No. 301, but had the still secret R-195 engines replaced by standard R-95Sh units. However, the infra-red suppression measures adopted for the R-195 were retained (i.e. the additional engine cooling air intakes and exhaust diffuser cone), which gave Western defence experts much scope for 'creative analysis' of their purpose on this airframe. This view also highlights the very short wheelbase of the Su-25. *(Sukhoi Design Bureau)*

cannon provided protection for the aircraft in the rear hemisphere, while a suite of active and passive countermeasures was included to protect the Il-102 from guided missiles and mobile anti-aircraft weapons. Bombs of 50–500 kg (110–1,100 lb) calibre could be carried on six underwing hardpoints and two underfuselage pylons, as well as on six wing mounts within the wing itself, although internal carriage was limited to 250 kg (550 lb) bombs. The wing pylons were also intended to carry unguided and guided air-to-air and air-to-surface weapons.

In spite of the fact that the Ilyushin 'shturmovik' was less elegant, from the aerodynamic point of view, the design of the airframe was chosen for cheap and simple series production. In terms of its combat load, the Il-102 was comparable with the American A-10 Thunderbolt II, while in terms of its radius of action it was similar to the Su-25. The maximum g-loading of the Il-102 was only 5, so its manoeuvring performance was rather poor compared with the Su-25, and even the forerunner of the Il-102, the Il-40, had a manoeuvring 5.45 g-limit. The Il-102 prototype did not have any special electronic equipment installed, but the designers said this could be fitted, to the 'customer's' specifications. (The 'customer', it will be recalled, is the rather coy Russian euphemism for the Soviet Air Force.) The Ilyushin 'shturmovik' had a better view from the cockpit for the pilot than from the Su-25, and like the latter it was also equipped with the standard Zvezda K-36 ejection seat.

The Il-102 was flown for the first time on 25 September 1982, by Ilyushin Design Bureau test-pilot S.G. Bliznyuk, and a total of 248 hours 35 minutes of flight-tests in 367 flights was amassed by the aircraft between that date and 29 December 1987. Maximum speed of the aircraft was limited to Mach 0.82, whereas the 1950s Il-40 had a Mach 0.9 limit. As already mentioned, the Il-102 was slightly inferior to the Su-25 in terms of manoeuvrability, but exceeded that of the Il-40, in spite of the lower g-limit of the more modern aircraft, thanks to the increased effectiveness of the airbrakes. On the prototype Il-40, it took one minute to slow the aircraft from maximum speed to half that figure, while for the Il-102 this only required 45 seconds. The minimum turn radius of the Il-102 did not exceed 400 m (1,312 ft).

An extremely persuasive factor in favour of the Su-25, when compared with the Il-102, was the absence of a rear gunner in the former, whose function, as demonstrated by the Sukhoi team, could be performed successfully by the pilot himself. Dispensing with a rear gunner enabled the weight of the aircraft to be reduced

and the effectiveness of fire to be increased. The overall performance of the Il-102 was only marginally inferior to that of the Su-25, but it was heavier than the Sukhoi design, although exceeding the latter in terms of its combat payload. However, the main factor leading to its rejection in the competition to find a new 'shturmovik' was that it was inferior to Sukhoi's design in manoeuvrability and combat survivability, in spite of its greater thrust-to-weight ratio. By the time the Il-102 had made its first flight, the Su-25 had already received its combat baptism in Afghanistan and had been put into series production. For the Il-102, the history of its predecessor, the Il-40, was being repeated, and in spite of its good overall performance, the aircraft was not what was required by the Soviet Air Force.

Although the Su-25 was officially accepted into Soviet Air Force service in 1981, the first details of this new Soviet attack aircraft had been published in the Western press, including photographs which had been obtained by spy satellites, as early as 1977. At that time the aircraft was given the provisional designation of RAM-J, under the system which allocated the letters of the test centre where it had been first sighted, plus a one-up suffix letter indicating each new type identified. In this case, it was RAMenskoye (the alternative name for the now more familiar Zhukovskiy), while the letter J indicated that it was the ninth aircraft so identified (the letter 'I' was not used, to avoid ambiguity between number and letter). The system was adopted in the 1970s by the United States Department of Defense to identify prototype and experimental aircraft detected at the Ramenskoye Flight-Test Centre, and it was eventually extended to cover missiles noted at Sary-Shagan (e.g. SH-01 ABM-1 *Galosh*) and aircraft at Taganrog (e.g. TAG-D for the Beriev A-40 *Albatross*). Once in service, the Su-25 was allocated the NATO code-name of *Frogfoot* by the Air Standardisation Coordinating Committee (ASCC), an international military organisation set up in 1948 by Australia, Canada, New Zealand, the United Kingdom and the United States. The principal objective of the ASCC is to 'ensure that member nations are able to fight side-by-side as airmen in joint and combined operations'; using standard nomenclature for the military equipment of their potential adversaries is an important part of such operations. The code-name system is one of many Air Standards developed by the ASCC's Working Parties, jet fighter names being two-syllable names beginning with the letter 'F', selected to be easily pronounceable by speakers from all of the partner countries' NATO and other allies.

3

Series Production and Experimental Modifications

The Series-Production Su-25 (T-8)

DURING the testing phase of the first two prototypes, T8-1 and T8-2, the Sukhoi Design Bureau's management had started to look around for a plant where series production of the Su-25 could be undertaken. The period coincided with burgeoning production of military aircraft for the Soviet Air Force, and there was little spare capacity anywhere in the Soviet Union. Factory No. 126 at Komsomolsk-on-Amur in the Russian Far East was heavily engaged in the manufacture of the Su-17 and its Su-20 and later Su-22 export variants, while Factory No. 153 at Novosibirsk and Factory No. 39 at Irkutsk also declined to be involved in the manufacture of the new Sukhoi design.

The former was working at full capacity producing the Sukhoi Su-24 *Fencer* swing-wing tactical bomber, while Irkutsk was heavily engaged in the production of the MiG-27 *Flogger-D* and other variants of the ground-attack *Flogger*. Factory No. 99 at Ulan-Ude, near Lake Baikal in Siberia, was at full capacity turning out helicopters, plus Antonov An-24 *Coke* and An-26 *Curl* transports, and Factory No. 30 (Znamya Truda – Banner of Labour) in Moscow was at full stretch manufacturing the latest variants of the MiG-23 interceptor. It was eventually decided to build the Su-25 at Smolensk, but this decision was later reversed when the plant received a more profitable order for the production of the Kh-55 (AS-15 *Kent*) strategic cruise missile.

Clearly, all this put the Sukhoi OKB in a very difficult position, and production of the Su-25 was thus placed in serious jeopardy by the lack of a suitable manufacturing plant. The only other remaining possibility was Factory No. 31, named after Georgiy K Dimitrov, at Tbilisi, in the Soviet Republic of Georgia, the major manufacturing base for the MiG-21UM *Mongol-B* trainer, production of which was winding down in fulfilment of its last export orders. Negotiations with the plant's management were long and difficult, but prospects were suddenly and unexpectedly improved after the demonstration of prototype T8-2D to the Georgian political leadership on 4 June

An early single-seat Su-25 outside the factory in Tbilisi, Georgia, painted in a non-typical camouflage scheme, without the light-coloured undersides. (*Sukhoi Design Bureau*)

1977. The flight demonstration had a decisive effect on the aircraft's further prospects, and only three days later, on 7 June, the order came from the Soviet Ministry of Aircraft Production authorising the manufacture of the Su-25 at the Tbilisi plant.

Factory 31's engineers quickly mastered the technique of welding the Su-25's titanium-armoured cockpit, made of ABVT-20 titanium alloy, using a new welding procedure which permitted the joining of titanium panels without the use of special equipment. This was conducted in the open air, with the panels of titanium armour being welded in a stream of inert argon gas. The factory's mastery of the production of the Su-25 enabled the first two aircraft to be handed over to the Soviet Air Force for commencement of flight-tests in 1979. After completion of all stages of the Joint State Trials, using the seven aircraft assigned to the programme, full-scale production of the Su-25 was then initiated at Tbilisi. As already described in Chapter 2, two of these development aircraft were used for trials in real combat conditions in Afghanistan, but series-production examples of the Su-25 differed from the first prototype T8-1 in a number of design details. These included, in particular, the following:

- the fuselage nose was lengthened by 210 mm (8.27 in), with a large single oblique window for the **Fon** (Background) laser rangefinder;
- different attachments for service access hatches;
- different lower fuselage nose panels, as a result of installing the VPU-17A cannon assembly and GSh-2-30 cannon;
- a different arrangement of the nosewheel undercarriage leg which was displaced 50 mm (1.97 in) to the left of the fuselage centreline;
- an absence of flat side panels and opening hatches in the area from Frame 20 to Frame 25;
- a lengthened rear fuselage, as a result of installing UV-26 infra-red flare dispensers;
- a different arrangement of the brake parachute cover;
- lengthened fairing for the tail antenna feeder system;
- the installation of an air intake at the base of the fin for cooling electrical generators;
- a greater cross-sectional area of the engine air intakes, which were of a different shape, with a rearward-sloping intake face;
- changes to the length and shape of the engine nacelle panels;
- changes to the shape of the fairings of the air intakes and engine nacelles where they joined the wing roots.

When compared with the first two prototypes, production Su-25s exhibited considerable differences, both in the geometry and in the actual construction of the wing and its components. The layout, design and composition of the aircraft's equipment underwent various changes as a consequence of experience gained during flight-tests, operational use on the squadrons and from analysis of the use of the Su-25 in Afghanistan. Some of these improvements were connected with the aim of reducing the labour intensity of manufacturing the aircraft, while some were attempts to increase the Su-25's combat survivability, as well as to increase its weapons effectiveness. An especially large range of modifications and improvements was introduced in aircraft batches manufactured from 1986. The changes to component layout, design and equipment took place in stages, from series to series, throughout the entire period of the type's manufacturing history. The main design changes and improvements included the following:

- the area of the wingtip airbrakes was increased from 1.2 m² to 1.8 m² (from 12.92 ft² to 19.38 ft²) in order to increase their effectiveness; the increase in area was itself the result of changing the design of the main brake surfaces, which split upwards and downwards into the airstream at an angle of 55° (total 110°); after modification, each brake section was provided with an additional surface which opened to an angle 90° relative to the external surfaces of the main brakes;
- the root portion of the third section of the leading-edge slats of each wing was extended to form a 'tooth' projection, slightly increasing the wing chord in that region;
- the main load-bearing elements of each wing cantilever section was strengthened to guarantee the defined limiting load factor of the aircraft;
- anti-glare shields were mounted on the wingtip airbrake fairings to prevent peripheral illumination from the landing lights affecting the pilot's vision;
- vortex generators were mounted on the wingtip airbrake housings;
- the wing centre-section panels were strengthened;
- the shape of the brake parachute housing was changed as a result of mounting additional infra-red flare dispensers in that area;
- additional flare dispensers were also mounted on the upper rear surface of the engine nacelles, alongside the engine compartment cooling air intake;
- the attachment points for the cannon were strengthened, an additional attachment was provided to

This unmarked Su-25 is finished in the camouflage scheme adopted for use in Afghanistan, with the pale blue-grey underside colouring extending right up to the mid-line of the fuselage. It carries a PTB-800 drop tank on the inner pylon and a mix of bombs and a B-8M1 80 mm rocket pod on the remaining pylons. *(Sukhoi Design Bureau)*

support the barrel and the structure of the fuselage nose around the cannon installation was also reinforced;

- the rear fuselage structure was strengthened;
- the horizontal stabiliser was modified with improved mass balancing of the elevator;
- an additional fire-extinguishing system was installed in the rear fuselage equipment bay, adjoining the engine bay;
- additional armour plating was applied to the sides of the rear fuselage tail boom, as a result of live combat experience; armour plating on the front fuselage was also increased;
- the undercarriage was strengthened and additional discs were installed in the braking system;
- a range of improvements was introduced, designed to reduce the labour intensity of the manufacturing process for certain airframe components, which led to a slight increase in the total mass of the airframe;
- a special fire-protective coating was applied to parts of the engine nacelles and rear tail boom;
- the aircraft's avionics were augmented by the inclusion of an R-828 FM/VHF radio to communicate with ground forces;
- clearance for the carriage of increased-capacity (1,150 litres/253 imp gal) PTB-1150, which permitted greater radius of action and longer ferry range;
- the aircraft was adapted for the installation of the R-195 engine, providing greater take-off thrust, increased time between overhauls and reduction of infra-red signature.

Production of the Su-25 at Tbilisi ended in 1989 with a total of 582 single-seat aircraft (commencing with prototype T8-3) having been manufactured from 1978, but not including the Su-25K (**Kommercheskiii**) export variant. This total breaks down as follows:

Year	Aircraft
1978	2
1979	4
1980	10
1981	13
1982	30
1983	55
1984	62
1985	78
1986	58
1987	100
1988	85
1989	85

During the course of its operational service and after a number of accidents that were caused by systems failures on the Su-25, attributed to salvo firing of weapons, or the launching of heavy-calibre unguided rockets, the use of its main armament, the 240 mm S-24 rocket, was prohibited. Its place as the main heavy weapon was taken by the FAB-500 500 kg (1,100 lb) general-purpose high-explosive bomb, which produced a similar effect, albeit from a markedly different delivery profile.

Work had already started in the Sukhoi Design Bureau on further developments and improvements to the Su-25, even during the early testing stages. In 1976, for example, the Soviet Air Force wrote up a long list of modifications to the aircraft and proposed that the single-seater should be modified to have two additional underwing hardpoints, plumbed for the carriage of two more auxiliary fuel tanks. More radical at the time, it was also proposed that the pilot should be provided with helmet-mounted sights (HMS) and the aircraft equipped with four R-73 (AA-11 *Archer*) air-to-air missiles for self-defence. The aircraft's performance would have been significantly improved by installing new R-295 engines, each of 5,000 kgp (11,023 lb st) thrust. Subsequently, the single-seat Su-25 was to undergo various modifications and receive certain improvements, albeit by a somewhat different route.

The Su-25K Export 'Shturmovik' (T8-K)

The Su-25 was used as the basis for a so-called 'commercial' export variant, known as the Su-25K (*Kommercheskiy*), and also built at Factory 31 in Tbilisi, Georgia. The aircraft differed from the Soviet Air Force version in certain minor details concerning internal equipment. Externally the export variant could be distinguished from the Soviet version by the presence of *Odd Rods* triple-bladed antennas of the older Russian IFF system, although many early Soviet Air Force Su-25s were also equipped with the original IFF equipment. The majority of Soviet Air Force Su-25s, however, were equipped with the later *Parol'* (Password) D-band IFF system, distinguished by the presence of small triangular-shaped blade aerials in front of the cockpit and under the rear fuselage.

A total of 180 Su-25Ks were built at Tbilisi between 1984 and 1989, made up of the following:

Year	Aircraft
1984	8
1985	36
1986	40
1987	40
1988	40
1989	16

The Su-25K was acquired by the air forces of the former Czechoslovakia, Bulgaria, Iraq, North Korea and Angola, and has subsequently been purchased, or acquired, by Armenia, Azerbaijan, Belarus', Democratic Republic of Congo, Ethiopia, Georgia, Kazakhstan, Macedonia, Peru, Turkmenistan, Ukraine and Uzbekistan.

The Su-25UB Combat Trainer (T8-UB)

The question of building a combat training variant (*Uchebno-Boyevoy*) of the Su-25 first arose in the mid-1970s, and a preliminary design for the T8-UB was drawn up in 1977. In the early 1980s, the Director of the Ulan-Ude aviation manufacturing plant, Yuri V. Konyshev, approached the management of the Sukhoi Design Bureau and the Ministry of Aircraft Production, with the suggestion that his enterprise should be involved in the manufacture of the Su-25. The reason for his approach was that production of the MiG-27 fighter-bomber was to cease at Ulan-Ude in 1981, freeing manufacturing capacity at the plant, which the Director wished to employ in continued production of another major aircraft programme. It was decided, therefore, that production of the Su-25UB would be transferred to Ulan-Ude. The factory was given the task of producing the first two prototypes, T8-UB1 and T8-UB2, and in 1982 a full set of engineering documents was sent to the plant.

After a change of management at the plant, work on the first two prototypes of the twin-seat version of the Su-25 was delayed, and by 1983 neither of the two aircraft had been completed, contrary to the original expectations. The Chief Designer of the Su-25, Vladimir Babak, had to intervene personally in the situation in order to establish a normal production rhythm for the assembly of the first prototype batch. In 1984, five fuselage sets of the two-seater had been assembled at Ulan-Ude, and were in various stages of completion. The first three of these, it was decided, were to be sent to the Sukhoi OKB, to be used as prototypes for their planned T8-M anti-tank upgrade, so the assembly of the first fully equipped prototypes of the combat trainer, using the two remaining fuselages, was not completed until the second half of 1985. The first prototype T8UB-1 (Red Bort No. 201) was rolled out in July 1985, and its maiden flight was carried out by Sukhoi test-pilot A.A. Ivanov at the Ulan-Ude factory airfield on 10 August. Another flight was conducted on 12 August, after which the aircraft was dismantled and flown by transport aircraft to Sukhoi's flight-test station at Zhukovskiy. At Zhukovskiy, T8UB-1 was fitted with a KZA recording device and all its systems were checked out before performing another test

The front cockpit of the Su-25UB is a far cry from that of the majority of modern Western combat trainers, and indeed no longer corresponds to Russian thinking on the best presentation of flight information to the pilot. *(Yefim Gordon)*

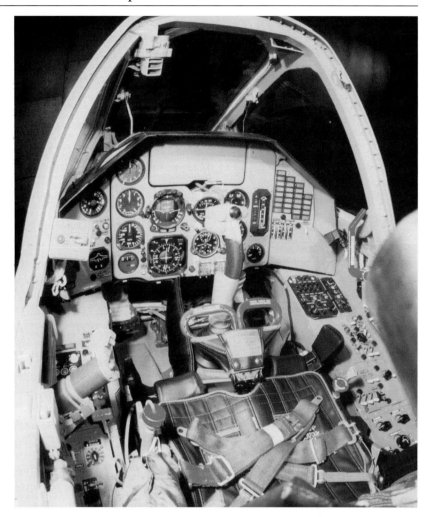

BELOW: A typical flight-line scene at Kubinka, with a pair of Su-25UB trainers and a pair of single-seaters being prepared for a mission. *(Yefim Gordon)*

ABOVE: Bulgaria has been an enthusiastic operator of the Su-25 for many years, here represented by one of the Bulgarian Air Force's four Su-25UB trainers. *(via Yefim Gordon)*

BELOW: An Su-25UB awaits its crew in a wooded dispersal area of the airfield. The Su-25UB does not have the built-in boarding ladder of the single-seater, probably because of weight considerations, so external ladders are used instead. *(Yefim Gordon)*

ABOVE: Taxiing the Su-25 on an icy airfield requires a delicacy of touch, since the narrow track and short wheelbase make ground manoeuvring difficult. With no weapons on the wing pylons, the pilots of this lightly loaded Su-25UB at Kubinka will not have to worry about the added inertia which results from weapons carriage. *(Yefim Gordon)*

BELOW: A standard Su-25UB of the Ukrainian Air Force seen at the Ukrainian naval airfield at Saki in the Crimea. Evidence of previous Russian ownership of the aircraft can be seen from the painted-over areas on the fuselage and the air intakes. Of particular interest is the cylindrical antenna array on top of the control tower in the background, which is identical to that installed on the aircraft-carrier *Admiral Kuznetsov*. The cylindrical assembly contains the transmitting and receiving elements of the *Cake Stand* antenna of the carrier's short-range navigation system, the equivalent of the land-based RSBN system, and provides an authentic 'naval' radio navigation environment for flight operations at Saki. *(Viktor Drushlyakav)*

flight on 10 October, again in the hands of A.A. Ivanov. A programme of factory tests was set up, although as a result of production delays with the two prototypes this was not conducted at the planned pace of development. Moreover, the aircraft was only configured as a pure training variant, and not as a combat trainer.

The leading engineer for the flight-test programme was V.P. Vasilyev, while the actual flying was carried out by Sukhoi test-pilots A.A. Ivanov, N.F. Sadovnikov and Oleg Tsoi. The first flight with two pilots on board was made on 7 December. The flight-tests were designed to check the aircraft's main performance criteria, including take-off and landing performance, as well as stability and control response of the new variant. The factory tests were completed on 13 December 1985, and at the end of the same month the second prototype, T8UB-2, made its maiden flight, enabling the two aircraft to be handed over in the early part of 1986 for the commencement of State trials. State trials of the combat trainer prototypes were conducted at a rapid pace

throughout 1986, and included use of the aircraft in its combat application, with weapons firing. Upon completion of the State trials, the aircraft was recommended to be accepted for service with the Soviet Air Force, with due note being taken of the need to correct certain minor problems recorded in the concluding document for the trials. Series production of the two-seat training variant, which was given the official designation Su-25UB, commenced at Ulan-Ude in 1986, and the first *'sparki'* (plural) were delivered to Soviet Air Force squadrons in 1987. ('*Sparka*' [singular] is the traditional Russian term for the two-seat variant of a single-seat fighter, and derives from the word '*para*', meaning a pair – in this context literally meaning 'with a pair [of seats]'). The Su-25UB replaced the Czech-built Aero L-39 Albatros jet trainer, which until then had been used in Soviet Air Force 'shturmovoi' regiments to train pilots selected to fly the single-seat Su-25. The first series-produced Su-25UBs manufactured at Ulan-Ude carried the factory's emblem on the nose, depicting a prancing brown bear.

The nose section of the mock-up of the Su-25UB two-seat trainer variant, marked here in Cyrillic letters as '8UB'. The Sukhoi Design Bureau 'winged archer' emblem on the nose was first known to have been applied to the Su-15TM *Flagon-F* prototype in 1971 and widely applied to the Su-17, Su-24 and Su-27 in Russian, but not foreign, service. Although seen on various Su-25s since the type entered service, it is not widely or consistently applied, and unlike its location on the other Sukhois, the symbol can be found on the nose or the fin of the Su-25, in a variety of sizes. Remarkably, after more than thirty years, no one in Russia, or anywhere else, seems to know anything of the origin of this emblem, or whether it was chosen or designed by Pavel Sukhoi himself. *(Sukhoi Design Bureau)*

After initially considering the possibility of using existing trainers such as the MiG-15UTI and a brief period using the L-39 Albatros as a conversion trainer for pilots assigned to fly the Su-25, a decision was taken to produce a dedicated training version at Ulan-Ude in Siberia. The prototype, T8-UB1, also introduced the practice of decorating the aircraft with a 'prancing bear' symbol, believed to be the Ulan-Ude factory emblem and applied to all twin-seat Su-25s (and Mi-8/17 helicopters) manufactured there. *(Sukhoi Design Bureau)*

The Su-25UB was intended for training and check flights of pilots on the squadrons and teaching cadets the techniques of aircraft handling in Soviet Air Force flying schools. It was also used to teach formation flying and flying as part of a combat group during conversion onto the single-seat Su-25, as well as the introduction to weapons application. The performance of the Su-25UB did not differ substantially from that of the single-seater. The navigation-attack, sighting devices and weapons-control system of the two-seater enabled it to be used for both routine training and weapons-training missions. The Su-25UB provided the following types of training tasks:

- development of flying techniques, both in daylight and night conditions, in Visual Meteorological Conditions (VMC) and Instrument Meteorological Conditions (IMC);
- instrument flying;
- attacks on ground targets, either simulated using a gun camera, or using cannon, unguided rockets and photo-bombing or live bombing techniques;

- teaching pilots how to handle systems malfunctions by simulating emergencies of the student's instruments from a special panel in the instructor's cockpit.

The Su-25UB was powered by two R-95Sh engines, as used in the single-seater, and the navigation-attack system was also identical with that of the Su-25. The Su-25UB did, however, differ from the single-seater in the following main respects:

- the forward fuselage was modified to take the new two-seat cockpit;
- installation of two separate hinged canopy sections over the cockpit;
- a slightly changed layout of equipment, particularly in the fuselage nose and fuselage spine compartments;
- installation of dual flight and engine controls, dual life-support systems and ejection seats, uprated air conditioning, electrical supplies and hydraulics;
- dual annunciator panels to signal in-flight systems failures, operation of the air conditioning and flight controls.

ABOVE: This direct overhead view of the Su-25UB reveals the aircraft's essentially cruciform shape. *(Yefim Gordon Archive)*

OPPOSITE PAGE:
TOP: Close-up of the nose of a standard Su-25UB showing the revised 'prancing bear' badge currently worn by aircraft and helicopters produced by the Ulan-Ude Aviation Plant. As with the Sukhoi winged archer symbol, the 'prancing bear' badge is only worn by aircraft and helicopters in Russian military service, and the history of its origin is unknown. *(Yefim Gordon)*

BOTTOM: An unmarked Su-25UBK finished in an unusual experimental camouflage scheme. This aircraft was built at Ulan-Ude and is seen here on a factory test flight. *(Ulan-Ude Aircraft Plant)*

The aerodynamic layout of the twin-seater differed from the single-seater in the shape and contours of the forward section of the fuselage, owing to the addition of the second cockpit. However, the length of the forward fuselage and the overall length of the aircraft did not differ. Changes connected with the increased height of the forward fuselage section led to a commensurate increase in the height of the central fuselage spine. The undercarriage of the Su-25UB was identical with that of the single-seat Su-25. The angle of view for the first pilot (student) was the same as that for the single-seater (17° looking forwards and downwards), while the angle for the second pilot (instructor) was 7° (in the same direction). The height difference between the instructor's seat and the student's position was 440 mm (17.32 in). The cockpit of the Su-25UB was equipped with two Zvezda K-36L ejection seats and the flight control system was identical with that of the single-seat aircraft. Obviously the cockpits differed from the Su-25 in the provision of a second pilot's position, with interconnected controls. The instructor position in the second (rear) cockpit had a sliding throttle control, the engine controls in both cockpits being directly interlinked, while the instructor's position giving him priority over a range of commands.

The electronic systems of the twin-seater differed slightly from those of the single-seater, in both their composition and purpose. These differences were primarily related to the installation of a second set of controls in the rear cockpit of the Su-25UB. A useful innovation on the Su-25UB, and typical of many Russian fighter designs, was that it was possible for the instructor to simulate malfunctions on the instrument panel of the student in the front cockpit. This was achieved by providing the instructor with special indicators, controls and warning lights, with which he could check and monitor the actions of the 'student' in the front cockpit, and in an emergency could transfer control of the aircraft from the front cockpit to his own position. The aircraft was fitted with an intercommunication (intercom) system which permitted two-way conversation between the two pilots, and there was also a cockpit voice recorder.

By the end of 1986 a total of 25 Su-25UBs had been produced at Ulan-Ude, although the twin-seater had been built at a time when the aircraft had not yet completed its State trials and had not been officially cleared for service with the Soviet Air Force. The two prototypes had been engaged in Joint State Trials throughout 1986.

The Su-25UB would not win any prizes for elegance of design, but it is a thoroughly practical aircraft, well proved in nearly two decades of service. *(Yefim Gordon)*

TOP: A view inside the assembly hall at Ulan-Ude, with a number of Su-25UB trainers in varying stages of construction. *(Ulan-Ude Aircraft Plant)*

ABOVE: Close-up of the detailed assembly work on an Su-25UB at Ulan-Ude. *(Ulan-Ude Aircraft Plant)*

The Czech Republic, when still part of the former Republic of Czechoslovakia, was the first Warsaw Pact recipient of the Su-25. Following the achievement of independence on 1 January 1993, the Czech Air Force continued to fly the Su-25 until 11 December 2000, when they were all retired and placed in storage at Přerov. Here, an Su-25UBK sits on the flightline at Námest-nad-Oslavou after a routine training mission. *(via Yefim Gordon)*

The Su-25UBK Export Combat Trainer (T8-UBK)

From 1986 to 1989, in parallel with the construction of the main Su-25UB combat training variant, the Ulan-Ude plant was also producing the so-called 'commercial' Su-25UBK (T8-UBK), which was intended for export to those countries that had already bought the Su-25K. The Su-25UBK differed from the Su-25UB only in minor details, in much the same way as the export Su-25K differed from the Soviet Air Force Su-25. Su-25UBKs were exported to the former Czechoslovakia, Bulgaria, Iraq, North Korea and Angola. Subsequently, the Su-25UBK was either acquired by, or purchased directly and indirectly by, Armenia, Azerbaijan, Belarus', Democratic Republic of Congo, Ethiopia, Georgia, Kazakhstan, Macedonia, Peru, Turkmenistan, Ukraine and Uzbekistan.

The Su-25B Project

While preparing the Su-25UB for production, the Sukhoi Design Bureau examined the possibility of providing the airframe of the two-seater with as much commonality as possible with the single-seat Su-25. While the two-seat Su-25UB was being built, operational experience with the single-seater was taken into consideration in a proposal to equip the Su-25 with more advanced equipment and increase its combat survivability. This study led to the development of a 'reversed application' (***obratnaya vozmozhnost'*** – literally 'reversed possibility') of using the airframe of the twin-seat Su-25UB as the basis for a more advanced single-seat project to be known as the Su-25B, with enhanced combat capabilities, which was given the factory code number T8-B. It was planned to equip the Su-25B with more advanced equipment, additional combat survival features and an increased combat payload. The R-195 would have been used as the powerplant for this variant. The concepts embodied in the Su-25B project were later to be used in the design of the even more advanced T8-M specialised anti-tank variant. (*See* Chapter 6.)

The Su-28 Basic Jet Trainer (Su-28M, Su-25UT, T8-UT)

The twin-seat Su-28 (also known as the Su-25UT, or T8-UT) basic jet trainer (***Uchebno-trenirovochnyy***) was designed on the basis of the Su-25UB as a private initiative of Sukhoi's Chief Designer for the Su-25 series, Vladimir Babak. However, the idea of building a basic trainer founded on the design of the Su-25 'shturmovik', to replace the Czech-designed and -built Aero L-39 Albatros used by DOSAAF, had first been put forward in 1981 by Marshal Aleksandr Yefimov. (DOSAAF [*Dobrovol'noye Obshchestvo Sodyeystviya Armii, Aviatsii i Flotu*] was the Communist-era Voluntary Society for the Support of the Army, Air Force and Navy, which offered pre-service training for young boys and girls in a variety of military disciplines, including flying training. It has now been replaced by ROSTO [*Rossiiskaya Oboronnaya Sportivno-Tekhnicheskaya Organizatsiya*], the Russian Defence, Sports and Technical Organisation, which has broadly similar aims.) The T8UB-1, the first prototype '*sparka*', was selected for conversion, with the objective of producing such a jet trainer variant. It was decided to lighten the aircraft as much as possible, in order to improve its performance. The modified aircraft, which received the factory code number T8-UT and the official designation Su-28 (or Su-25UT), differed from the basic Su-25UB by the absence of the following:

- a weapons control system;
- a sighting system;
- a built-in cannon;
- weapons hardpoints and pylons;
- armour screening of the engines;
- electrical supplies which powered removed items of equipment;
- duplicated control rods for the elevator circuit;
- polyurethane foam in the fuel tanks.

Redundant elements of the fuel system were also removed on conversion to the Su-28 (Su-25UT) standard. A balance weight was installed to compensate for the aircraft's change in centre of gravity after removal of heavy items such as the cannon, while blanking plates were placed over the apertures left by removal of certain indicators and panels in the cockpit. The laser rangefinder window, the cannon compartment and the apertures of all other removed systems were blanked off externally with aluminium panels. The Su-28 carried the red Bort

Once hoped to become an indigenous replacement for the huge numbers of Czech-built L-29 and L-39 jet trainers used for military pilot training in the former Soviet Union, the Su-28 was essentially a demilitarised Su-25UB and was also referred to as the Su-25UT and Su-25M. The sole example of the Su-28 carried DOSAAF titles on the fin, and had it not been for the demise of the USSR in 1992 it is likely that this organisation would have received large numbers of this rugged trainer. Here, the aircraft is seen wearing its international air show Bort No. 302, being prepared for flight. *(Sukhoi Design Bureau)*

number 07 and DOSAAF titles in blue lettering on the fin. The aircraft was intended to be used for basic training, navigation training, formation flying and the teaching of aerobatics. In sum, it was able to offer the following training procedures:

- basic jet training;
- aircraft handling and navigation both in daylight and at night, in VMC and IMC conditions;
- instrument flight using a 'blind flying hood' (*shtorka*) for the student;
- teaching the student how to handle certain malfunctions, using a special malfunction simulator in the instructor's (rear) cockpit; malfunctions of the navigation instruments, engine and various aircraft systems could be simulated.

The Su-28 (Su-25UT) had maximum commonality with the Su-25UB and Su-25 in terms of handling, performance and cockpit equipment, but differed from the latter two types in its greater manoeuvrability and its improved ability to take off, land and carry out normal flight on one engine. It could operate on diesel fuel and be based on grass airfields, the undercarriage could better withstand hard landings with the lightened airframe, and the aircraft was capable of performing up to 18–20 take-offs and landings in one sortie. It also exhibited high reliability and safety, with minimum expenditure on servicing. For ferrying to other airfields, the Su-28 (Su-25UT) could be equipped with four 800-litre (176 imp gal) PTB-800 auxiliary fuel tanks, which could be jettisoned in an emergency.

Conversion of the Su-28 (Su-25UT) was completed towards the end of July 1987, and the aircraft performed its maiden flight in August of that year. It was then made ready to take part in the annual air show held in that month at Tushino, on the outskirts of Moscow, to celebrate Air Force Day. For this demonstration, the Su-28 (Su-25UT) carried out a trial landing on a grass airfield (Tushino also has only a grass surface) and once again confirmed its excellent airfield performance. The General Designer of the Sukhoi Design Bureau, Mikhail Simonov, himself took the decision to authorise the landing on the grass airfield. However, despite the success of the grass-strip landing, the Su-28's flight at Tushino did not take place, since the air show was cancelled. Nevertheless, the new trainer took part in a sports aerobatic competition in the city of Volgograd and achieved third place overall. A little later, in June 1989, the aircraft was displayed at the 38th International Air Salon at Le Bourget, Paris, with the new designation Su-28M, and was also demonstrated at air shows in the

When airborne, the Su-28 assumed a slightly more elegant appearance than the standard Su-25 since the wing did not require weapons pylons for the pure training role. *(Sukhoi Design Bureau)*

This view clearly shows the substantial tail hook of the Su-25UTG and the locally strengthened fuselage attachment point, designed to accept retardation loads of up to 5 *g* on landing. *(Sukhoi Design Bureau)*

Philippines, Dubai and Abu Dhabi. For its participation in the Paris Air Show it was given a new Bort number, Blue 302.

Su-25UTG (T8-UTG) Naval Trainer

In the summer of 1984, almost coincident with the commencement of 'ski-jump' trials with the Su-27 at the 'Nitka' complex on Saki airfield in the Crimea, a programme of similar tests was being carried out with the T8-4 prototype of the Su-25. (Nitka is an acronym from *Nauchno-issledovatyel'skii trenirovochny kompleks aviatsii*, meaning 'Aviation scientific-research complex', which, although giving no clue to the nature of the actual 'research' conducted, was used to describe the simulated carrier deck and ski-jump used for training Soviet Navy carrier pilots at Saki.) The tests demonstrated the possibility of using the Su-25 for ski-jump take-offs, which persuaded the Sukhoi OKB to set about the task of designing a carrier-capable trainer, which received the designation T8-UTG, or Su-25UTG, meaning Su-25 *Uchebno-Trenirovochnyy s Gakom*, or 'Trainer with a Hook'!

Development work on the T8-UTG started in 1987 on the initiative of Mikhail Simonov and Vladimir Babak. It was based on the Su-25UB combat trainer and was designed specifically to train pilots in the techniques of taking off from, and landing on, a land-based simulated carrier deck complex, with a sloping ski-jump section and arrester wires. (The Russian term for the ski-ramp is *tramplin*, meaning both ski-jump and springboard, the latter term describing the take-off action perfectly.) It could also be used for training and check flights for pilots on ordinary squadrons or the training of students in military flying schools. At the beginning of 1988, one of the standard Su-25UB combat trainers was converted into the prototype T8-UTG1 trainer at Ulan-Ude, equipped with an arrester hook, and was given the blue Bort number 08. In March of the same year, the aircraft flew from Ulan-Ude to Sukhoi's flight-test station at Zhukovskiy, where after some minor adjustments to the arrester hook and installation of a KZA flight data recorder, it was test-flown by Igor Votintsev in September 1988. Leading flight-test engineer for the factory flight-tests was N.P. Petrukhin. In October, the aircraft was ferried down to Saki, where a programme of arrested landings was carried out. These flights were performed by Sukhoi OKB

The tail hook of the Su-25UTG retracts against the rear fuselage and is locked in place against a transverse stabilising bar. Note that the hook locks into place very close to the triangular blade antenna of the Parol' IFF system. *(Sukhoi Design Bureau)*

Blue Bort No. 08 was the prototype Su-25UTG, making its first carrier landing on board the aircraft-carrier SNS *Tbilisi* in November 1989. The ship's name was changed in 1991 to *Admiral of the Fleet of the Soviet Union Kuznetsov*, and remains Russia's only aircraft-carrier, its name now shortened to *Admiral of the Fleet Kuznetsov*. *(Sukhoi Design Bureau)*

test-pilots Igor Votintsev, Viktor Pugachov, Evgyeny Frolov and Sergei Myelnikov, while A.V. Krutov of the Flight-Test Institute at Zhukovskiy and military test-pilots A.B. Lavrikov and A.I. Fokin were also involved in the programme. On 1 November 1989, the prototype T8-UTG1, piloted by Votintsev and Krutov, carried out the first-ever normal aircraft-style landing on a Russian aircraft-carrier, when it landed on the Heavy Aircraft Carrying Cruiser *Tbilisi*, preceded by Su-27K and MiG-29K carrier-borne versions of the *Flanker* and *Fulcrum* fighters. (*Tbilisi* was later to be renamed *Admiral of the Fleet Kuznetsov*, and it remains the Russian Navy's sole aircraft-carrier). Flight-testing of T8-UTG1 to establish the viability of basing the aircraft on the Soviet aircraft-carrier extended into 1991 and was completed in 1992, when the carrier was relocated to its new home port of Severomorsk in the far north of Western Russia.

A small batch of Su-25UTG trainers was built at Ulan-Ude in 1989–90. Five of them, which remained at Saki airfield after the break-up of the Soviet Union, were eventually transferred to the Ukrainian Naval Air Arm. One was subsequently destroyed in an accident attributed to pilot error and a further four currently serve with Russian Naval Aviation at Severomorsk. Such a small number of aircraft was insufficient to serve the training needs of Russia's carrier air group, so an additional batch of around ten Su-25UB trainers were converted into Su-25UTGs, these aircraft also being known by the alternative designation Su-25UBP (*Uchebno-Boyevoy Palubny*). The adjective '*palub-nyy*', meaning 'deck', indicated that these aircraft had a naval function. Thus, Russian Naval Aviation received a total of around 20 Su-25 trainers configured to UTG standards.

The overall performance of the Su-25UTG differs little from that of the basic Su-25UB. Its flight instrumentation allows the normal range of training activities and check flights to be carried out in all weather conditions. The aircraft shares maximum commonality with the Su-25UB in terms of its aerodynamic layout, weight and dimensions, powerplant and related systems and the airframe structure, including the

This Su-25UTG is not slowly sinking into the sea off the end of the carrier's ski-jump, but has just taken off from the angled deck in the bottom right of the picture! Russian carrier-borne aircraft are not catapulted off the deck, as is customary, but instead rely on high specific excess power and wind over deck effects to perform 'standing start' take-offs. (*Sukhoi Design Bureau*)

One of the advantages of being a pilot in the Russian Navy is the occasional deployment to Saki on the temperate Crimean peninsula, where naval aircrew can practise the art of taking off and landing on the simulated carrier deck (NITKA) laid out on this airfield. Perhaps not appreciated by the Su-25UTG pilots at the time, these deployments, with their early-morning sorties during the summer months, provide some breathtaking moments as the flying programme gets under way just as dawn is breaking. The early starts are designed to take advantage of the best wind conditions on the airfield, whereas the carrier can always create its own favourable flying conditions by sailing into wind. Note the deployed airbrakes on this aircraft, which has just performed a simulated wave-off. *(Yefim Gordon)*

BELOW: A general study of the prototype Su-25UTG with its arrester hook deployed. This aircraft has conducted a large percentage of the carrier qualification trials, both for the Su-25UTG itself and for pilot training and evaluation. *(Yefim Gordon)*

OPPOSITE PAGE:

TOP: The prototype Su-25UTG seen on one of the side deck-lifts of the *Admiral Kuznetsov*. With below-deck space being at a premium and with the inability to fold its wings, the aircraft was probably taking part in compatibility trials when the photograph was taken. The yellow tractor alongside is one of a comparatively small number of specialised wheeled vehicles developed for use on the carrier deck and inside the hangar. *(Yefim Gordon Archive)*

BOTTOM: A dramatic shot of the Su-25UTG prototype coming to rest on the carrier deck with the assistance of the arrester wire. *(Sukhoi Design Bureau)*

A fine study of a series-production Su-25UTG performing an overshoot, or simulated wave-off, at Saki. It is a peculiar feature of the *Frogfoot* family that the wingtip airbrakes are kept open during overshoots. *(Yefim Gordon)*

One of the small number of Su-25UTGs inherited by Ukraine and used initially by both Ukrainian Navy and Russian Navy pilots at Saki. The aircraft was eventually transferred to the Russian Navy base at Severomorsk in northern Russia. *(Yefim Gordon)*

Decorated with both the Russian Navy St Andrew's Cross emblem and a double-headed eagle badge on the fin, symbolic of the Russian Federation, this standard Su-25UTG begins its unassisted take-off run down the main deck of the *Admiral Kuznetsov*. *(Roman Kondrat'ev)*

BELOW: During one of the summer training periods at Saki naval air station, pilots of the 279th Shipborne Fighter Aviation Regiment (279 KIAP) from Severomorsk hone their deck-landing skills on the simulated carrier deck (NITKA) marked out on the airfield. *(Yefim Gordon)*

ABOVE: Caught just at it descends onto the wet runway at Saki, this Su-25UTG is well set up to take the wire of the NITKA complex, with 'everything down'. *(Yefim Gordon)*

A deck-level view of Su-25UTG Red 11 taking the wire on the deck of the *Admiral Kuznetsov*. Note that retardation is effected largely by the arrester wire and that there is little evidence of the 'nose dipping' seen on Western carrier aircraft, which tend to use heavy braking in addition to being slowed by the arrester wire. *(Roman Kondrat'ev)*

BELOW: Resting between sorties, a trio of Su-25UTGs bask in the Crimean sunshine during their deployment to the Ukrainian base in the summer of 2000. The middle aircraft, Red 11, carries a badge on the side of the engine nacelle with the legend '[Award] for a Long-range Cruise' (**Za Dal'niy Pokhod**), commemorating the fact that it was deployed on board the *Admiral Kuznetsov*. on one of its rare out-of-area deployments. *(Yefim Gordon)*

In addition to using the imitation deck at Saki for simulated carrier approaches and arrested landings, pilots can also practise taking off from the ski-jump runway, which simulates the effect of departing the carrier's ski ramp at the appropriate angle of attack. A limitation of such an installation at a land-based site is that the wind-over-deck effect is entirely dependent upon local weather conditions. *(Yefim Gordon)*

undercarriage and internal equipment. The Su-25UTG can be used for the following training tasks:

- take-off from the ski-jump of the carrier simulator at Saki;
- arrested landings using the aircraft's retractable arrester hook;
- basic aircraft handling, in daylight and at night, in VMC and IMC conditions;
- instrument flight, including the use of the 'blind flying hood' for the student;
- simulation of malfunctions as on the Su-25UB;
- basic flight training in military flying schools and training centres.

The Su-25UTG differs from the Su-25UB by the absence of the following items of equipment and systems:

- targeting and sighting equipment;
- weapons control units;
- a built-in cannon;
- weapons hardpoints and pylons;
- armour screening of the engines;
- the R828 radio for communicating with ground forces;

- self-protection systems (chaff/flare dispensers, etc.).

When compared with other variants of the Su-25, the Su-25UTG exhibits the following differences:

- a retractable arrester hook, with a damper, retracting/extension jack and lateral stabilisers;
- a modified rear fuselage, strengthened to take the increased loads created by the arrester hook during deck landings; the brake parachute housing is faired over with a rounded cap;
- a forward-looking periscope installed in the rear cockpit;
- blanking plates fitted over removed indicators and panels of the weapons system.

Additionally, a number of other minor changes were incorporated, including:

- the laser rangefinder window is blanked off, as are other apertures created by removal of equipment, including removal of the antennas for the SPO-15 **Beryoza** (Birch) radar warning receiver (RWR);
- armour-plated hatches protecting the fuel collector tank have been replaced by an aluminium alloy structure, to reduce weight in the central fuselage area;

A fairly typical carrier deck scene, with the prototype Su-25UTG being prepared for take-off on the main flight deck. What is not typical, however, is the presence of the mobile crane parked near the 'island'. Although a number of specialised towing and servicing vehicles were developed for the carrier, the Soviet (and later Russian) Navy has had to 'make do' with a number of standard airfield support vehicles in order to support air operations at sea. In spite of the country's extensive military experience and technological prowess, the attempt to build a carrier-borne aviation capability from scratch has been an almost impossible task, exacerbated by permanent funding shortages in the wake of the collapse of the Soviet Union. *(Sukhoi Design Bureau)*

- the empty compartment left by removal of the cannon is skinned over with aluminium panels.

For ferry purposes, the aircraft retains the capability of carrying four 800-litre (176 imp gal) PTB-800 auxiliary fuel tanks, two under each wing and each being jettisonable in an emergency.

During take-off from a ski-jump ramp (at Saki, or off the carrier), the aircraft assumes the correct take-off attitude because of the curvature of the ramp. This reduces considerably the length of the take-off run. Before take-off, the pilot taxis out and positions the aircraft's main wheels over a special restraining chock device, selects maximum thrust and holds the elevators in the take-off position. On receipt of permission to take off, the aircraft is released from the chocks and begins to accelerate down the runway (or deck) to enter the ski-jump ramp. After entering the ramp, the aircraft's angle of attack quickly reaches the normal take-off value, and after two to three seconds accelerates to take-off speed and becomes airborne as it crosses the edge of the ramp. During the landing process, the Su-25UTG is guided into the visual zone of the *Luna-3* (Moon-3) optical landing system, and upon entering the guidance beam of the system the pilot establishes the aircraft on its assigned glide slope. Descent on the glide slope, right down to contact with the runway (deck), is held at the required angle of attack, maintaining the optimum approach speed. At touchdown, the arrester hook makes contact with the runway (deck) surface and picks up one of the arrester wires positioned across the runway (or deck), the aircraft travelling around 90 m (295 ft) before stopping, experiencing a maximum of 4–5 g in the longitudinal axis during the process.

The Su-25BM Target-Towing Variant (T8-BM)

Development of the Su-25BM (*Buksirovshchik Misheney*) target-towing variant began in 1986. (The Russian designation means literally 'tug aircraft for targets'). Two alternative projects were examined when this concept was initially defined: the first was to have been based on the Su-25UB, while the second involved development of the single-seat Su-25. Preference was eventually given to the latter solution. In 1989, a standard production Su-25 from the Tbilisi factory (c/n [255.081].10489) was converted into the T8-BM1 (Red Bort No. 12), as the first prototype of the target-towing variant. The aircraft was flown for the first time on 22 March 1990 by V.P. Korostiev. It was ferried from Tbilisi to the Sukhoi flight-test station at Zhukovskiy by factory test-pilot A.N. Komarov on 30 May of that year, and had completed a total of nine test flights at Tbilisi by that time. The factory flight-test programme for T8-BM1 was flown by Sukhoi OKB test-pilots Oleg Tsoi and E.G. Revunov. Later, some of the flight-tests of the target-towing variant were carried out using another airframe, T8-15. Other pilots taking part in the programme were A.P. Petrov from GKNII VVS, who was also the leading test-pilot for the T8-BM project, V.N. Muzyka, S.A. Lushin, V.N. Voronov, V.Eh. Dakhtler, N.F. Diorditsa, Y.A. Bezhevyets and several others. After successful completion of the test phase, the aircraft, which was given the service designation Su-25BM, was put into series production at Tbilisi. The aircraft was also sometimes referred to as the Su-25BMK (*Buksirovshchik Misheney 'Kometa'*), where *Kometa* (Comet) refers to the aircraft's towed target. The suffix 'K' of this designation should not be confused with the same letter denoting an export variant (*Kommercheskii*), the target-towing Su-25BM never having been offered for export.

The Su-25BM target-tower was designed to provide towed target facilities for training ground forces and naval personnel equipped with ground-to-air or naval surface-to-air weapons. It is powered by the R-195 engine and is equipped with the RSDN-10 (*Radio Sistema Dal'ney Navigatsii*) long-range navigation system, which is analogous in operation to the Western LORAN (Long-Range Air Navigation) equipment. For the specific role of target towing it was also equipped with a control system for the deployment and monitoring of the targets, with a winch for reeling them out and hauling them back in at the end of a sortie. As mentioned briefly above, the actual towed target of this variant is the *Kometa*, while the PM-6 (*Pikiruyushchyaya Mishen'*) gliding target (literally 'diving target') and M-6 parachute-retarded target can also be used when required. The M-6 target is basically a cylindrical 'bomb-shaped' canister, 1,167 mm (3 ft 10 in) long and 280 mm (11 in) in diameter, packed with a magnesium/sodium nitrate mix held in a binding agent and weighing 98 kg (216 lb) on release. Release height is from 2,500 m (8,200 ft) up to 17,000 m (55,775 ft), the target descending at a speed of between 4 and 15 m/sec (13–49 ft/sec) and producing a light intensity of greater than 2 million international candlepower in the initial

The prototype Su-25UTG takes the substantial arrester wires on the deck of SNS *Tbilisi* in 1989.
(*Sukhoi Design Bureau*)

The prototype Su-25BM (T8-BM1) with a *Kometa* towed target in its TL-70 podded winch housing under the port wing and a counterbalancing inert FAB-500 bomb under the starboard wing. This standard production aircraft was converted at Tbilisi and renumbered (as Bort 12 Red) for the trials programme to prove the viability of the Su-25 as a target-towing platform. *(Sukhoi Design Bureau)*

burn period of 3–6 seconds. The M-6 is detectable by a target-tracking radar up to 40 km (21 nm) away, and is visible to an infra-red tracking device up to 35 km (19 nm) distant. The types of targets used permit ground forces and naval gunners to practise detection and tracking of targets in the optical, infra-red and radar portions of the electromagnetic spectrum and live firing of anti-aircraft artillery and other weapons using those modes of detection.

The *Kometa* towed target is designed to imitate the aggregate values of the reflected and radiating properties of real targets in the optical, infra-red and centimetric radar wavelengths. The *Kometa* is equipped with a miss distance recorder capable of recording the passage of shells from a distance of 50 m (164 ft) down to zero. Miss distances and information about the number of shells passing the target are transmitted to the *Planer-M* (Glider), a ground-based device for recording the ground-to-air gunnery results. The *Kometa* target is towed behind the Su-25BM on a towline played out by the winch to a distance of 2,300–3,000 metres (7,546–9,843 ft). It is deployed from a podded TL-70 (*Turbolebyodka*) winch, which reels out and retracts the target via a mechanism which is powered by a wind-driven turbine mounted on the nose of the TL-70 itself. Control of the winch can be either manual or automatic. The TL-70 turbo-winch provides extension and retraction of the tow line, preliminary extraction of the target

from the main body of the winch on its parallelogram arm, receiving of the target, attachment to the tow hook and braking (retardation) of the tow line during target-towing. The *Kometa* target is 2.13 m (7 ft) long, and has a diameter of 0.2 m (0.66 ft) and a tailplane span of 0.71 m (2.33 ft). The Su-25BM and the *Kometa* towed target are generally used some distance away from built-up areas over specially equipped firing ranges. When the *Kometa* target and its associated TL-70 winch assembly is mounted on the Su-25BM, it is usual to suspend an aerodynamic counterweight under the opposite wing. This is very often an inert bomb of equivalent weight. The TL-70 pod and the *Kometa* target are usually suspended from the port middle wing pylon.

The PM-6 free-flying gliding target is equipped with radar wavelength corner reflectors and smoke/flare tracers to imitate a diving target, descending after release at an assigned angle between 30° and 70°. At the end of its flight, the PM-6 makes an automatic parachute-assisted landing on the ground or on a water surface. The Su-25BM can carry four PM-6s at the same time, two under each wing on the second and fourth pylons. The aircraft can carry two 1,150-litre (253 imp gal) PTB-1150 auxiliary fuel tanks to increase range and endurance when equipped with the *Kometa* or PM-6 targets, but in this configuration only two PM-6s can be carried.

As already mentioned, production of the single-seat Su-25 'shturmovik' ceased in 1989 at Tbilisi, and it was originally planned to build 170 Su-25BMs at the plant as a follow-on to the pure combat variant. However, in 1990, only 50 aircraft were completed, which were distributed to 'shturmovik' regiments already operating the basic Su-25. Twelve Su-25BMs were delivered to the 368th Independent 'Shturmovoi' (Assault) Regiment (*368-oy Otdyel'nyy Shturmovoy Aviatsionnyy Polk*), which formed part of the Group of Soviet Forces in Germany (GSFG), based at Demmin-Tutow. Deliveries took place between 1990 and 1992. These aircraft, not being fully equipped with the TL-70 winch pod, were never actually used for target-towing, but at that time, in the early 1990s, they were the most up-to-date versions of the Su-25, equipped with R-195 engines and an improved navigation system, incorporating RSDN.

Su-25K Catapult-launched Carrier-based 'Shturmovik'

At the beginning of the 1970s, the Soviet Defence Minister, Marshal Dmitriy Ustinov, when reviewing questions concerning national defence, put forward a proposal to update the design of the Project 1123 large anti-submarine cruisers, *Moskva* and *Leningrad*. His suggestion was that a third vessel of this class should be built, with a larger displacement than the previous two, to take an embarked group of vertical take-off and landing (VTOL) fighters and helicopters. He also suggested that a further two vessels should be designed to take catapult-launched versions of the MiG-23, the MiG-23K (*Korabyelnyy*) and the Su-25, as the Su-25K (*Korabyelnyy*), where *Korabyelnyy* indicated that they were shipborne, from the Russian for ship – *korabl'*. This project received the designation Heavy Aircraft Carrying Cruiser (*Tyazholyy Avianesushchiyy Kreiser* – TAKR), the word 'Project' itself being the conventional Soviet/Russian style of describing naval ship developments. A number of organisations subordinate to the Ministry of the Shipbuilding Industry of the USSR began detailed studies of these designs, with prospects of building two such vessels with nuclear powerplants in 1985.

In connection with these proposals and commencing as far back as 1972, the Sukhoi Design Bureau had conducted studies concerning the development of the Su-25K shipborne variant, designed for catapult launching from an aircraft-carrier. (Later, it will be recalled, the designation Su-25K was used for the export variant of the basic Su-25 'shturmovik'). Preliminary drawings of the naval Su-25K were produced in 1976. It was to have been developed from the standard single-seat Su-25

and intended for operations against small naval targets, anti-naval landing defences, neutralisation of naval air defence systems and anti-AWACS operations. It was planned to equip the Su-25K with an all-weather navigation-attack system, TV- and radar-guided air-to-surface missiles, a 'hold-back' device for carrier take-offs and an arrester hook for deck landing. The Su-25K was to have had a normal tricycle undercarriage, allowing the aircraft to be based on a carrier equipped with a catapult system and arrester wires. The nose undercarriage leg was to have had trailing-link suspension and twin-wheels, while the wing would have folded to reduce the aircraft's dimensions for parking on the deck. It was also planned to equip the Su-25K with an in-flight refuelling system to increase its radius of action, and the preliminary studies also envisaged the building of a two-seat combat training variant, intended for teaching naval pilots the techniques of taking off from, and landing on, an aircraft-carrier. It would also have been used for general handling and continuation training of pilots in open ocean conditions during normal cruise deployments, as well as weapons application training.

Su-25R Tactical Reconnaissance Variant (Project)

In 1978, design studies were undertaken for a tactical reconnaissance version of the Su-25, to be known as the Su-25R (*Razvedchik*), based on the single-seat Su-25 and intended to be used for reconnaissance support of the ground forces and Army Aviation. The reconnaissance variant was to be equipped with podded photo- and electronic reconnaissance systems, carried on the standard hardpoints on the wings and fuselage. The proposed reconnaissance equipment was quite comprehensive and included day and night cameras, plus a system for the management and transmission of acquired data. The use of modular reconnaissance apparatus was envisaged which was common to other types of tactical reconnaissance aircraft then in service.

Su-25U3 'Russian Troika' Three-seat Basic Trainer (Project)

In 1991, The Sukhoi OKB initiated studies for a highly original three-seat basic training aircraft which was given the project designation Su-25U3, where the suffix indicated its three-seat trainer layout (*Uchebny 3-myestny*). It was also known within the design bureau as the Russian Troika (*Russkaya Troika*), 'troika' deriving from the Russian word for three and used as a collective noun for any group of three items or people. The aircraft was based on the two-seat Su-25UB. The Su-25U3 was intended to be used for basic pilot training, aircraft handling, formation flying and aerobatic training. The distinguishing features of this three-seat variant included:

- a novel approach to the training process, where it was possible to teach two students on the same sortie, using the principle of 'teaching by others' mistakes' ('*Uchitsya na chuzhikh oshibkakh*');
- a 30–40% reduction in the cost of pilot training as a direct consequence of reducing the number of sorties required in the normal training cycle;
- advanced aerodynamics, developed for the original Su-25 'shturmovik' and the Su-25UB trainer;
- a high level of maintainability;
- high reliability (not a single Su-25 had been lost, or involved in a fatal accident because of technical failure, throughout the entire operating life of the Su-25);
- the capability of flying and landing with one engine shut down;
- the capability of using diesel fuel;
- the capability of being based on grass or packed-earth airstrips;
- an undercarriage designed to take heavy landings.

The Su-25U3 was to be capable of providing:

- basic jet training;
- basic aircraft handling and navigation training during the day and at night, in VMC and IMC conditions;
- instrument flight training using a 'blind flying hood' for the two students;
- instruction in the handling of certain malfunctions, using the special malfunction simulator in the instructor's (rear) cockpit; malfunctions of the navigation instruments, engine and various aircraft systems could be simulated.

The aircraft was developed from the basic layout of the Su-25UB, but differed from the two-seater in the following details:

- the shape of the forward and part of the centre section of the fuselage was changed as a result of installing the three-seat 'tandem' cockpit;
- all weapons pylons were removed from the wings, along with the wingtip-mounted airbrakes;

- the air intakes and intake ducts were modified in shape and size as a consequence of using less powerful engines.

The powerplant was to have been a suitable engine in the 2,200 kgp (4,850 lb st) class, and in accordance with a customer's request, foreign-built engines of similar power could also be installed. (In this case, the 'customer' was not just the Russian Air Force, as in the old Soviet convention, but any interested export client wishing to purchase this novel design.) It would also have had a standard avionics suite capable of supporting its training role, and this too could be specified by the customer. Later in 1991, work on the project was suspended as a result of lack of available financing.

Su-25 Test-Bed

It is known that one Su-25 was used as a flying test-bed for research into the properties of a new anti-radar coating, identical work also being performed with a MiG-29 *Fulcrum* and other fighter types. No details of these programmes have ever been released.

Su-25U Trainer

After the break-up of the USSR in 1992, Factory 31 at Tbilisi had almost ceased series production of the Su-25. However, between 1989 and 1996, the plant had produced a small batch of Su-25T variants, which will be described in detail in a separate chapter. The Su-25T was a single-seat anti-tank version developed from the twin-seat Su-25UB built at Ulan-Ude, but never manufactured at Tbilisi. Having become an independent state following the collapse of the Soviet Union, the new Republic of Georgia 'inherited' a small number of single-seat Su-25s, which formed the basis of the Georgian Air Force. However, the Air Force required a training version in order to be able to teach new students and maintain the proficiency of existing pilots. Engineers and designers from the Tbilisi plant provided a very enterprising solution to this problem. Using some of the engineering drawings for the Su-25T, they 'designed' and built three twin-seat variants, which they referred to simply as the Su-25U (*Uchebnyy*), turning out one Su-25U each year in 1996, 1997 and 1998, the first of which was handed over to the Georgian Air Force at the end of 1996.

4

Design of the Su-25 and its Variants

T HE Su-25 has a normal aerodynamic layout with a shoulder-mounted trapezoidal wing and a conventional tailplane and rudder. The specific mass of materials used in the construction of the airframe is made up of the following metals: aluminium alloys – 60% (D16, V-95, AK4-1, VAL-10, AMg3 and Amg6); steel – 19% (VNS-2, 30KhGCA, VIL-3, 12Kh18N10T); titanium – 13.5% (OT4-1, VT20, VT5L); magnesium alloy – 2% (MA 8, MA 14T, ML 54); other materials 5.5%. The overall weight of armour protection for the airframe makes up 7.2% of the aircraft's normal take-off weight.

Fuselage. The fuselage of the Su-25 has an ellipsoidal section and is of semi-monocoque, stressed-skin construction, whose primary structure consists of a longitudinal load-bearing framework of longerons, beams and stringers and a transverse load-bearing assembly of frames. Structurally, the fuselage is made up from the following major sub-assemblies:

- the front fuselage section with an upward-hinged nose cap, sideways-hinged canopy (opening to the right) and the nosewheel undercarriage doors;
- the mid-section with the main undercarriage doors and the air intakes;
- the tail section, comprising the fin, rudder and tailplane.

The fuselage does not have any production breaks. The nose section can be further broken down into the following sections:

- the compartment in front of the forward edge of the cockpit canopy, housing avionics equipment, of stressed-skin construction and joined directly to the cockpit section;
- quick-release panels which are located on the sides of the fuselage nose, permitting easy access to the radio equipment housed inside;

- the upward-hinged nose cone, which is locked into position by means of guide pins and fasteners;
- the unpressurised, dust-filtered cockpit, forming an armoured 'tub' made out of ABVT-20 aviation-quality titanium, whose thickness varies between 10 and 24 mm (0.4–0.94 in), the pilot being further protected by 65 mm (2.6 in) thick TSK-137 armour-plated triplex glazing on the canopy.

The cockpit also has a 6 mm (0.24 in) thick steel headrest, mounted on the rear bulkhead. The titanium sheets of the cockpit armour are welded, with transit ports in the walls of the cockpit allowing control rods and wiring looms to pass through, while a transverse beam mounted under the cockpit floor takes up the loads from the nosewheel undercarriage mounting. Guide rails for the ejection seat are mounted on the rear wall of the cockpit. The pilot has a standard instrument panel and side consoles and normal flight and engine controls and sits on a Zvezda K-36 ejection seat. Outside the cockpit, on the left-hand side of the fuselage, there is a square-section folding footrest, to ease pilot access. Cockpit overpressure, used as a protective measure against nuclear, biological and chemical contaminants, is between 0.03 and 0.05 atmospheres (0.44–0.74 lb/in^2).

There is a compartment underneath the cockpit which houses the cannon and magazine, a link collector and a shellcase ejection system. The cannon is mounted on a load-bearing beam, attached to the cockpit floor and the forward fuselage support structure.

The nosewheel housing is located partially in the area under the cockpit floor and partially in the area behind the cockpit. The recess has a supporting framework around the edge. Two hinged doors cover the lower part of the nosewheel bay in flight. A protective cover is attached to the inside of the nosewheel bay to prevent FOD (foreign object damage) and spray from entering the avionics compartment. This is detachable to facilitate access by the ground crew to the line-replaceable electronics units (LRUs) in the avionics bay.

The area behind the cockpit, located between the cockpit itself and the forward fuel tank, is a dust- and gas-filtered avionics compartment. Access to equipment installed in the forward section of the fuselage is facilitated by panels with quick-release fasteners on the top and sides. On the left-hand side of the cockpit, towards the rear, there is a built-in ladder for access to the cockpit, the upper part of the engine nacelles and the wing. This obviates the need for additional ground-support equipment. The ladder comprises three telescoping sections.

DIMENSIONS AND PERFORMANCE CHARACTERISTICS OF THE Su-25 VARIANTS

	Su-25	*Su-25UB*	*Su-25UT*	*Su-25UTG*	*Su-25BM*	*Su-25T*	*Su-25TM*
Crew	1	2	2	2	1	1	1
Powerplant	2×R95Sh	2×R95Sh	2×R95Sh	2×R95Sh	2×R195	2×R195	2×R195
Take-off thrust, kgp (lb st)	2×4,100 (2×9,040)	2×4,100 (2×9,040)	2×4,100 (2×9,040)	2×4,100 (2×9,040)	2×4,300 (2×9,480)	2×4,300 (2×9,480)	2×4,300 (2×9,480)
Length overall, including Pitot tube, m (ft)	15.36 (50' 4.72")	15.36 (50' 4.72")	15.36 (50' 4.72")	15.36 (50' 4.72")	15.33 (50' 3.54")	15.33 (50' 3.54")	15.33 (50' 3.54")
Wingspan over airbrake fairings, m (ft)	14.36 (47' 1.32")	14.36 (47' 1.32")	14.36 (47' 1.32")	14.36 (47' 1.32")	14.36 (47' 1.32")	14.36 (47' 1.32")	14.36 (47' 1.32")
Wingspan with wings folded, m (ft)	–	–	–	9.32 (30' 6.92")	–	–	–
Height on ground, m (ft)	5.2 (17' 0.72")	5.2 (17' 0.72")	5.2 (17' 0.72")	5.2 (17' 0.72")	4.8 (15' 8.97")	5.2 (17' 0.72")	5.2 (17' 0.72")
Wing area, m² (sq ft)	30.1 (324)	30.1 (324)	30.1 (324)	30.1 (324)	30.1 (324)	30.1 (324)	30.1 (324)
Maximum take-off weight, kg (lb)	17,600 (38,800)	18,500 (40,785)	16,560 (36,508)	16,500 (36,376)	18,500 (40,785)	19,500 (42,989)	20,500 (45,194)
Normal take-off weight, kg (lb)	14,600 (32,187)	15,300 (33,730)	13,320 (29,365)	13,000 (28,660)	15,300 (33,730)	16,580 (36,552)	16,990 (37,456)
Empty weight, kg (lb)	9,315 (20,536)	10,240 (22,575)	10,290 (22,685)	9,790 (21,583)	9,660 (21,296)	10,670 (23,523)	10,740 (23,677)
Take-off weight with *Kometa* target and two auxiliary fuel tanks, kg (lb)	–	–	–	–	15,300 (33,730)	–	–
Internal fuel, kg (lb)	3,000 (6,614)	2,750 (6,063)	2,750 (6,063)	2,915 (6,426)	3,000 (6,614)	3,840 (8,466)	3,840 (8,466)
Normal ordnance load, kg (lb)	1,400 (3,086)	1,400 (3,086)	–	–	1,400 (3,086)	2,000 (4,409)	2,000 (4,409)
Maximum ordnance load, kg (lb)	4,400 (9,700)	4,400 (9,700)	–	–	4,400 (9,700)	6,000 (13,228)	6,000 (13,228)
Maximum speed, km/h (kts)	950 * (513)	950 * (513)	950 * (513)	950 * (513)	950 * (513)	950 * (513)	950 * (513)
Landing speed, km/h (kts)	210 (113)	210 (113)	210–220 (113–119)	210 (113)	210 (113)	230 (124)	240 (130)
Service ceiling, m (ft)	7,000 (22,966)	7,000 (22,966)	7,000 (22,966)	7,000 (22,966)	7,000 (22,966)	10,000 (32,808)	10,000 (32,808)
Maximum altitude in combat configuration, m (ft)	5,000 (16,404)	5,000 (16,404)	5,000 (16,404)	5,000 (16,404)	5,000 (16,404)	30–5,000** (100–16,404)	30–7,000** (100–22,966)
Range with normal ordnance load, without auxiliary fuel, km (nm)							
– at sea level:	495 (267)	450 (243)	450 (243)	560 (302)	500 (270)	400 (216)	400 (216)
– at altitude:	640 (345)	950 (513)	750 (405)	–	950 (513)	700 (378)	900 (486)
Range with normal ordnance load and 4 auxiliary fuel tanks, km (nm)							
– at sea level:	750 (405)	750 (405)	1,250 (675)	–	750 (405)	750 (405)	750 (405)
– at altitude:	1,250 (675)	1,250 (675)	2,150 (675)	–	1,250 (675)	1,250 (675)	1,250 (675)
Ferry range, km (nm)	1,950 (1,053)	–	–	–	2,000 (1,080)	2,500 (1,350)	2,500 (1,350)

	Su-25	Su-25UB	Su-25UT	Su-25UTG	Su-25BM	Su-25T	Su-25TM	
Take-off run, m (ft):								
– on concrete runway	550 (1,804)	550 (1,804)	450 (1,476)	500 (1,640)	550 (1,804)	550 (1,804)	550 (1,804)	
– on packed earth runway	600 (1,969)	600 (1,969)	500 (1,640)	–	600 (1,969)	600 (1,969)	600 (1,969)	
– from 'ski jump'	–	–	–	190 (623)	–	–	–	
Landing run, m (ft):								
– on concrete runway, using brake chute	400 (1,312)	400 (1,312)	400 (1,312)	–	400 (1,312)	400 (1,312)	400 (1,312)	
– on concrete runway, without brake chute	600 (1,969)	600 (1,969)	500 (1,640)	450 (1,476)	600 (1,969)	600 (1,969)	600 (1,969)	
– on packed earth, without brake chute	700 (2,297)	750 (2,460)	700 (2,297)	90 *** (295)	750 (2,460)	750 (2,460)	750 (2,460)	
Maximum g limit with normal combat load	6.5	6.5	6	6.5	6.5	6.5	6.5	6.5
Maximum g limit with maximum combat load	5.2	5.2	–	–	5.2	5.2	5.2	5.2

Notes:
* at 5,000m (16,404 ft); maximum speed at sea level is 850 km/h (459kts).
** normal range for combat operations.
*** using arrester wires.

This view shows the curved steel protective plate around the ejection seat head-rest and the mounting of the rear-view mirror in the centre of the canopy. Also clearly shown here is the deployed boarding ladder and footrest and the gun-gas exhaust louvres behind the cannon installation.
(Sukhoi Design Bureau)

The centre section of the fuselage comprises:

• the forward fuel tank, made up of riveted panels (except for the lower part, which is milled), access to which is facilitated by a removable side panel. Elements of the fuel system, including the filling nozzle, are mounted on top of the tank. The collector tank is located behind the forward tank and has a panel mounted on its lower side for access to the interior when required. The upper part of the tank is made of protective armoured sheet; the rear wall of the tank has a circular access hatch;

- the wing centre-section, which serves as the attachment point for the wings, forming an integral fuel tank and consisting of upper and lower milled panels joined to each other by ribs. The centre section torsion box has front and rear walls, with engineering access hatches, and each wing cantilever section is fixed to the torsion box with bolts attached to load-bearing ribs;
- the mainwheel wells, located under the forward fuel tank on the left and right of the fuselage's axis of symmetry. The upper parts of the wells are bounded by the air intake ducts, and while in flight the wells themselves are covered by three undercarriage doors;
- a fairing, covering the upper part of the fuselage over the forward fuel tank and the wing torsion box, which serves as a housing for elements of the fuel system, control rods of the flight control system and other services; the fairing is divided into three sections by two longitudinal walls, forming a central and two lateral compartments;
- the air supply ducts, which pass through the central part of the fuselage, from the air intakes to the engine compartment, which are positioned in the fuselage with clearance between the ducts and the fuel tanks and are attached to the fuselage frames.

The tail section of the fuselage is structurally divided into the following:

- a tail beam forming a platform on which the vertical and horizontal tail units are mounted, the load-bearing primary structure of the beam being formed from a transverse assembly of frames and a longitudinal assembly of upper, central and lower longerons and stringers. The tail section consists of compartments housing aircraft and engine control equipment, plus the booster unit for the tailplane incidence control system and the brake parachute. The upper skin of the fuselage tail-beam structure, in front of the fin, comprises a series of access hatches. On the underside of the structure there are more access hatches, retained by quick-release fasteners. Along the sides of the rear fuselage structure there are access panels to the engine mounts. The hinge points for the rudder and tailplane are mounted on load-bearing frames of the tail beam, while the engine fairing panels are attached to the sides of the fuselage structure;
- the two engine nacelles, located on either side of the rear fuselage, each nacelle comprising a fixed element, firmly attached to the fuselage with rivets,

plus a detachable rear section. The engine mountings are bolted to load-bearing frames of the nacelles. The side walls of the rear fuselage serve as the inner walls of the engine nacelles. The lower surface of the non-detachable parts of the nacelles consists of front and rear hinged cowlings, permitting access to the engines. An air intake is mounted on top of the rear part of each engine nacelle to provide cooling airflow to the engine compartment.

In order to increase the aircraft's survivability, armour plating is applied to the sides of the rear fuselage, to the engine exhaust zone and on the underside of the forward cowlings of the engine nacelles. Armour plating is also included in the construction of the detachable rear parts of the engine nacelle. The container for the PTK-25 brake parachute assembly forms the tail cone of the rear fuselage. The container houses a brake chute and a spring release mechanism, a second parachute and a corresponding link attachment, the two cruciform-shaped chutes having a combined area of 25 m² (269 ft²). The parachute container is attached to the periphery of the rearmost load-bearing fuselage frame. The inner part of the container forms a cylinder into which the parachutes are packed, and the extreme tip of the assembly hinges upwards when the brake chutes are deployed on landing.

The cockpit canopy is mounted on the forward fuselage and consists of a fixed windshield and a sideways-opening canopy, hinged on the right. The opening section of the canopy is fitted with locks which mate with appropriate attachments on the main canopy frame, and opening and closing is achieved manually. A periscope is mounted on the top of the canopy frame to provide a rear hemisphere view for the pilot. Mirrors are also mounted on the canopy arch for the same purpose, one on each side.

The aircraft is equipped with fixed-geometry laterally mounted air intakes with an oblique elliptical intake entrance, which form the forward part of the air supply ducts to the engines. The intakes have a comparatively thick leading edge. Between the sides of the fuselage and the air intakes there are subsonic boundary-layer splitters.

The air intakes are of stressed-skin construction, and the leading edge has longitudinal spacers to increase structural rigidity at the intake entrance. The internal panels of the air intakes are reinforced with circular frames, which take up the pressure variations within the intake duct. In the upper part of each air intake,

External close-up of the cockpit of an Su-25 (actually prototype T8-11), showing the rear-view mirror over the canopy, plus an internal mirror and the armoured metal fairing to the rear of the transparency. The canopy has armoured triplex glazing. *(Yefim Gordon)*

above the air ducts, there are equipment compartments which are accessed via detachable hatches. Above the right-hand air intake there is an auxiliary intake for the air-conditioning system.

The twin-seat variants of the Su-25, i.e. the Su-25UB (Su-25UBK), Su-25UT (Su-28) and Su-25UTG, have a modified forward fuselage to accommodate the second crew-member, with a new cockpit and two separately hinged canopies. The angle of view of the pilot in the front cockpit is the same as on the single-seater – 17° in the forward and downward direction – while the angle of view for the rear seat crew-member is only 7° in the same direction. The height differential between the two seats is 440 mm (17.32 in). The rear cockpit is equipped with a forward-looking periscope to assist the pilot's vision on take-off and landing. The naval Su-25UTG has, in addition, an arrester hook with a special damping and retraction mechanism and a lateral mechanical stabilising bar which allows the hook to move either side of the central position without striking the fuselage. The rear fuselage primary structure was modified to accommodate the additional loads from the hook, and the rear fuselage was shortened slightly as a consequence of removing the brake parachute system, no longer required for the naval training role. The mid-section of the fuselage of the Su-25UT (Su-28) and the Su-25UTG has the armour plating protecting the underside of the collector tank replaced by aluminium alloys.

Wing and empennage. All versions of the Su-25 have an all-metal cantilever wing of moderate sweep and high aspect ratio, equipped with high-lift devices. The wingspan is 14.36 m (47.11 ft), aspect ratio is 6, area is 30.10 m² (324 ft²), leading-edge sweep is 19° 54' and dihedral angle is 2.5°. The wing consists of two cantilever sections, attached to a central torsion box forming a single unit with the fuselage. At the tips of each wing there are separate gondola-type fairings which house the airbrakes.

The wing torsion box absorbs all external loads and transmits them to the central torsion box. The wing is attached to the centre section by bolts and flanges along the contours of the inner wing rib. It consists of front and rear spars, upper and lower skin panels and ribs. The internal part of the torsion box, bounded by the spars and ribs, forms a hermetically sealed integral fuel tank, filled with polyurethane foam in order to increase the aircraft's combat survivability.

Each wing has five hardpoints for weapons carriage, with the attachment points mounted on load-bearing ribs and spars. The wing leading edge houses control rods for the ailerons, controls for the slats, wiring looms for the weapons pylons and other electrical services. The load-bearing assembly of the wing leading edge consists of the profiled nose section and upper and lower skin panels. Part of the leading-edge structure is designed to take the mountings for the guide

ABOVE: The cockpit canopy of the Su-25UB trainer has a more cumbersome framework than the single-seater, with additional strengthening frames to cope with additional aerodynamic loading over the larger cockpit aperture. Note the built-in 'blind-flying hood' in the front cockpit, to enable the pilot to carry out full instrument flight procedures in an authentic flight environment. The majority of combat trainer variants of Russian fighter aircraft incorporate such hoods (**shtorki**) and effectively compensate for the lack of flight simulators in the Soviet and Russian Air Forces. *(Yefim Gordon)*

Key to the Su-25's excellent airfield performance and combat manoeuvrability is the 'highly mechanised' wing of modified SR-16 profile. The inner and outer sections of the double-slotted flaps are interchangeable. *(Sukhoi Design Bureau)*

rails for the slats and absorb the loads introduced during their extension and retraction.

The rear torsion box houses the high-pressure pipes and tube assemblies of the hydraulic system which operates the flaps, airbrakes and ailerons. The load-bearing assembly of the rear torsion box consists of spacers and upper and lower skin panels. The hinge brackets of the flaps and ailerons are also mounted in the rear part of the torsion box.

Airbrakes are mounted at the wingtips in profiled gondola-type fairings. The airbrake panels are installed in the rear part of the fairing and are effectively an

Detail view of the four identical pylons for the carriage of offensive stores, with the smaller pylon for the self-defensive R-60 (AA-8 *Aphid*) missile outboard. The pylons make a convenient hanger for the pilot's seat harness. *(Yefim Gordon)*

extension of the fairing. The upper and lower brake panels are mechanically linked and open up and down to an angle of 55° for each panel and are hydraulically activated. The upper and lower main brake sections themselves have supplementary panels which are mechanically linked to the body of the airbrake fairing. On extension of the main airbrakes, the supplementary panels are also extended. When the main brakes are deployed to their full 55° the supplementary panels open up to an angle of 90° relative to the external surfaces of the main panels.

Each wing has a five-section leading-edge slat, a two-section flap and an aileron. The slat occupies the entire leading edge of the wing, and each section has two guide rails for attachment to the front of the forward wing spar. Slat operation is achieved by means of six actuating jacks. At the root of the third section of the leading-edge slat there is a projection following the contour of the slat's profile, which forms a 'tooth' on the leading edge. The structure of the slat consists of spacers (including load bearers, to which are attached the guide rails) and upper and lower skin surfaces. Sections of the slats are linked to each other by connector pins. Both sections of

the trailing-edge flaps on each wing are double-slotted and the inner and outer sections are interchangeable. The flaps are mounted on brackets on the rear spar on steel sliders and rollers. The load-bearing element of each flap section consists of a spar, two load-bearing rails, a load-bearing supporting rib, spacers and upper and lower skin surfaces. A fixed deflector is attached to the forward part of the flap.

The ailerons are of trapezoidal shape and are located near the wingtip. They have three hinge points and the load-bearing element consists of longerons, a spar, a false spar, a leading-edge and rib structure, upper and lower skin surfaces, plus leading-edge protector strips with mass balances. The mass balances are attached to the forward edge of the aileron.

The wing's main components have the following geometric characteristics: overall area of the flaps is 4.44 m^2 (47.80 ft^2), area of the leading edge slats is 2.6 m^2 (27.98 ft^2), area of the ailerons is 1.51 m^2 (16.25 ft^2) and the area of the wingtip airbrakes is 1.8 m^2 (19.59 ft^2). On the first series of aircraft the area of the wingtip airbrakes was 1.2 m^2 (12.92 ft^2).

INSET: Close-up of the wingtip airbrake fairing, showing the landing light and the anti-glare shield. The additional antenna in the middle of the fairing is non-standard (this aircraft being the T8-15 prototype), but has been installed on some of the Su-25T development aircraft and is believed to be part of the *Pastel'* electronic surveillance measures suite. *(Sukhoi Design Bureau)*

MAIN PIC: The unique wingtip airbrakes of the Su-25 seen in the fully open position, revealing this novel solution to providing a larger surface area without actually increasing the size of the brakes themselves. *(Sukhoi Design Bureau)*

The horizontal tailplane is a one-piece unit and has three selectable angle-of-incidence positions, dependent upon the flight regime, controlled by a hydraulic jack. The tailplane is attached at two mounting points to a load-bearing frame on the rear fuselage tail beam and has a 5° dihedral angle. The overall area of the tailplane is 6.47 m^2 (69.64 ft^2), while the area of the elevators is 1.88 m^2 (20.24 ft^2).

The longitudinal structure of the tailplane consists of two fixed spars, false spars and stringers. The transverse tailplane structure comprises normal and reinforced ribs. Tailplane hinge elements and drive rods are mounted on the reinforced ribs. Fixed leading-edge fairings are attached to the front spar of the tailplane. The elevators consist of two separate halves, connected via a universal joint shaft. A servo-compensator is mounted on each elevator and a trim tab is also mounted on the right elevator section. The elevator has aerodynamic compensation and mass balancing and is linked to the tailplane through an elevator horn mounted on the universal joint shaft, with a spring balance. Each elevator is attached to the tailplane by three suspension points. The trimmer and servo-compensator also have aerodynamic compensation and mass balancing.

The fin is constructed using a three-spar layout and carries the rudder and yaw damper. The fin comprises a central load-bearing structure, a leading edge and a dielectric tip. The longitudinal structure of the fin comprises three spars, false spars and stringers. The transverse structure consists of ribs, including a load-bearing rib at the junction of the dielectric fin-tip. The fin is attached to the fuselage at three points and is bolted to load-bearing frames. The leading-edge is detachable and is bolted to the forward load-bearing element of the fin. At the top of the fin, a navigation light is mounted under the dielectric tip. Elements of the 'Tester' flight data recorder are installed inside the fin structure. An air intake is mounted at the base of the fin to feed the generator cooling system. The rudder has aerodynamic and mass balancing and is attached to the fin at three hinge points. It has a trimmer, a servo-compensator and a yaw damper element and has balance weights mounted on the trailing edge. The overall area of the fin is 4.65 m² (50.05 ft²), while that of the rudder is 0.75 m² (8.07 ft²).

Undercarriage. The undercarriage is of tricycle layout, with the mainwheels attached to the central part of the fuselage, retracting forwards into wells in the air intake ducts. The nosewheel retracts backwards into a housing which lies just behind the cockpit area. The nosewheel leg is displaced slightly (50 mm/1.97 in) to the right of the central axis of the fuselage in order to facilitate the installation of the aircraft's built-in 30 mm cannon, which is mounted below the cockpit on the left side of the fuselage. The wheelbase, when the aircraft is parked, is 3.95 m (12.96 ft) and the track is 2.5 m (8.20 ft).

The mainwheel and nosewheel wells are fully covered by doors when the aircraft is in flight. Each main undercarriage unit has a KT-136D (**Kolyeso Tormoznoye**) wheel with integral braking, fitted with 840 × 360 mm (33 × 14 in) wide-profile tyres, while the nose unit has a KN-21 (**Kolyeso Netormoznoye**) unbraked wheel with a 660 × 200 mm (26 × 8 in) tyre. The levered suspension main undercarriage and the semi-levered nosewheel unit provide adequate shock

absorption of both vertical and side loads on the undercarriage. Nosewheel steering is employed to facilitate manoeuvring on the ground. A mudguard is fitted to the nosewheel to protect the engines from FOD ingestion during take-off, landing and while taxiing.

Powerplant. Early aircraft of the Su-25 family were equipped with two R95Sh non-afterburning turbojet engines, each developing 4,100 kgp (9,040 lb st) of static thrust at sea level, although from 1989 the R195 engine was introduced, which offered a thrust of 4,500 kgp (9,920 lb st), the two engine types being interchangeable. The engines are installed in separate compartments on either side of the rear fuselage, air being supplied via two cylindrical ducts which are fed by two oval-shaped subsonic, fixed-geometry air intakes. The gap between the front end of the engine and the end of the air intake duct is protected by a rubber sealing ring. The engines are mounted on load-bearing frames within the engine nacelles at two points, forward and rear. The forward attachment comprises three location points, consisting of two lateral link pins, adjustable in length, and an upper engine-mounting trunnion. The link pins absorb the vertical loads and the trunnion takes the longitudinal and lateral loads. The rear attachment point also comprises three location points and consists of two lateral link pins, adjustable in length, to absorb vertical loads, and an upper horizontal attachment pin to absorb lateral loads.

Cooling of the engines, sub-assemblies and surrounding fuselage structure from local heating is provided by air from the cooling air intakes on top of the engine nacelles, blown through the engine compartment at comparatively high speed and pressure when the aircraft is in flight. The air is expelled from the engine compartment through the annular slot formed between the engine nacelles and the exhaust nozzles.

A drainage system ensures that fuel, oil and hydraulic fluid residues can be collected after the engines are shut down after flight, or in the event of an unsuccessful start. The engine control system permits autonomous operation of each engine and comprises throttles mounted on a control panel on the left-hand side of the cockpit, throttle cables and cable support rollers, cable tensioners and auxiliary drive assemblies on the engines.

The lubrication system is of the closed-loop type, autonomous and intended to support the normal temperature criteria of the engines' rotating parts, as well as to guarantee reduction of wear and tear and of friction losses. The engine starting system provides for autonomous and automatic start-up of the engines and establishing stable running parameters after start-up. Engine starting on the ground can be carried out on the aircraft's internal battery or by using an airfield power source.

The fuel system guarantees properly sequenced fuel flow from the tanks to the engines at all power settings and in all flight regimes, regardless of the spatial orientation of the aircraft. The system includes the fuel tanks, sub-assemblies and fuel pipes for fuelling the aircraft on the ground, plus sub-assemblies and pipes for fuel delivery from the tanks to the engines. It also includes a system for fuel delivery in zero and negative g conditions, instruments for checking the working of the fuel system on the ground and in flight, plus sub-assemblies for creating over-pressure or drainage of the tanks, as required.

Fuel is carried in: two fuselage tanks, Tank No. 1 (forward) and Tank No. 2 (rear); in a tank in the wing centre-section, mounted above Tank No. 2; and in single wing tanks in each wing. There is, therefore, a total of five internal fuel tanks in the Su-25. Four auxiliary fuel tanks can also be mounted on underwing pylons. These can be 800-litre (176 imp gal) PTB-800 (*Podvesnoy Toplivny Bak*) or PTB-1150 of 1,150-litre (253 imp gal) capacity and are mounted singly or in pairs under each wing on the pylons nearest the fuselage. Number 2 Tank is the collector tank, located on the aircraft's centre of gravity. The fuselage and wing tanks are hermetically sealed and are integral elements of the structure of the aircraft's fuselage and wing.

On the lateral surfaces of Tanks Nos 1 and 2, separated from the air intake duct by a structural clearance between the lower surfaces of the centre-section tank and Tank No. 1, there is a special protective shield. This substantially reduces the leakage of fuel if the aircraft suffers bullet or shell damage and reduces the likelihood of fire. The double layer of protective material has a thickness of 20 mm (0.79 in). In order to provide a measure of protection from ballistic explosions in the fuselage, wing, centre section and underwing fuel tanks, the tanks are all filled with porous polyurethane foam. Polyurethane foam is also used to protect adjacent compartments from fire, which includes the areas alongside the first and second fuselage fuel tanks, the space around and between the air intake ducts and around and between the fuel tanks. Laying the polyurethane foam inside the tanks is performed via maintenance access hatches. The drainage and fuel pressurisation system supplies an over-pressure in the wing and fuselage tanks under all flight conditions. To

this end, all tanks are connected via drainage pipes fed by air under pressure from external air intakes, as well as the over-pressure system.

Filling the fuel tanks is achieved by two separate methods:

- centralised gravity filling;
- gravity filling using the filler nozzles of each tank.

Using the centralised gravity filling method, refuelling of the fuselage and wing tanks is carried out through the filler nozzle of Fuel Tank No. 1. The sequence of fuel consumption is determined by the requirement to maintain the centre of gravity within the design limits under all flight conditions. Since Tank No. 2 is the collector tank, it is emptied last and is kept full at all engine operating settings by virtue of pumping fuel from the fuselage and wing tanks. Fuel is pumped to the engines by three different means:

- from Tank No. 2 under all flight conditions, when there is no indication of zero or negative g conditions;
- delivery from the accumulator (collector) tank when operating under zero or negative g conditions;
- by gravity flow through non-return valves in the case of pump failure.

The capacity of the accumulator tank is sufficient to guarantee 5–15 seconds of fuel delivery under zero or negative g conditions. Under normal operating conditions, the accumulator tank is full of fuel. Fuel from the wing tanks is pumped to the collector tank by a jet pump.

The overall capacity of the fuel system of the Su-25 is 3,660 litres (805 imp gal), but the maximum fuel weight in the internal tanks differs according to the aircraft variant, and for the Su-25, Su-25K and Su-25BM is 3,000 kg (6,614 lb). It is 2,750 kg (6,063 lb) for the twin-seat Su-25UB, Su-25UBK and Su-25UT, and 2,850 kg (6,283 lb) for the twin-seat naval Su-25UTG.

Fuel transfer from the underwing tanks is achieved by over-pressure, and fuel from these tanks is consumed first. The underwing tanks are constructed in the form of a cylindrical casing, reinforced by frames which are electrowelded to the casing. In order to improve their transportability and for ease of storage, the underwing tanks are made of three detachable sections, a nose section, a mid-section and a tail section, joined by bolted attachment rings. The tail section of each underwing tank is fitted with a stabiliser, consisting of two small horizontal winglets. The central part

Although not as formidable a weapon as the A-10's GAU-8 Avenger, the Su-25's 30 mm GSh-30 cannon is accurate and hard hitting. The paintwork in the vicinity of the barrels appears to have been affected by gun gas erosion, but the aircraft structure is protected from acoustic fatigue damage during weapon firing by the use of titanium reinforcing plates attached to the skin. This is an early-model Su-25, as evidenced by the two-piece muzzle assembly. *(Yefim Gordon)*

of the underwing fuel tank is load-bearing and contains the suspension lugs which attach to the wing pylons and also contains the fuel feed pipe from the tank to the aircraft's main fuel system. The Su-25UT (Su-28) and Su-25UTG differ from the basic Su-25 and Su-25UB by the absence of armour plating between the engines, while some elements of the fuel system have been removed from the Su-25UT (Su-28). A balance weight replaces the removed components in order to restore the aircraft's centre of gravity to its normal locus.

Armament. The cannon armament of the Su-25 (Su-25K), Su-25UB (Su-25UBK) and Su-25BM (Su-25BMK) consists of a fixed built-in Gryazev and Shipunov GSh-30 30 mm cannon, which has a rate of fire of 3,000 rounds per minute. The ammunition box holds 250 rounds. The cannon is mainly intended for the destruction of lightly armoured targets such as, for example, armoured personnel carriers. The weapon is mounted in the nose of the aircraft under the cockpit area, offset to the right. Apart from the built-in cannon, it is also possible to mount SPPU-22 paired 23 mm gun pods on the underwing pylons, the barrels of this weapon being depressible to an angle of 30° and each gun having a total of 260 rounds.

External armament is carried on five hardpoints under each wing of the Su-25. Eight of the total of ten suspension points have interchangeable weapons attachments, each capable of carrying all types of bombs and unguided rockets up to a weight of 500 kg (1,100 lb). For self-defence, a single R-60 (AA-8 *Aphid*) short-range air-to-air missile can be carried on each of the two outermost underwing pylons.

Unguided bomb armament of the Su-25 consists of standard aviation bombs of calibres from 100 to 500 kg

(220–1,100 lb), KMGU (*Konteiner Malogabaritnykh Gruzov Unifitsirovanny*) pods, 250 kg (550 lb) RBK (*Razovaya Bombovaya Kasseta*) cluster bombs and incendiary (napalm) bombs. Unguided rockets of various calibres can also be used by the Su-25, including 130 mm rockets in B-13 pods, 85 mm S-8 rockets in B-8M-1 pods and 340 mm S-25 rockets mounted in O-25 containers. The aircraft can also carry air-to-surface guided missiles, the principal type being the Kh-25 (AS-14 *Kedge*). The following is the complete list of the weapons normally used on the Su-25:

- up to two KAB-500Kr TV-guided 'smart bombs';
- up to ten AB-100 or AB-250 bombs;
- up to eight AB-500 bombs;
- up to eight RBK-250 or RBK-500 cluster bombs;
- up to eight KMGU pods
- up to eight ZB-500 napalm tanks;
- up to four Kh-25ML (AS-14 *Kedge*) laser-guided ASMs;
- up to eight B-8M-1 rocket pods with S-8KOM (*Kumulyativno-oskolochny*) cumulative charge or S-8T (*Tankovy*) anti-tank rockets (a total of 160 rockets);
- up to eight B-13 pods with S-13OF (*Oskolochno-fugasny*) fragmenting high-explosive rockets or S-13T (*Tankovy, oskolochno-pronikayushchiy*) anti-tank fragmenting/penetrating rockets, the number of rockets in each pod being five, giving a maximum total of 40 rockets in eight pods;
- up to eight unguided S-24B or S-240OFM 240 mm high-explosive fragmentation rockets;
- two SPPU-22 detachable cannon pods with a GSh-23L twin-barrelled cannon (rate of fire 3,400 rounds

A typical weapons load of four B-8M-1 80 mm rocket pods and a single R-60 (AA-8 *Aphid*) air-to-air missile. The Russian Air Force is still an enthusiastic user of unguided rockets for air-to-ground attacks, and this load of 160 80 mm rockets would have a devastating effect on 'soft' targets on the battlefield. *(Yefim Gordon)*

per minute, 260 rounds per pod. Barrels can be depressed up to 30° in the forward hemisphere and 23° when firing to the rear);
• up to two R-60 (AA-8 *Aphid*) short-range air-to-air missiles for self-protection.

The normal combat payload of the Su-25 is 1,400 kg (3,086 lb), while the maximum load is up to 4,400 kg (9,700 lb).

The Su-25UT (Su-28) and Su-25UTG differ from the single-seat combat and twin-seat combat training variants by the absence of the cannon installation and weapons pylons. The cannon mounting bay is skinned over on the pure training variants.

The specialised target-towing Su-25BM variant dispenses with the standard armament of the combat version in favour of the target systems generic to its role. The Su-25BM can carry a ***Kometa*** (Comet) towed target, PM-6 (***Pikiruyushchaya Mishen***) gliding targets and M-6 infra-red heat-source targets which have a slow descent profile incorporating a parachute mechanism. Four PM-6 targets can be carried simultaneously on the Su-25BM/Su-25BMK, on the second and fourth underwing pylons of each wing, reading outwards from the fuselage. When the ***Kometa*** target and its associated winch pod is mounted on the aircraft, an

aerodynamic counterbalance is carried under the opposite wing, the ***Kometa*** target and winch mechanism being mounted on the third wing pylon outboard of the fuselage, usually under the port wing. When using the ***Kometa*** and PM-6 targets, the Su-25BM/Su-25BMK can carry two PTB-1150 auxiliary fuel tanks on the inboard pylons, to increase range and/or endurance, although the number of PM-6 targets that can be carried is reduced to two in this configuration.

Equipment. The avionics equipment installed on the Su-25 (Su-25K) consists of the following:

• a weapons-aiming system which provides targeting data for attacks on ground targets, using rockets, bombs and cannon armament, as well as targeting of aircraft and helicopters with rockets and cannon in visual flight conditions; the sighting unit comprises the ASP-17BTs-8 (***Aviatsionny strelkovo-bombardirovochny pritsel***) weapons sight (which permits the automatic calculation of the ballistic profile of all classes of weapons used by the Su-25) and the ***Klyon-PS*** (Maple-PS) laser-designator and distance-measuring system;
• a navigation complex which permits flight in day and night conditions, both in VMC (visual meteorological conditions) and IMC (instrument meteorological

conditions), and which inputs navigation and flight data into the weapons-aiming system and the aircraft's flight instruments;
- radios for air-to-ground communications and communications with other aircraft;
- a weapons control system;
- a self-defence suite, incorporating infra-red flare and chaff dispensers, capable of launching up to 256 flares and dipole chaff, plus an SPO-15 **Beryoza** (Birch) radar warning receiver (RWR).

The navigation system comprises the KN23-1 navigation complex, including:

- the KN-23-1 navigation complex, including;
- an IKV-1 inertial navigation unit;
- an RSBN-6S short-range navigation system;
- a DISS-7 Doppler navigator providing ground speed and drift measurement;
- an ARK15M automatic radio compass;
- an A-031 radio-altimeter;
- a UUAP-72 angle-of-attack indicator and accelerometer;
- an SVS-1-72-18 air data computer system.

The radio communications system comprises:

- an R-862 transmitter-receiver;
- an R-828 low-VHF transmitter-receiver for communication with ground forces;
- IFF;
- an MRP-56P marker-receiver;
- an SO-69 transponder.

The avionics equipment of the twin-seat Su-25UB (Su-25UBK), Su-25UT (Su-28) and Su-25UTG differs from the single-seater both in its application and composition. In the main, these differences relate to the presence of a second crew-member in the cockpit. A capability for inputting simulated equipment failures was introduced for the instructor in the rear cockpit who can select specific malfunctions to be displayed to the student in the front cockpit. The instructor's cockpit is provided with an override and warning indicator system, through which he can monitor the actions of the student and where necessary can switch control from the first cockpit (student) to the second (instructor).

The aircraft has an intercom system enabling two-way conversation between the two crew-members, plus a cockpit voice recorder which is intended to record the crew's intercom and radio conversations.

A view showing the window of the **Klyon-PS** laser rangefinder and marked target seeker. To the right of the window is the main pitot tube with the rather complex antenna array of the RSBN short-range navigation and ILS system. To the left of the window is the secondary, or standby, dynamic pressure probe. *(Yefim Gordon)*

The equipment layout of the twin-seat variants is partially altered with respect to the single-seat Su-25s, mainly in the nose section of the aircraft and in the dorsal fairing, and the central warning panel is duplicated in each cockpit.

The Su-25T (Su-28) and Su-25UTG differ from the basic Su-25UB (Su-25UBK) by the absence of the following equipment:

- weapons aiming sights;
- weapons control panel;
- the R-828 low-VHF FM radio;
- the **Beryoza** RWR.

Blanking panels are installed in the cockpits of the Su-25UT (Su-28) and Su-25UTG to cover the empty spaces left by removal of combat-related control panels. The airframes of these trainer variants also have blanking panels over the location of the laser-designator window, as well as over the area occupied by the radar warning receiver antennas on the combat variants.

On the Su-25BM target-towing variant, a system for the operation and monitoring of the winch and deployment and retraction of the **Kometa** target has been installed.

All variants of the Su-25 are equipped with the *Tester* flight data recorder system.

Visible under the rear fuselage is the handle-shaped antenna for the R-828 FM radio set used to communicate with troops on the ground. The radio operates in the standard 30-88 MHz range of many Russian combat sets and is normally used over short ranges and in line-of-sight. Also visible is detail of the combined rudder and yaw damper, the latter comprising the upper section of the split rudder. *(Yefim Gordon)*

Flight control system. The flight control system of the Su-25 consists of the normal three-axis controls common to all conventional aircraft. These comprise foot-operated rudder pedals, aileron and elevator control via a standard control column, three-axis trimmers, servo-compensators, an adjustable all-moving tailplane, flaps, slats and electrically actuated airbrakes.

To reduce loads on the control column, a spring-loaded servo-compensator is installed in the longitudinal control circuit, while a hydraulic booster performs this function in the roll channel. The ailerons have an electromechanical trim system to relieve loads on the control column in the rolling axis, while the rudder has a kinematic servo-compensator to reduce loads on the rudder pedals. Input forces to and from the control column and rudder pedals are transmitted directly via a system of control rods and bellcranks. Loads from the ailerons are not transmitted to the control column, these being taken up by a hydraulic actuator, which fully absorbs the pivoting moment arising from aerodynamic loads on the ailerons. The aileron control circuit contains a spring loading mechanism to simulate the loading on the control column, changing the loading on the stick as a function of the angle of deflection of the ailerons.

The elevator control linkage is duplicated and carried along each side of the fuselage in order to increase the aircraft's combat survivability.

The twin-seat variants of the Su-25 each have duplicated controls in the instructor's cockpit.

Hydraulic system. The hydraulic system of the Su-25 consists of two circuits which are totally independent of each other.

The primary hydraulic system provides control of the nosewheel steering, retraction and extension of the airbrakes, extension and retraction of the leading-edge slats and trailing-edge flaps, control of the position of the all-moving tailplane, control of the ailerons, emergency lowering of the undercarriage, automatic braking of the mainwheels during undercarriage retraction and emergency braking of the main undercarriage wheels.

The secondary hydraulic system provides main undercarriage extension and retraction, main undercarriage braking, control of the ailerons and control of the nosewheel steering.

Each hydraulic system has its own pressurisation source, pumps, jacks, pipes and reservoir tanks. The pressure in the hydraulic system is 210 kg/cm^2 (3,000 lb/in^2) and both systems are pressurised from accumulator tanks.

Air conditioning system. The aircraft's air conditioning system provides the following:

- the required operating environment for the pilot (or pilot and student in the training variants), including the optimum pressurisation and temperature values;
- cabin ventilation;
- prevention of condensation on the inside of the cockpit transparencies;

- the required temperature in the avionics bays of the aircraft.

Additionally, air from the conditioning system is used to supply the anti-*g* suits of the pilot (and crew of the twin-seat variants) and ventilation of their flight clothing. The air supplied for these functions is tapped from the last compressor stages of the engine and cooled in a heat exchanger.

Fire extinguishing system. The aircraft has two fire warning systems, one in each engine compartment. The fire warning indication comprises an actuating unit and two groups of sensors which are linked to it, with fire-warning indicators on the main instrument panel in the cockpit. There are two fire extinguishers and the associated distributing manifolds for the extinguishant. The fire extinguishers are mounted in each engine compartment and the spray manifolds and associated pipes are installed around the frames of the engine bay structure.

Emergency escape system. The Zvezda K-36L ejection seat is installed in the Su-25, two such units being installed in the twin-seat variants. The K-36L guarantees safe ejection of the pilot at speeds up to 1,000 km/h (540 kt) at all normal operational altitudes, including the take-off and landing phase. In flight, the pilot is held in the seat by an individual harness system, and fully variable adjustment for a pilot's height provides a comfortable seating position in the cockpit and good visibility outside. The pilot is protected from *g*-forces and dynamic air loads during ejection by high-altitude flight clothing and a protective helmet, a fixed position in the seat and the K-36's aerodynamic stabilisation system. The ejection sequence is initiated by pulling the seat pan handles, after which all of the seat's own systems and the aircraft's cockpit canopy jettison mechanism work automatically, in synchrony, right up to the moment of deployment of the pilot's parachute and separation of the pilot from the seat. The pilot's survival after landing, or coming down

Viewed from above, the cockpit of the *Frogfoot* trainer, here a naval Su-25UTG, is quite narrow, dominated by the bulky but highly reliable Zvezda K-36L ejection seat. *(Sukhoi Design Bureau)*

on the sea or other water surface, is assisted by equipment and supplies contained in his NAZ (*Noseemyy Avariynyy Zapas*) individual survival pack, which translates literally as 'portable emergency kit'. The NAZ is installed in the seat but attached to the pilot's parachute harness, and separates from the seat at the same time as the pilot, hanging slightly below the level of his feet during the descent. Cockpit canopy jettison can be accomplished either by actuating the ejection handle on the K-36L seat, or by using the autonomous jettison handle. Operation of the hinged, opening section of the canopy is carried out using two separate methods – 'Normal' and 'Emergency'. The twin-seat variants of the Su-25 have canopy jettison and ejection sequences designed to take account of the presence of the second crew-member.

Oxygen system. The oxygen system of the Su-25 comprises a main supply and a seat-mounted unit.

The main oxygen system consists of an oxygen regulator, plus oxygen bottles and fittings, and is intended to supply the pilot with oxygen during flights at all altitudes within the operating capability of the aircraft. The on-board oxygen reserve of the main system is contained in four 5-litre (1.32 gal) bottles in gaseous form, at a pressure of 150 atmospheres (2,205 lb/in²). Oxygen is delivered to the pilot's oxygen mask under normal conditions via an individual regulator in his aircrew equipment assembly, once a height of 2,000 m (6,560 ft) has been reached.

The seat-mounted oxygen system consists of a bottled oxygen supply, pipes and connections and selectors for automatic and manual supply. The system is intended to supply the pilot with oxygen during the ejection sequence at high altitude and subsequent descent. It can also be used in the event of failure of the main system and to permit underwater breathing after landing on water (and remaining afloat) for a period of three minutes after switching the supply on.

The oxygen system of the twin-seat Su-25s is designed to cater for the presence of the second crew-member.

Field maintenance. Since the aircraft had been designed with ease of maintenance in mind, for operation from austere sites, the project team had also developed a special field maintenance kit for the Su-25, capable of sustaining autonomous operations by a flight of four aircraft for a period of five days. The anticipated scenario was that the flight would deploy to a forward operating location (FOL) which had already been surveyed and supplied with fuel and ammunition, either by airdrop, helicopter or vehicle delivery. The

Su-25s themselves would be equipped with a set of four special pods, based on the design of the PTB-800 drop tank and mounted in place of the fuel tanks on the underwing pylons. The whole system was called AMK-8 (*Aeromobilnyy Kompleks Samolyota [T]8*, meaning, literally, the 'airmobile complex for the T8 aircraft', i.e. Su-25). Each pod was given a separate designation, pod K-1E being designed to carry environmental covers for the cockpit, engine blanks, wheel chocks, crew chief's toolkit, a folding ladder, an electrically powered winch for weapons loading and a set of tools and essential spares. The latter is referred to by Air Force personnel as ZIP (*Zapchasti, Instrument i Prinadlezhnost'*, the first word meaning 'spare parts', while the second and third words describe two different standards of tool sets). The second pod, K-2D (*Dozapravshchik*, or 'refueller'), carried a fuel pump capable of refuelling the aircraft from any appropriate container, plus cans of oil, hydraulic fluid and oxygen bottles.

Pod K-3 was the GPU (ground power unit), equipped with a small gas-turbine engine, driving a generator, which provided sufficient electrical power to run all essential systems for pre- and post-flight checks, start the engines and also power the electromechanical weapons-loading winch. The fourth pod of the AMK-8 set was the K-4KPA (*Kontrol'no-Proverochnaya Apparatura*, or test equipment pod) for checking the Su-25's main systems. During the project definition stage, the Sukhoi designers also proposed a fifth pod, intended to carry an aircraft technician, although they considered that this would only ever be used in time of war and he would not, therefore, be provided with a personal survival parachute. The 'customer' (i.e. the Soviet Air Force) insisted on the provision of a separate survival capability for the technician, but neither side was able to come to an acceptable agreement about this issue, and work on the fifth pod was discontinued. Although this might seem to have been a rather bizarre concept, it was to be taken up again in the mid-1990s by Avpro in the United Kingdom, who designed the EXINT (Extraction/Insertion) pod for use on the Boeing Apache helicopter and the Harrier V/STOL fighter. Avpro obtained clearance in 2000 for the transport of cargo in the EXINT pod, but clearance for the carriage of personnel is still awaited and the project is currently believed to be 'in suspension' (!). The four-pod AMK-8 maintenance support system, however, was built and successfully completed factory and special State trials, but was not put into production because the Tbilisi plant lacked spare capacity owing to its commitment to the manufacture of the Su-25 itself.

5

Su-25 Operators

FOR many years, the former Soviet Union had been involved in the export of military equipment, with aviation materiel and aircraft heading the 'league table'. The Su-25, which had gained a strong reputation from its use in the Afghan conflict, figured largely among the types sold to a number of 'friendly' foreign states. Only two variants were ever offered for export, the single-seat Su-25K and the twin-seat Su-25UBK combat trainer. However, following the break-up of the Soviet Union, the standard 'Soviet'-configured Su-25 was also acquired by a number of the former component republics of the Soviet Union, these aircraft being virtually identical to those operated by the newly reorganised Air Force of the Russian Federation.

The Su-25s delivered to many of the countries listed here are still operated by their air forces and are held in high regard by their pilots.

Russian Federation

According to data provided by the Russian side during the talks in Paris in 1990 leading to the Treaty on Conventional Armed Forces in Europe, there were 385 Su-25s in the European part of the former Soviet Union in October 1990. After the collapse of the Union, some of these aircraft remained in the old constituent republics, forming the core of their newly independent air forces.

Today, the Russian Federation (Russia) possesses a reduced fleet of Su-25s which are operated by Shturmovoi (Assault) Regiments based in a number of different regions of the country. The major variants used are the single-seat Su-25, the twin-seat Su-25UB and the Su-25BM target-towing version, the latter generally used as a pure attack aircraft, rather than in its designed role. In addition, the Russian Air Force also received a small number of Su-25T dedicated anti-tank variants for trials and evaluation, which have been tested with notable success in real combat situations in Chechnya. The Su-25 is also operated by the Russian Navy, both in standard land-based Su-25 and Su-25UB guise, as well as in the

specialised Su-25UTG role as a carrier-operable trainer.

The most combat-ready units are considered to be those based in southern Russia in the North Caucasus region, plus the regiment based at Buturlinovka in central Russia, between Voronezh and Saratov. The most experienced Su-25 pilots are to be found in the 4th Combat Application and Aircrew Conversion Centre at Lipetsk in central Russia and at the Russian Air Force Flight-Test Centre at Akhtubinsk in the Astrakhan region, some 1,300 km (800 miles) to the south-east of Moscow.

Overall, the number of Su-25s in current service with the Russian Air Force is thought to be around 180 aircraft, with a further fifty aircraft operated by Russian Naval Aviation.

Known Russian Navy Su-25s			
Side Number	C/n	Variant	Notes
08 Blue		Su-25UTG	Prototype
07 Red		Su-25UTG	
08 Red		Su-25UTG	
11 Red		Su-25UTG	
12 Red		Su-25UTG	
14 Red		Su-25UTG	
15 Red		Su-25UTG	
16 Red		Su-25UTG	

Afghanistan

It is believed that small numbers of Su-25s were handed over to Afghanistan by the Soviet Union in the period 1986–1990 and in open-source newspaper reporting the number varied between twelve and sixty aircraft. The actual number of Su-25s acquired by Afghanistan has never been established, nor indeed whether any remain in Afghan Air Force service. Since no evidence of Afghan operation of the Su-25 has emerged during recent allied operations related to the ousting of the Taleban regime in Afghanistan, it is likely that the *Frogfoot* was never actually acquired by the country.

Angola

An agreement was reached at the beginning of 1988 between the Soviet Union and Angola for the delivery of a squadron of Su-25s, comprising twelve single-seat Su-25Ks and two Su-25UBK trainers. Later, these numbers were augmented by at least a further three two-seaters. Up to this time, for a period of around fourteen years, a major civil war had been raging in this former Portuguese colony, and the country had been effectively divided into two separate factions. One was controlled by the pro-Communist regime of José Eduardo dos Santos and the other by elements of the UNITA organisation, led by Dr Jonas Savimbi. (UNITA stands for União Nacional para la Independencia Total de Angola, or National Union for the Total Independence of Angola.) With the aid of Soviet weapons deliveries and the use of Cuban military personnel, the government was able to gain control of the central region of the country, while the UNITA rebels were driven into the provinces. From their new provincial 'bases', the latter were able to conduct a successful partisan war against government forces. The struggle to control these rebel groups, who skilfully exploited the natural cover of the African bush lands of Angola, required round-the-clock support from the air, providing reconnaissance, resupply with weapons and food and the conduct of tactical air strikes on rebel groups and their camps. The government forces had decided to rely heavily on the use of air assets, hoping to achieve a decisive turning point in the long-standing confrontation. In the opinion of the chief military adviser to the Soviet Military Mission in Angola, Lieutenant-General Pyotr Gusyev, 1989 was to be marked as a turning point in the war. The Su-25 was to be brought into the conflict as a 'Weapon of Victory', along with armoured vehicles, tanks and artillery, plus the legendary Mi-24 *Hind*, which had acquired such a fearsome reputation in counter-insurgency operations in other parts of the world.

The delivery of Su-25s to Angola was achieved relatively quickly – the Tbilisi factory was, at the time, turning out six to eight aircraft per month, and by March 1988, all the Su-25s had been crated up for delivery by sea from the port of Novorossiisk to Luanda. The particular export variant for Angola differed from standard in the provision of certain 'tropicalised' items of equipment, including some of the avionics. For example, all the Angolan aircraft had the old SRO-2 *Odd Rods* IFF system, instead of the later **Parol'** (Password) fitted to later Russian Su-25s, and they were not capable of launching guided missiles or precision guided bombs.

A group of Russian specialist air- and groundcrews was formed in the Soviet Union to assist the Angolans to master the Su-25. The fourteen-man group included three pilots and a team of technicians and engineers from the 80th Independent Shturmovoi Air Regiment

(**80-y Otdyel'nyy Shturmovoy Aviapolk – OShAP**) based at Sital-Chai, on the edge of the Caspian Sea, as well as from 90 OshAP, based at Artsiz (now Artsyz) in the Odessa region of the Ukraine. At the time, the latter was in the process of disbanding. Major Rafis Gumyerov was appointed Commanding Officer of the group, with Major Leonid Chernov as Flight Planning Navigator (**Shturman Programmist**) and Captain Vladimir Kornyev as Flight Commander. The engineering support team was led by Major Viktor Yesik. All members of the training support group were experienced Afghan veterans.

The selection of the members of this group was well founded, and it would have been difficult to find anyone to equal these officers in terms of their knowledge of the Su-25, or active combat experience. The two above-mentioned regiments were the first to acquire the Su-25, and the pilots selected for the Angolan mission had carried out the type's initial proving trials in squadron service. Their early experience on type had also been exploited to form the famed 'Afghan' 378 OshAP, through which all Su-25 pilots assigned to the Afghan theatre had had to pass.

On 26 November 1988, a Boeing 707 of the Angolan airline TAAG was used to deliver the group to Luanda. The operating base selected for the Su-25 was situated near the port of Namibe, some 170 km (105 miles) from the border with the South-African-administered territory of Namibia. (In 1990 the territory achieved independence from South Africa, to become the Republic of Namibia.) Already based at Namibe was the 26th Fighter-Bomber Regiment of the Angolan Air Force, equipped with the MiG-21MF *Fishbed-J*, plus the Su-22M4K *Fitter-K* and Su-22UM3K *Fitter-G* export variants of the ubiquitous Sukhoi ground-attack fighter. The Su-25 was to form the third squadron of this composite regiment. Also based here was a squadron of Cuban MiG-23ML *Flogger-G* interceptors, deployed to provide air cover for the southern region of Angola.

Conversion courses were organised at Namibe to train Angolan Air Force technical personnel, and as they generally had a fairly good command of the Russian language they had mastered the main servicing tasks for the Su-25, and some simple repair work, by February 1989. By this time, and after various delays, the Su-25s themselves were finally assembled. Assembly and test-flying of the aircraft was carried out by teams from Tbilisi (for the Su-25) and from Ulan-Ude (for the two-seat Su-25UBK).

After familiarisation flights on the two Su-25UBK '*sparki*', the Angolan students went on to general aircraft handling, navigation training, formation and group flying and were introduced to weapons application. By August 1989, two flights of the new squadron were ready for solo flying, but basic training continued up to the autumn of the following year, since the Angolans did not show any special desire to get involved in combat. The low qualification level of the Angolan pilots was soon to show itself, and three of the Su-25s fell victim to the actions of their own pilots. Surprisingly, these accidents did not occur on landing, as might be expected, but during take-off. (Because the aircraft had a short wheelbase and narrow track and had a tendency to skid, or dip a wing during hard braking, the Su-25 was quite difficult to handle on the runway and required a particular skill during the ground run.) In February 1990, one Angolan pilot decided to raise the undercarriage before he had reached take-off speed; the nosewheel 'dutifully' retracted into the wheel well, the aircraft dug its nose into the runway, and having scraped the cannon along the full length of the concrete strip, ran off the end and exploded. Three months later, two other Angolan 'aces', taking off in a pair and having scarcely got airborne, started to perform a banking turn, wingtip to wingtip. The aircraft collided, breaking up in mid-air, and crashed on the edge of the airfield. In all three cases the pilots were lucky to escape with their lives, managing to eject just in time. In the first accident the pilot ejected on the ground only seconds before the aircraft exploded, while the two who collided in mid-air ejected at very low level. One punched out as soon as he felt the jolt of his wingman and the other ejected as his aircraft, which had lost a wing, started tumbling sideways.

By October 1990, the Su-25 squadron had flown a total of around 1,500 hours. Only one flight had completely mastered the weapon's application phase of training on the aircraft, including the Squadron Commander, Captain Jaime. Bombing and air-to-ground gunnery were practised not far from the airfield at a range situated about 7 km (just over 4 miles) north of Namibe, where targets were made out of old automobile tyres and burned-out vehicles dragged off the highway.

In order to augment its air force, Angola received fourteen brand-new Su-22M4K *Fitter-K* and Su-22UM3K *Fitter-G* fighter-bombers from the USSR in the spring of 1990. They replaced the MiG-21MF *Fishbed-J*s formerly based at Namibe, but later transferred to Lubango, after which the regiment at Namibe became a purely ground-attack regiment.

It was decided to involve the regiment in operations which had been planned to take place in the summer of 1990. The UNITA rebels had undertaken a number of successful raids in the central provinces of Angola and in the vicinity of the capital Luanda, and the Angolan military leadership thought that it was now time for the Su-25s to become involved in the 'war'. They decided to set the Su-25 the task of destroying rebel positions with heavy assault strikes against their deployed groups and bases, to clear the way for the advance of government forces. It was further decided that the Su-22M4Ks and MiG-21MFs should operate from the forward base at Minonge, supporting operations on the eastern front. A flight of Su-25s was deployed to a base near Luanda, with everything needed for their operations, including spares, weapons and ammunition, being flown from Namibe by chartered Lockheed C-130s or Air Force Antonov An-26 transport aircraft, when required.

The Angolan pilots prudently maintained a safe altitude when conducting combat sorties, flying no lower than 5,000–7,000 m (16,500–23,000 ft) and avoiding diving in order not to be picked off by ground anti-aircraft fire. Bombing raids involved the use of OFAB-100-120 and OFAB-250-270 high-explosive fragmentation bombs and RBK-500 cluster bombs loaded with small-calibre fragmentation bomblets. When conducting attacks on road-vehicle convoys, UNITA rebel camps and settlements occupied by guerrillas, the Su-25s sometimes employed 57 mm unguided rockets launched from UB-32-57 pods. Angolan use of the Su-25 was contrary to the recommended procedures defined in the Soviet 'Manual for the use of "Shturmovoi" (Assault) Aviation', and it turned out that the manoeuvrability, accuracy of weapons delivery and striking power of the aircraft, so essential in this particular combat situation, was not actually exploited. Even worse, in the opinion of the Angolan pilots the Su-25 was inferior to the high-speed 'MiGs', which were capable of unloading their bombs and disappearing from danger in a matter of seconds. It was not so much a question of the aircraft's combat effectiveness, but rather of the preparedness for combat of the Angolan pilots themselves. After having flown twenty-five combat sorties in a month, the Angolans refused to take part in any further combat activity, flew the Su-25s back to Luanda Airport and stayed there.

In October 1990, some of the Soviet pilots and the majority of the technical personnel were rotated, but their actual work level was also reduced. After the unsuccessful 'trial' of the Su-25 in the abortive Luanda operation, the Angolan Air Force practically ceased to involve the type in combat operations at all. The Angolan pilots flew very little, and as a result quickly lost even the not particularly high level of flying competence which they had accumulated over the past months. A gradual reduction in the size of the Soviet advisory group in Angola began from around December 1990. By March 1991, flying activity on the Su-25 squadron had ceased and the aircraft were left unprotected, to rust in the humid climate. Also by this time, the Cuban contingent had left the country, and President dos Santos, who had been unable to deal with his opponents by military means, also declared his 'disillusionment with, and condemnation of Marxism'. The Su-25 did not take any further part in military operations and did not even fly after this time. However, a little later, Angola acquired an additional batch of Su-25s, both to augment its inventory of combat aircraft and for the training of pilots of the Angolan Air Force.

The following serial numbers are known for Angolan Air Force Su-25s:

Side Number	C/n	Variant	Notes
B-600		Su-25K	
B-601		Su-25K	
B-603		Su-25K	
B-604		Su-25K	
B-605(?)		Su-25K	
B-606		Su-25K	
B-608		Su-25K	
B-609		Su-25K	
B-610		Su-25K	
I-40		Su-25UBK	
I-41		Su-25UBK	
I-44		Su-25UBK	
I-45		Su-25UBK	
I-48		Su-25UBK	

Armenia

Following the break-up of the Soviet Union, Armenia had no Su-25s in its inventory, but after the start of the conflict in Nagorno-Karabakh in 1991–2, the newly independent Republic of Armenia 'unofficially' acquired a small number of aircraft (believed to be four or five single-seaters and two Su-25UBs). These aircraft were organised into a single flight, and one aircraft is known to have been shot down during combat operations. (Nagorno-Karabakh is a disputed region inside Azerbaijan with a majority Armenian population. The two main nationalities are divided on religious grounds. The Karabakhi Armenians say that they are prepared to be part of Azerbaijan, providing they have 'horizontal' links with the Azeri government in Baku. The Azeris want an unconditional return of all occupied areas of Azerbaijan and refuse to talk directly to the Karabakhi Armenians. A stalemate exists at the present time.)

Azerbaijan

Like Armenia, Azerbaijan did not inherit any Su-25s after the break-up of the Soviet Union, but a single aircraft was obtained in April 1992, as the consequence of a pilot defecting from the Russian Air Force base at Sital-Chai. Later, this republic acquired at least five Su-25s through 'secret channels', although one aircraft is known to have been obtained as the result of yet another defection, this time from the Georgian Air Force. Other Su-25s must have been acquired later, since at the beginning of 2001 the Azerbaijan Air Force still had three of the type in its inventory, although it is believed that around four Su-25s had been shot down in combat operations against Armenia relating to Nagorno-Karabakh.

Belarus'

Following the collapse of the Soviet Union, the newly independent Republic of Belarus' became the second member state of the Commonwealth of Independent States (CIS), after the Russian Federation, to possess a significant number of Su-25s. Information varies widely on the actual number of Su-25s on the Belarus' inventory. According to one official source (for 1996), two independent 'shturmovoi' regiments remained on the territory of Belarus' at the time of the creation of the CIS: 206 OShAP at Lida and 378 OShAP at Pastavy (i.e. the slightly different Byelorussian spelling of the former Russian base at Postavy). The 1996 figures claimed forty-four Su-25 *Frogfoot-A*s and six Su-25UB *Frogfoot-B*s at Lida, while at Pastavy there were forty-three Su-25s and four Su-25UBs. Currently available information confirms that all the Su-25s remaining in Belarus' are concentrated at Lida air base, forming a dedicated 'shturmovoi' group, with a total of eighty-one Su-25 *Frogfoot-*

As and nineteen Su-25UB *Frogfoot-B* two-seaters. Under the restructured organisation of the Belarus' Air Force, the Su-25 unit at Lida is designated **206 Shturmovaya Aviabaza** (206 Attack Air Base) and comprises elements of 206 OShAP from Lida itself, 378 OShAP from Pastavy and 397 OShAP from Kobrin. Belarus' also retained the 558th Aviation Repair Plant in Baranovichi, which carries out major overhauls on the Su-25. Recently, the 558th Repair Plant has also developed a special SEAD (Suppression of Enemy Air Defences) package for the Su-25UB, which incorporates a small rectangular pod mounted on the under-fuselage centre-line pylon. The pod, designated KRK-UP, is the targeting interface for the Kh-58 (AS-11 *Kilter*) anti-radiation missile selected for this role and contains the L-150 *Pastel'* electronic surveillance measures (ESM) system which is used to identify and locate appropriate radiating targets. Also located in the pod is the launch-control equipment for the Kh-58E/U missile. Target information from the *Pastel'* is displayed in the rear cockpit on a specially installed IM-3M-14 monochrome CRT screen, which is then interpreted by the rear crew-member to programme the seeker head of the *Kilter* missile prior to launch. The widely reported sale in 1999 of eighteen Su-25s (single- and twin-seaters) to Peru is believed to have included Su-25UBs modified to this new standard. All eighteen aircraft were reported to have been sold at a price below their commercial value in order to obtain much needed foreign currency.

Bulgaria

Bulgaria was the second Warsaw Pact country to obtain the Su-25, acquiring its first examples of both the Su-25K and the Su-25UBK in 1985. The aircraft were intended to replace obsolete MiG-17F *Fresco-C* ground-attack fighters which had been the backbone of the Bulgarian Air Force's fighter-bomber fleet for many years. Soviet ferry pilots delivered the new aircraft to the Bulgarian base at Bezmer, deliveries taking place in three stages between 1985 and 1986. Eventually, they were formed into a dedicated attack regiment, equipped with a total of 36 Su-25Ks, with conversion training of both pilots and groundcrews being conducted by Soviet instructors.

When training first commenced in 1985 there were some difficulties resulting from the fact that no Su-25UBK twin-seaters had been delivered in the first batch. Consequently, training was carried out on ageing UTI-MiG-15 *Midget* trainers which had similar qualities to the new Sukhoi, particularly in terms of simplicity and handling. After the delivery of six Su-25UBKs in 1986–7 the pace of training the Bulgarian pilots was

Bulgaria is a highly experienced operator of the Su-25, and with the country's recent accession to NATO the once adversarial *Frogfoot* of the Bulgarian Air Force's Bezmer wing is now a valued addition to the Alliance's European combat forces. *(Yefim Gordon)*

accelerated. One single-seat *Frogfoot* was lost during the conversion-training phase.

Currently, the Bulgarian Air Force Su-25s are deployed in two separate squadrons, subordinate to the **Korpus Takticheska Aviatzia**, whose Headquarters are at Plovdiv.

They comprise the following units at Bezmer:

- **1/22 Eskadrila** – Su-25K, Su-25UBK, L-29;
- **2/22 Eskadrila** – Su-25K, Su-25UBK.

The following side numbers are known for Bulgarian Air Force Su-25s:

Side Number	C/n	Variant	Notes
002		Su-25UBK	
017		Su-25UBK	
099		Su-25K	
102		Su-25K	
103		Su-25K	
104		Su-25K	
105		Su-25K	
109		Su-25K	
147	38220113147	Su-25UBK	
196		Su-25K	
205		Su-25K	
207		Su-25K	
209		Su-25K	
211		Su-25K	
241		Su-25K	
246	(25508110046?)	Su-25K	
249	(25508110049?)	Su-25K	
252	25508110052	Su-25K	
254	25508110054	Su-25K	
255	(25508110054?)	Su-25K	

Czechoslovakia

The first country to receive the new Soviet 'shturmovik' was Czechoslovakia, in 1984. (The country was to separate into the Czech and Slovak Republics less than ten years later.) The 30th Ostravsky Attack Regiment, based at Hradec-Kralove, was selected to operate the Su-25K, followed some time later by the first of the two-seat Su-25UBKs.

The Su-25s were flown from the USSR by Soviet delivery pilots, the first four aircraft touching down at Hradec-Kralove on 2 April 1984. The aircraft initially wore black side numbers, but as these blended into the overall camouflage colours of the Su-25, the numbers were painted white in 1986.

In the summer of 1984, a group of Czechoslovak pilots started to convert onto the new aircraft, and on 11 June of that year Major František Novák completed his first familiarisation flight in an Su-25K (Side No. 5007), which lasted forty minutes. Training of the pilots and preparation of the aircraft was accomplished with the assistance of a specialist team from the factory in Tbilisi, Georgia. A further eight aircraft were delivered to Czechoslovakia during the course of 1985, and in the same year the regiment was relocated to Pardubice. The regiment's first squadron was formed with a total of twenty aircraft of the first series, which did not have hydraulic boosters in the aileron circuit.

After delivery of a second batch of ten Su-25Ks in 1986 (these aircraft were equipped with boosted ailerons), the Czechoslovak Air Force started to form a second squadron, and in September that year all of the Czechoslovak Su-25s took part in the Warsaw Pact Exercise 'Friendship-86' (*Druzhba-86*). Another two batches of Su-25s were delivered in 1987, the first comprising six aircraft and the second eight. Three attack squadrons were formed in the Czechoslovak Air Force, all equipped with the Su-25K. (It is not strictly correct to call the Czechoslovak squadrons 'shturmovoy', since this term was not understood in the original Russian sense outside of the Soviet and Russian Air Forces.) From 1986 to 1987 the Czechoslovak Republic reportedly received an additional delivery of six Su-25UBK combat trainers. Each squadron was thus equipped with twelve single-seat Su-25Ks and two Su-25UBKs, the Czechoslovak Air Force having received a total of 42 of the new aircraft.

At the end of 1992, the Czechoslovak Republic split into the present-day independent Czech and Slovak Republics, and all military equipment operated by the Army and Air Force was divided between the two new states in the ratio of 2:1 in favour of the Czech Republic. As a result, the Czech Republic acquired twenty-four Su-25Ks and one Su-25UBK, while the Slovak Republic received twelve single-seat Su-25Ks and one Su-25UBK. The sharing out of these two Su-25UBKs ties in with other sources that claim the Czechoslovak Air Force only ever received two trainers in the first instance.

From 1 January 1993, both of the newly formed Czech Air Force's Su-25 squadrons relocated to the 32nd Tactical Air Base at Námest-nad-Oslavou.

The first four Su-25s of a batch of ten were delivered to the Democratic Republic of Congo in November 1999, and are seen here on board the An-124 which delivered them. Since arriving in the Congo, little has been heard about their operations. *(TAM)*

BELOW: Czechoslovakia was the first non-Soviet country to operate the Su-25, receiving its first aircraft in 1984. With the eventual break-up of the Soviet Union and the Warsaw Pact, the Czechoslovakian aircraft were split between the newly independent Czech Republic and Slovakia in 1993, the Czech Su-25s being retired from service and placed in storage at Přerov in December 2000. *(via Yefim Gordon)*

Side Number	C/n	Variant	Notes
5003	25508105003	Su-25K	Stored Přerov
5006	25508105006	Su-25K	Stored Přerov
5007	25508105007	Su-25K	
5008	25508105008	Su-25K	Stored Přerov
5039	25508105039	Su-25K	
5040	25508105040	Su-25K	
6019	25508106019	Su-25K	Stored Přerov
6020	25508106020	Su-25K	Stored Přerov
8076	25508108076	Su-25K	
8077	25508108077	Su-25K	
8078	25508108078	Su-25K	
8079	25508108079	Su-25K	
8080	25508108080	Su-25K	
9013	25508109013	Su-25K	
9014	25508109014	Su-25K	
9093	25508109093	Su-25K	
9094	25508109094	Su-25K	
9098	25508109098	Su-25K	
9099	25508109099	Su-25K	
1002	25508110002	Su-25K	
1003	25508110003	Su-25K	
1004	25508110004	Su-25K	
1005	25508110005	Su-25K	
3348	38220113348	Su-25UBK	

In 1994, Su-25K 1003 was damaged during landing when testing the brake parachute system. The aircraft was restored for use as a ground instructional airframe at the military training college at Vyškov.

On 23 September 1994, the Slovak Air Force formed its squadron of Su-25s at the 33rd Air Base located at Malacky-Kuchyna.

Side Number	C/n	Variant	Notes
5033	25508105033	Su-25K	
5036	25508105036	Su-25K	
6017	25508106017	Su-25K	
6018	25508106018	Su-25K	
8072	25508108072	Su-25K	w/o
8073	25508108073	Su-25K	
8074	25508108074	Su-25K	
8075	25508108075	Su-25K	
1006	25508110006	Su-25K	
1007	25508110007	Su-25K	
1008	25508110008	Su-25K	
1027	25508110027	Su-25K	
3237	38220113237	Su-25UBK	

One Su-25K, 8072, was written off charge after a landing accident at Sliac on 27 May 1993.

Congo

In late 1999, the Tbilisi Aerospace Manufacturing (TAM) plant (formerly Factory 31 and the Tbilisi Aircraft State Association [TASA]), signed a contract with the Democratic Republic of Congo (formerly Zaire), for the delivery of ten Su-25Ks to the Force Aérienne Congolaise. The deal was reported to be valued at US$6 million, and the first four aircraft were delivered on board an An-124 in November 1999. The remaining six aircraft were delivered in January 2000.

Ethiopia

A batch of four Su-25s were delivered to Ethiopia in the first quarter of 2000, comprising a pair of Su-25Ts and two Su-25UBK combat trainers. The twin-seaters were withdrawn from Russian Air Force service and modified in accordance with a special request from the Ethiopian Air Force. The single-seat Su-25T specialised anti-tank variant was transferred from the 4th Centre for Combat Application and Aircrew Conversion at Lipetsk, and is the first known export of this variant, which has only seen limited service in Russia itself. Pre-delivery modifications were carried out by the 121st Aviation Repair Plant at Kubinka, which specialises in the overhaul of the Su-25. After modification, the aircraft were delivered to Ethiopia by Russian Air Force An-22 *Cock* and Il-76 *Candid* transports, probably representing one of the last such delivery flights by the Antonov heavylifter. Since acquiring the four aircraft, the Ethiopian Air Force has used them in combat operations against Eritrean insurgent groups. According to information published in at least one handbook of combat aircraft of the world, a total of ten Su-25s is believed to have been supplied to Ethiopia.

Georgia

Georgia, which during the Soviet era had produced hundreds of MiG-21U/UM/US *Mongol* trainers and

Although brightly painted for their aerobatic display role, the Su-25s of the now defunct Celestial Hussars aerobatic team retained the aircraft's combat function and regularly practised air-to-ground attacks using the *Frogfoot's* standard armament. Here Hussar Black 90 is seen equipped with B-8M1 80 mm rocket pods taxiing out at snow-covered Kubinka, not long before the team disbanded. *(Yefim Gordon)*

ABOVE: One of the Czech Air Force's best known Su-25s, painted to represent the mottled colours of a frog, with a fiendish representation of the amphibian on the fin, crushing a tank with a large hammer. The aircraft was painted in this amusing colour scheme just before its visit to RAF Boscombe Down in the summer of 1992, when it was operated by the 2nd Squadron of the 30th Attack Regiment, based at Pardubice. *(via Yefim Gordon)*

RIGHT: A lone Su-25 heads off to the range armed with a pair of Kh-25ML (AS-10 *Karen*) laser-guided air-to-surface missiles. The aircraft is one of a group of 899 OShAP Su-25s which deployed to Kubinka from Buturlinovka, near Borisoglebsk, in March 1998. *(Yefim Gordon)*

ABOVE: An armed Su-25 of 368 OShAP seen at Budyonnovsk in the summer of 1996, armed with six OFAB-250 bombs and a pair of AA-8 *Aphid* AAMs, awaiting its next sortie over Chechnya. The regiment was previously based at Demmin-Tutow in the former German Democratic Republic. *(via Yefim Gordon)*

An Su-25 of 899 OShAP caught just at the point of lift-off from its base at Buturlinovka, lightly armed with 80 mm rockets and underwing fuel tanks for the long transit to the range. *(Yefim Gordon)*

Flight operations at Russian military airfields are often carried out in fairly harsh conditions in the winter, as witnessed by these four Su-25s of 899 OShAP at Kubinka in March 1998, being prepared for a ground-attack programme at a weapons range in the Moscow area. The box in the foreground is probably the storage and transport container for the AA-8 *Aphid* self-defence missile, which has a high tolerance of extreme storage conditions, from the highest summer temperatures to the lowest temperatures of a typical Russian winter. *(Yefim Gordon)*

The Su-25 maintains an initial level altitude following unstick. *(Vyacheslav Martynyuk)*

ABOVE: During the transitional changes that the Russian air forces experienced before the final break-up of the Soviet Union in 1992, a number of Su-25s were assigned as shore-based assets of the Soviet Navy. The aim of this was to circumvent the CFE treaty limitations on total numbers of allowable Soviet Air Force aircraft based 'west of the Urals'. The treaty did not apply to naval combat aircraft. Here, Red 12, wearing the Soviet Navy ensign on its air intake, is parked in the 'un-nautical' setting of Panevezhys airfield in Lithuania. In addition to the single UB-32-57 and the two B-8M1 rocket pods, the aircraft also carries a SPPU-22-01 cannon pod on the inboard pylon. *(Yefim Gordon)*

RIGHT: The comparatively high aspect ratio of the Su-25's wing is evident in this take-off view.

(Vyatcheslav Martynyuk)

RIGHT: One of the prototype Su-25Ts (01 outline) parked on the flightline at Akhtubinsk. The aircraft is equipped with the **Merkuriy** (Mercury) electro-optical pod on the fuselage centreline station. Note the conical exhaust-gas cooling device protruding from the rear of the jet pipe of this variant's R-195 engine. *(Yefim Gordon)*

MIDDLE: A development Su-25T (Red 16) being prepared for a range programme from the State Flight Test Centre at Akhtubinsk. Evident in this view is the long cylindrical pod at the base of the fin which normally houses the **Sukhogruz** (Cargo Vessel) active infra-red jammer of the improved *Frogfoot* variants. The housing is probably an engineering mock-up on this aircraft, with a blanking plate over the jammer's window and no built-in chaff and flare dispensers in the upper part of the cylindrical body. The finned container inboard of the AA-8 *Aphid* training round is a KMG-U weapons dispenser, while further inboard is a pack of **Vikhr-M** anti-armour missiles. *(Yefim Gordon)*

BELOW: A production Su-25T (Red 08) banks away from the camera aircraft over the desert area in the vicinity of the State Flight Test Centre at Akhtubinsk, showing to good effect the external location of the barrel of its 30 mm cannon. *(Yefim Gordon)*

LEFT: Banking sharply away from the 'camera ship' near Akhtubinsk, this Su-25T displays its weapons load of four Kh-25ML (AS-10 *Karen*) laser-guided missiles. It also provides an excellent study of the *Frogfoot*'s overall layout.
(Vestnik Aviatsi i Kosmonavtiki)

BELOW: Not yet assigned a Bort number, this development Su-25TM wears the 'naval style' blue camouflage scheme in which the type was presented at several Moscow Air Shows. Note in this view that the larger cockpit canopy of the modified single-seat *Frogfoot* has two additional strengthening frames, similar to those on the Su-25UB.
(Ulan-Ude Plant)

BELOW: This Su-25T is 'armed' with an ideal, but probably impractical, arsenal of air-to-ground weapons, including a dummy Kh-31 (AS-17 *Krypton*) ASM, eight **Vikhr-M** anti-armour missiles on APU-8 launchers, an S-25L laser-guided 340 mm rocket and a five-tube B-13L launcher for the heavy 122 mm S-13 rocket. Self-defence of the aircraft is provided by the AA-8 *Aphid* on the outer pylon. An identical weapons load was mounted on the starboard side. Note also the **Merkuriy** electro-optical pod on the fuselage centreline. *(Yefim Gordon)*

ABOVE: An Su-25UB trainer taxies out of dispersal with four underwing fuel tanks for an extended-range navigation exercise (Navex). *(T. Shia)*

LEFT: An unmarked Su-25UBK, wearing an unusual camouflage scheme, seen on a sortie from the factory airfield at Ulan-Ude in the Buryat Republic, Siberia, where it was built. *(Ulan-Ude Plant)*

BELOW: An Su-25 taxiing past a Russian Army BMP-2 AFV at Grozny Airport during the first Chechen campaign in 1996. Along with its stable-mate the Su-24 *Fencer*, the Su-25 has borne the brunt of Russian Air Force fixed-wing action over Chechnya in the continuing struggle to regain control of the breakaway republic. Like many modern 'asymmetrical' conflicts, it is unlikely that possession of superior firepower alone will achieve anything other than prolonged misery for both sides, and no end is in sight almost a decade after the start of hostilities.

The final mock-up of the LVSSh had been radically transformed into an aircraft much closer to the final appearance of the Su-25. Here the mock-up is seen with a mix of dummy bombs and rockets outside Sukhoi's design facilities at Zhukovskiy in 1972.

BELOW: The pilot's cockpit of the Su-25 is well protected and he sits inside a titanium 'bath tub', with additional protection from armour-plated glazing of the canopy. However, the canopy itself is still vulnerable to direct hits from the side from heavy-calibre guns at low level.

RIGHT: Su-25 prototype T8-10 (Blue 10) was used in trials of rearward-firing rockets and in the evaluation of the use of the SPPU-22-01 cannon pod mounted to fire to the rear. It was also used on trials of the asymmetric application of the airbrakes as part of the aircraft's clearance for service. Here, the aircraft is seen armed with conventional forward-firing 80 mm rockets in B-8M1 pods.

This view of T8-1 reveals the shorter wingspan and smaller main wheels of the Su-25 prototype.

This forward underside view of T8-15 shows the eventual location of the ten underwing pylons, the GSh-30-2 cannon and the slightly offset nosewheel. The square dielectric panel covers the antenna of the DISS-7 Doppler navigation system, and the downward-deflected window of the **Klyon-PS** laser designator/rangefinder is visible in the nose cone. *(Yefim Gordon)*

After initially considering the possibility of using existing trainers such as the MiG-15UTI and a brief period using the L-39 Albatros as a conversion trainer for pilots assigned to fly the Su-25, a decision was taken to produce a dedicated training version at Ulan-Ude in Siberia. The prototype, T8UB-1, also introduced the practice of decorating the aircraft with a 'prancing bear' symbol, believed to be the Ulan-Ude factory emblem and applied to all twin-seat Su-25s (and Mi-8/17 helicopters) manufactured there. *(Ulan-Ude Plant)*

scores of single-seat Su-25s at the Tbilisi plant, was left with virtually no air force or aircraft following the break-up of the Soviet Union. Only a very small number of single-seat Su-25s were actually taken on to the inventory of the newly formed Georgian Air Force, these aircraft being examples which were left in the factory at the time of the declaration of independence. In addition to these, three 'hybrid' twin-seat Su-25U trainers were built at the Tbilisi factory between 1996 and 1998, only one of which was handed over to the Georgian Ministry of Defence. According to Russian information in the open press, Georgia has at its disposal up to eight Su-25s of various modification standards, both in the Air Force and remaining on factory territory. In a Russian television report in August

2002, at least four Su-25s were shown at an unnamed Georgian Air Force base. It is believed, however, that a handful of Su-25s are operated by a Composite Air Unit at Tbilisi-Marneuli, a former Soviet Air Force Su-15TM *Flagon-F* base. Additionally, an unknown fighter-bomber regiment is said to be equipped with both the Su-25 and Su-25UB and located at Kopitnari near Tbilisi, this airfield being a former Soviet Air Force Su-24 *Fencer* tactical bomber base.

Currently, Georgia is developing an upgraded version of the Su-25 with Israel, known as the Su-25KM Scorpion (*see* next chapter), and is also offering a number of 'developing' nations small batches of both single-seat and twin-seat Su-25s. The Su-25KM upgrade brings together Tbilisi Aerospace Manufacturing (TAM), the

One of the Georgian Air Force's Su-25s is seen here at Tbilisi-Marneuli in the summer of 2000, wearing Soviet-era camouflage and a bird of prey squadron badge ahead of the Bort number. The aircraft is equipped with the early *Odd Rods* IFF system, as revealed by the three-bladed antennas in front of the cockpit and under the tail unit. (*Stenio Bacciocchi*)

One of the Su-25U trainers built by TAM engineers in the Tbilisi factory, using drawings for the single-seat Su-25T to convert three standard Su-25 airframes to this interim trainer configuration for the Georgian Air Force. The aircraft wears an interesting non-standard camouflage scheme and is equipped with the later standard of IFF, with triangular blade aerials at front and rear of the fuselage. (*Stenio Bacciocchi*)

new name for the former Tbilisi Aircraft State Association (TASA), Elbit Systems Ltd and Elgad Inc. According to some defence experts, the factory at Tbilisi has enough component parts and structural elements to assemble up to seventy-five Su-25s. Unfortunately, however, Georgia is not yet capable of producing a modern upgrade of the *Frogfoot* on its own, which is why it has arranged to work in partnership with Israel on the Su-25KM. The following Georgian Air Force Su-25s are known to exist:

Side Number	C/n	Variant	Notes
07 Red		Su-25	
16 Red		Su-25	
21 Red		Su-25U(?)	
316 (Blue – Paris Show No.)		Su-25KM	

Iran

On 21 January 1991, seven Iraqi Air Force Su-25s were flown to Iran, seeking a temporary 'safe haven' from Operation *Desert Storm* attacks on major Iraqi military installations. In effect, these Iraqi aircraft were considered by the Iranians to be a 'gift' from their former long-term adversary, although as a result of lack of spare parts, documentation and, more importantly, training, these aircraft were never flown by the Islamic Republic of Iran Air Force. The current status of the seven Su-25s is not known, but they are believed to be in protected storage.

Iraq

During the course of the early phase of the Iran–Iraq War from 1980 to 1988, Iraq approached the Soviet Union with a request to purchase a wide variety of military equipment. As a result, Iraq become the first non-Warsaw Pact country to obtain the Su-25K and Su-25UBK. Russian press reports claim that Iraq received a total of seventy-three Su-25s, of which four were the Su-25UBK combat trainer. The aircraft were delivered to Iraq by sea transport in 'knocked-down' form and reassembled by Soviet technicians. Pilot training was carried out by Soviet instructors in parallel with the deliveries. The first Iraqi Air Force Su-25 regiment was formed in 1986, followed by a second in 1987. During the Iran–Iraq War, the Su-25 represented the main strike force of the Iraqi Air Force, and they were deployed according to a mobile

basing philosophy, which involved operating from the many airfields around the country on an irregular rotation cycle. As noted in the brief Iran section, seven Su-25s were flown to Iran in January 1991, ostensibly for 'safe haven', and they have remained there up to the present time. On 6 February 1991, two Su-25Ks were shot down by USAF F-15 Eagles.

According to press information in January 1998, Iraq still possesses twelve Su-25s, and at least three Su-25Ks were seen in a flypast over Baghdad in December 2002.

The following serial numbers are known for the Iraqi Air Force aircraft:

Side Number	C/n	Variant	Notes
8220		Su-25K	
25590	(255081)09041	Su-25K	
25591		Su-25K	

Note: Some, but not all, Iraqi Air Force aircraft of Russian origin used the type number as part of the side number, as in the two examples above, with **25**590 and **25**591. The Su-22s had five-figure numbers commencing with **22**xxx, MiG-23BNs used the **23**xxx series and MiG-29 serials were in the **29**xxx block.

Kazakhstan

The Kazakh Air Force received twelve single-seat Su-25s and two Su-25UB trainers in December 1995, as 'compensatory' payment for the return of the Tu-95MS *Bear-H* strategic bombers which had been rapidly flown out of the republic at the time of the collapse of the Soviet Union. The Kazakh Su-25s are located at Chimkent air base in the south of the country. The camouflage scheme chosen for operation in mountainous and desert regions has been retained, but the side numbers have been changed.

Macedonia

Macedonia purchased three single-seat Su-25s and one Su-25UB following incursions and attacks on Macedonian villages and security forces by Albanian separatists in early 2001. The aircraft were supplied to Macedonia by the Ukrainian organisation '*Ukrspetseksport*', having been withdrawn from Ukrainian Air Force

Soon after Iraq acquired its first batch of Su-25Ks, they were displayed at a military equipment exhibition in Baghdad. Here 25590 is seen exhibited in an otherwise empty dispersal area, with none of the explanatory placards which would be seen at a Western air show.

BELOW: Wearing the Macedonian flag on the nose, Su-25 serial number 122 was presented for inspection by senior military personnel at Petrovec air base near the capital, Skopje, in November 2001. The aircraft, newly refurbished in the Ukraine, as evidenced by its mint condition, was displayed with a representative selection of weapons, including the AA-8 *Aphid*, OFAB-100 bombs on MBD-267U bomb racks, plus 57 mm and 80 mm rockets. In front of the aircraft is a FAB-500ShR bomb and a B-13L 130 mm rocket launcher. *(MIA via Igor Bozinovski)*

Silhouetted against a grey sky background, one of the Macedonian Air Force's three single-seat Su-25s (serial number 121) is seen during a special air display on 1 November 2001 to present the aircraft to a military audience. *(MIA via Igor Bozinovski)*

service and overhauled prior to delivery. They were flown to Macedonia on 20 June 2001, by delivery pilots, from Odessa to Petrovec air base, just outside the Macedonian capital Skopje, overflying Romania and Yugoslavia en route. The Su-25s were immediately assigned to the Macedonian Air Force's 101 Aviation Company (**101 Avijaciska Četa,** or **101 A?**), based at Petrovec, and the first aircraft went into action on 24 June monitoring the action around Aračinovo village, where heavy fighting was taking place. This was the first time in the brief post-independence history of the Macedonian Air Force that a fixed-wing combat aircraft had operated from a Macedonian Air Force base. However, it was not until 10 August 2001 that the Macedonian Su-25s were involved in actual combat themselves, when they were used in attacks against Albanian terrorists located in the villages of Raduša, where sixteen Macedonian soldiers had been ambushed and killed in the previous two days. The Su-25s operate in close co-operation with the Air Force's Mi-24V *Hind-E* gunships, using tactics developed by the Russians during the Afghan conflict. It seems, however, that Macedonia's operation of the Su-25 will be comparatively short-lived, since a US government advisory team suggested in October 2002 that the four aircraft in the Air Force's inventory should be sold and its transport helicopter force expanded instead. The Macedonian Army is reportedly unwilling to dispose of the Su-25s before 2004, but does recognise the need to build up its transport helicopter capability in preparation for future NATO membership, an objective it is keen to achieve at the earliest possible opportunity.

The Macedonian Air Force Su-25s carry the following serials:

Side Number	C/n	Variant	Notes
120		Su-25UB	
121		Su-25	
122		Su-25	
123		Su-25	

North Korea

North Korea was the first Asian country to obtain the Su-25. In the 1950s the North Korean Air Force had accumulated useful experience of operating the Su-25's piston-engined predecessor, the Ilyushin Il-10 *Beast* during the Korean War. This fact might have been the impetus which led the North Korean government to decide to purchase a small batch of Sukhoi's jet-powered successor to the Il-10. In the period from the end of 1987 until 1989 the Korean People's Democratic Republic acquired a total of thirty-two single-seat Su-25Ks and four Su-25UBKs. The aircraft are based at Sonchon (some 80 km from Pyongyang), which has heavily fortified natural hangars cut into the rock face of the surrounding hillsides, equipped with blast-proof doors capable of protecting the aircraft from conventional and nuclear explosions. The North Korean Air Force operates a single regiment of Su-25s, comprising three squadrons, organised along former Soviet lines.

Peru

Peru received eighteen ex-Russian Air Force Su-25s in late 1998 from the Republic of Belarus', which refurbished them prior to delivery. The total was made up of ten single-seat Su-25 and eight Su-25UB trainers. The overhaul was carried out by the 558th Aviation Repair Plant at Baranovichi, which specialises in the Sukhoi types. It is thought that the aircraft were all built just before the downfall of the Soviet Union and thus represented the latest equipment standard for the Su-25. Both the Su-25 and the Su-25UB operated by the **Fuerza Aérea del Peru** (FAP) retain, for example, the small blade antennas of the *Parol'* (Password) D-band IFF system, although it is not known whether FAP surveillance radars are themselves compatible with this equipment. The single-seaters are also equipped with chaff/flare dispensers on top of the rear engine cowling. According to unconfirmed reports, Belarus' also supplied a number of AS-10 *Karen* and AS-14 *Kedge* air-to-surface missiles with the aircraft. The Peruvian Su-25s are based at BA Capitán Victor Montes at Talara, near the border with Ecuador, and are operated by **Escuadrón Aéreo 112** of **Grupo Aéreo 11** at this base, which also houses **Escuadrón Aéreo 111**, operating the Su-22M2 *Fitter-F* single-seat fighter-bomber and the Su-22UM2 *Fitter-E* trainer. With the reduced threat of military action from neighbouring Ecuador, following the signing of a Peace Treaty in October 1998, the Su-25s have been reassigned to operations to counter the illegal drugs trade which blights this South American republic's economic and social stability. It is believed that up to December 2000 at least twenty-five light aircraft transporting cocaine had been shot down by the Peruvian Su-25s. Although acquired initially for its reputed assault capabilities, in response to frequent border clashes with Ecuador, the

Frogfoot has proved to be an ideal 'drug-busting interceptor', with stable handling at low speeds and a useful weapons capability against light-aircraft targets.

Known Peruvian Su-25 serials are:

Side Number	C/n	Variant	Notes
074 Yellow		Su-25	
080 Yellow		Su-25UB	

Turkmenistan

After the November 1990 signing of the Treaty on Conventional Armed Forces in Europe, the air base at Kizyl-Arvat in the then Soviet Republic of Turkmenia was selected as the storage base for Su-25 aircraft withdrawn from the European part of the Soviet Union. Following the downfall of the Soviet Union, the newly independent Republic of Turkmenistan was given the forty-six Su-25s which had been assembled for storage on its territory up to that time. It is known that in accordance with an agreement between Georgia and Turkmenistan in 1999, Tbilisi Aerospace Manufacturing (TAM) refurbished six of these aircraft for the new Turkmenistan Air Force. Altogether, TAM planned to refurbish forty-five Su-25s for the Turkmenistan Air Force by way of payment owed by Georgia to the Asian republic for the delivery of natural gas by Turkmenistan in the years 1992–4. The refurbished aircraft were relocated at Ak-Tepe air base, and by 2001 a total of eighteen Su-25s were known to be based there.

Ukraine

Ukraine retained a total of ninety-two Su-25s, of differing variants, following independence in the wake of the break-up of the Soviet Union. However, data from a variety of sources relating to the current numbers of Su-25s held by Ukraine do not tally. According to the most reliable information available, Ukraine currently possesses around sixty Su-25, Su-25UB and Su-25UTG variants, which are operated by the 299th Independent Assault Regiment (**299 OShAP**), based at Saki in the Crimea, and the 456th (452nd?) Assault Regiment (**ShAP**) at Chortkiv (formerly Chortkov). The Su-25UTGs at Saki (some four or five aircraft), which are intended for training carrier-based personnel, are flown (by agreement) by Ukrainian and Russian Navy pilots. It is also known that up to twenty-five to thirty Su-25s are in storage at the 4070 Reserve Base, where they had been assembled after the disbandment in 1989–90 of **90 OShAP** at Artsyz (formerly Artsiz). Evidently, three of the Su-25s which were sold to Macedonia came from this reserve pool, although it is impossible to confirm this precisely, and it is equally likely that the aircraft were withdrawn from an operational unit of the Ukrainian Air Force.

One of the newly independent countries of the Commonwealth of Independent States to adopt radically different national markings from those worn in the Soviet era is the Central Asian Republic of Turkmenistan. Here a line-up of four Su-25s is seen wearing the new markings at Ak-Tepe air base in 2001. *(via Yefim Gordon)*

Outside Russia, Ukraine is probably the largest operator of the Su-25. One of its aircraft is seen here wearing the Ukrainian Air Force's blue and gold trident fin marking. This aircraft also wears the **grach** (rook) symbol initially applied to the Su-25 in Soviet Air Force service in Afghanistan. *(Yefim Gordon)*

On 24 August 2001, a military parade was held to celebrate the 10th Anniversary of Ukraine's Independence, during which the Air Force took part for the first time, and a formation of Su-25s was included in the fly-past over Kiyiv (Kiev). Troops, armoured vehicles and tanks paraded down the capital's historic Kreshchatik Avenue, while overhead, Su-24s, Su-25s, Su-27s, as well as Tu-22M3 bombers, escorted Antonov transports in the mixed military and civil flypast.

The following side numbers are known for Ukrainian Air Force Su-25s:

Side Number	C/n	Variant	Notes
37 Red		Su-25	
63 Blue		Su-25UB	Saki
17 Blue		Su-25	Chortkiv
17 Red		Su-25	
10 Red		Su-25	Saki

Uzbekistan

Until 1990, a Soviet Air Force pilot training centre was located at Chirchik air base in Uzbekistan, equipped with around twenty Su-25, Su-25UB and Su-25BM variants of the Sukhoi 'shturmovik'. In 1991, a small number of

Su-25s were also located at Dzhizak air base, but after 1991 all the Su-25s in Uzbekistan were concentrated at Chirchik, operated by the 59th Fighter-Bomber Aviation Regiment (**59-y Aviapolk Istrebiteley-bombardirovshchikov**, or **59 APIB**) of the Soviet Air Force. After the collapse of the Soviet Union, all the Su-25s on the territory of the now independent Republic of Uzbekistan became the property of the new government.

In the spring of 1999, the Minister of Defence of Uzbekistan, Lieutenant-General Khikmatula Tursunov discussed the prospect of military co-operation with Georgia. Later, the Uzbek minister met the President of Georgia, Eduard Shevardnadze, in Tbilisi, along with a number of other Georgian ministers, including his counterpart, David Tevazadze, and expressed interest in acquiring several upgraded Su-25s, which would be supplied by Tbilisi Aerospace Manufacturing. What the Uzbek Defence Minister had in mind in particular was the Su-25T dedicated anti-tank variant, although the deal did not actually come to fruition, since the Uzbek side wished to obtain the Su-25s in a barter arrangement. Georgia, on the other hand, wished to sell the aircraft for hard currency. However, an eventual agreement cannot be ruled out, since Georgia is also interested in acquiring various items of military equipment manufactured by Uzbekistan's military-industrial enterprises.

6

The New Generation
of 'Shturmoviks'

The Su-25T (T8-M) Tank Killer

THE employment of the Su-25 in the Afghan war not only confirmed the correctness of the chosen configuration of the new 'shturmovik', but also accelerated design work on a variant capable of round-the-clock operation, armed with anti-tank weaponry. Initially, a 45 mm calibre cannon of advanced design was considered as the main armament of the upgraded Su-25, the barrel of which was to be capable of being depressed in the vertical plane. However, because of difficulties arising during the development of this weapon it was decided to equip the new aircraft with a fixed 30 mm twin-barrelled cannon instead. The Sukhoi OKB design team started work on the development of the new weapons complex for the

Su-25 in 1980. Preliminary design of the new variant was completed in 1981, and it was given the factory designation T8-M and the official Soviet Air Force designation Su-25T. The suffix letter 'T' stands for *Tankovy* (Tank), although in essence this should have been *Protivotankovy* (Anti-tank) to more accurately reflect its intended role as a 'tank killer'. The Su-25T represented a significant development of the mass-produced Su-25 (T-8) and incorporated all of the improvements inspired by years of operational experience with the latter, including actual combat experience. The new, specialised strike variant of the aircraft was intended for the destruction of:

- tanks on the move and other armoured vehicles;
- bridges, shelters and other hardened targets;
- troops in the field and fire positions;
- anti-aircraft defences;
- helicopters and transport aircraft;
- high-speed patrol boats, frigates, destroyers and landing craft.

It was envisaged that the Su-25T (T8-M) would be used in day and night conditions over the battlefield, up to 450 km (240 nm) behind the FLOT (Forward Line of Own Troops), within a height band extending from 30–50 m (100–165 ft) up to 5,000 m (16,400 ft).

During the Su-25T flight-test phase, between 1984 and 1988, the three trials aircraft were painted with false cockpits on the raised fairing behind the real cockpit. The objective of the deception was to confuse US analysis of satellite photography of the prototypes: making the aircraft look like ordinary trainers would divert attention away from the real purpose of these potent developments of the *Frogfoot*. The effectiveness of the deception on T8M-1 is very obvious here, and for an appreciable length of time it probably worked, the true identity of the new variant only becoming obvious some way into the test programme. *(Yefim Gordon)*

The high combat survivability of the new variant was to be guaranteed by:

- effective use of a built-in jamming system directed against enemy radars, and the dispensing of decoy flares and chaff to counter the threat from missiles with infra-red and radar seeker heads;
- the use of the full capabilities of a modern navigation and attack system (Nav-attack) and modern weapons;
- the use of engines with a reduced infra-red signature;
- the employment of a basing philosophy using packed-earth airfields and other airfields with limited support facilities, with bearing strengths of 6–7 kg/cm^2 (85–99 lb/in^2), as well as the use of highway strips.

High combat survivability has become one of the decisive factors in the overall survivability and effectiveness of this type of aircraft when operating in conditions of heavy anti-aircraft defences deployed by an adversary. The Sukhoi designers adhered to this concept when developing the integrated combat survival complex embodied in the Su-25T (T8-M), and took account of the widened range of combat tasks foreseen for the new aircraft. In particular, much attention was focused on the fact that the Su-25T would be able to spend a greater amount of time over an adversary's territory and subjected to more capable air defence systems. The design work on the Su-25T (T8-M) was completed in 1982, with work commencing on the construction of the first prototype of the upgraded aircraft in the following year.

The aerodynamic layout of the Su-25T (T8-M) is practically identical with that of the twin-seat Su-25UB (T8-UB) trainer version, with *c.*85–90% commonality in the airframe and aircraft systems of the two variants. The Su-25T differs externally from the Su-25UB by having a slightly longer nose and the absence of glazing in the aft 'cockpit' area. The cannon installation was also changed on the Su-25T, compared with earlier variants, in that the barrels of the gun project into the airflow below the fuselage skin panels. Additional equipment and avionics were installed in the enlarged fuselage spine area behind the cockpit (inherited from the original Su-25UB layout), this area also being somewhat strengthened compared with the trainer.

An early production Su-25T parked on the flightline at Akhtubinsk. The aircraft is equipped with the **Merkuriy** (Mercury) electro-optical pod on the fuselage centreline station. *(Yefim Gordon)*

Introduced to the flight-test programme in 1986, the third prototype Su-25T (T8M-3), modified from a standard Su-25UB, was the first to have the *Sukhogruz* active jammer installed. As mentioned elsewhere in the text, the three Su-25T prototypes had 'false' rear canopies painted on to deceive satellite imagery analysts. The deception is shown to good effect here, although the reflectivity of the two 'canopies' is noticeably different from that on the other two prototypes. *(Sukhoi Design Bureau)*

Since the Su-25T was based on the design layout of the Su-25UB and at that time the airframe of the first flying example of the T8-UB trainer was already under construction, converted from a standard Su-25, it was decided to use this as the basis for the new variant. This was done with the agreement of the Ministry of Aircraft Production in order to accelerate the construction and transition to the test phase of the first prototype of the T8M-1 anti-tank 'shturmovik'. The modifications associated with this were:

- the installation of a new forward fuselage and nose section, with a single-seat armoured cockpit;
- changing the VPU-17A gun assembly and its twin-barrelled GSh-2-30 cannon (often referred to simply as the GSh-30) to the NPPU-8M system (*Navesnaya Podvizhnaya Pushechnaya Ustanovka* for the T8-M aircraft), albeit using the same cannon. Meaning literally 'mounted movable cannon installation', the weapon was relocated from the housing just in front of the cockpit, below the aircraft nose, to the central part of the fuselage, and displaced slightly to the right of the fuselage central axis;

- modification of the tail section of the fuselage to take a fin of increased area, of the type used on the Su-25UB.

The armoured cockpit (a so-called titanium bath-tub) itself remained the same as on the Su-25. Elements of the **Shkval** (Squall) TV sighting system were installed in the redesigned equipment compartment in front of the cockpit, along with other items of electronic equipment, in order to exploit the additional space freed by relocating the cannon. The compartments below and behind the cockpit, although seemingly externally identical to the Su-25UB, were redesigned and built as new structures. The only difference was that on the first flying example (T8M-1), it was decided not to install the supplementary fuel tanks Nos 3 and 4 in the space behind the cockpit, as envisaged in the original design of the T8-M. This was done in order to accelerate the development of the new aircraft and get it into the test phase as quickly as possible. As a result, the fuel system of T8M-1 remained identical with that of the standard single-seat Su-25, in terms of both volume (3,500 litres/770 imp gal) and the disposition of the

A production standard Su-25T launches a Kh-25ML (AS-10 *Karen*) laser-guided ASM over one of the trials ranges associated with the Akhtubinsk Flight-Test Centre. *(Vesnik Aviatsii i Kosmonavtiki)*

The cockpit of the Su-25T and Su-25TM incorporated a TV screen in the upper right quadrant of the instrument panel, to present the pilot with imagery from the **Shkval** (Squall) electro-optical sensor system. *(Sukhoi Design Bureau)*

fuel tanks themselves. Additional equipment was housed in place of the flexible Nos 3 and 4 tanks.

Relocation of the cannon under the central part of the fuselage and its more 'solid' attachment to the fuselage allowed the acoustic loading and airframe vibration to be reduced when firing the weapon. This resulted in lower vibration levels for the sensitive target-sighting equipment in the forward fuselage, and significantly reduced the effects of gas ingestion by the engines. The change of location for the cannon and its associated ammunition box led to the need to slightly offset the nosewheel to the left, similar to the solution adopted for the earlier Su-25 variants. The first flying example of the T8M-1 anti-tank aircraft carried test and measuring equipment in place of the NPPU-8M, which was also used later during the flight-test stage. The T8M-1 was equipped with BU-45A hydraulic boosters in both the lateral channel (ailerons) and the longitudinal channel (elevators), the latter not being fitted on the standard Su-25 single-seater.

The powerplant of the Su-25T (T8-M) comprises two R-195 engines, which, as mentioned in earlier chapters, are developments of the original R95Sh, with increased thrust (4,300 kgp/9,480 lb st instead of 4,100 kg/9,040 lb st), longer overhaul life, improved performance and reduced infra-red signature. If necessary, the R-195 on the Su-25T can be replaced by the R95Sh without any changes to the airframe. The new engines improve the take-off performance of the aircraft and have led to an increase in maximum speed. Four PTB-1150 auxiliary fuel tanks can be carried on the Su-25T, each with a capacity of 1,150 litres (253 imp gal), mounted on the innermost pylons of each wing. The use of four auxiliary fuel tanks, along with the increased capacity of the internal tanks, permits the radius of action to be increased significantly, as well as extending its ferry range.

The armament which can be carried by the Su-25T is mounted on ten underwing hardpoints, and comprises:

- sixteen AT-16 (no NATO code-name) *Vikhr* (Whirlwind) anti-tank missiles, in two launch packs of eight under each wing (mounted on the second pylon from the fuselage), with a range of up to 10 km (5.4 nm) and capable of penetrating armour of up to 1,000 mm (39.37 in);
- air-to-surface guided missiles, such as the Kh-29T (AS-14 *Kedge*) TV-guided weapon, or the Kh-25ML (AS-10 *Karen*), Kh-29L (AS-14 *Kedge*) and the 330 mm S-25LD rocket, all with laser guidance, plus the

Kh-58 (AS-11 *Kilter*) anti-radiation missile, within the weight range 150–650 kg (330–1,430 lb);
- unguided folding-fin rockets of calibres from 57 mm and above, as well as unguided rocket projectiles up to 370 mm;
- bombs from 100 kg to 500 kg calibre (standard 'dumb' bombs, plus 'smart' laser-guided bombs);
- R-60M (AA-8 *Aphid*) and R-73 (AA-11 *Archer*) short-range infra-red air-to-air guided missiles, carried on the outermost wing pylons;
- two pod-mounted 30 mm cannon installations, on the outer pylons.

The most spectacular weapon carried by the Su-25T is the AT-16 *Vikhr* laser-guided anti-tank missile, which can be carried in addition to other ground-attack weapons on the same sortie, with a pair of short-range air-to-air missiles for self defence. The maximum combat load of the Su-25T is in excess of 4 tonnes (8,800 lb), and bombing accuracy is of the order of 2–5 m (6–16 ft) CEP (Circular Error Probable).

The avionics installation on the Su-25T permits effective destruction of a range of ground targets, including small manoeuvring armoured vehicles. The avionics complex consists of an integrated navigation attack system comprising:

- an electro-optical (television) sighting system with 23× magnification of the target and surrounding terrain;
- an anti-tank missile guidance system;
- a night-capable electro-optical sighting system for target identification and prosecution of attack;
- a system for the projection of target information on the head-up display (HUD);
- an integrated electronic surveillance measures (ESM) and attack system, capable of identifying and destroying enemy radars, launching of flares and chaff to jam infra-red and radar-guided missiles; an automatic flight-control system;
- a television monitoring system which checks the actions of the pilot when carrying out targeting activities, plus a range of other systems.

The aircraft's weapons controls system guarantees the following:

- laser guidance of the AT-16 *Vikhr* anti-tank missile and other anti-tank weapons onto tank-sized targets and similar armoured vehicles, with a kill probability

(Pk) of 0.85–0.90 (85–90%) over flat terrain, in mountains and over broken terrain;

- the use of guided weapons against several targets from a single pass;
- the use of guided weapons from high altitude with a steep dive angle;
- the use of guided weapons without entering an adversary's air defence operations zone and without loss of delivery accuracy;
- the launch of AT-16 laser-guided missiles while the aircraft is manoeuvring;
- target search and detection of ground targets using the integrated day/night sighting systems, followed by the launch of unguided weapons against them;
- the detection and destruction of ground radars.

The avionics equipment is mounted in compartments in the aircraft's nose, in the compartment behind the cockpit and in the tail section (tail boom) of the fuselage. The SAU (*Sistema Avtomaticheskovo Upravlyeniya*) automatic flight-control system is used to provide the following:

- increased weapons effectiveness as a direct consequence of automatic control;

- increased flight safety;
- improved stability and control;
- heightened effectiveness of the pilot's actions and reduction of fatigue.

The process of navigation to the target, and subsequent attack, with the Su-25T, has been automated to the highest possible degree. The aircraft has been designed to fly out automatically to the target zone, then at a distance of *c.*10–12 km (5.5–6.5 nm) switch on the television tracking system, which has been aligned to look in the appropriate direction, after which the pilot checks the selection and automatic lock-on of the target, followed by the system's transfer to automatic tracking mode. When the pilot presses the firing button, the computer selects the appropriate weapons and carries out either their launch (if it is a missile) or their release (if it is a bomb). The Su-25T can also carry out a second approach in automatic mode or, if the pilot chooses, he can return to base (also in automatic mode) and can take over manual control of the aircraft just before touchdown. Navigation accuracy in automatic mode has been demonstrated to show no more than a 0.3% deviation over the entire distance flown, while the accuracy of automatic tracking of a small-sized moving target at a range of 8 km (4.3 nm)

A production Su-25T wearing the appropriate Bort number 01 in white outline and an original camouflage scheme, seen on the ground at Akhtubinsk during the early test phase. The aircraft carries the suitcase-style *Merkuriy* (Mercury) LLTV/FLIR pod on the fuselage centreline pylon. *(Yefim Gordon)*

This aircraft was presented in the West as the prototype of the export Su-25TK, although no actual flying prototype of an export version of the Su-25T was ever built. It is more likely that this airframe is actually T8M-10, hence the Bort number 10 on this example. *(Yefim Gordon)*

is 0.6 m (2 ft). Overall, the Su-25T represents a significant step forward when compared with the first Su-25 from the early 1980s.

Apart from the first flying prototype of the Su-25T, which, as mentioned earlier, received the factory designation T8M-1, it had also been planned to construct a further two prototypes, T8M-2 and T8M-3, as well as a static test airframe, T8M-0. It was decided that the airframes of these aircraft would be built by modifying the airframes of the first trials batch of Su-25UBs already completed at Ulan-Ude. (Series production of the Su-25UB *sparka* had already begun at the Ulan-Ude Aviation Plant in 1984.)

The first flying example, T8M-1 (with Blue Side No. 01) was completed in June 1984, after which it was transferred from the factory to the Sukhoi flight-test station at Zhukovskiy. V.I. Popov was designated Leading Engineer for the initial flight-test phase of the Su-25T. Ground-tests were carried out on the aircraft during July, with all systems being thoroughly checked, and on 13 August 1984 Sukhoi OKB test-pilot A.N. Isakov twice conducted high-speed taxiing tests in order to establish its controllability and braking effectiveness. After these two 'interrupted take-offs' Isakov performed a successful maiden flight in the new anti-

tank 'shturmovik', which also initiated the factory flight-test stage. The second (T8M-2 Blue Side No. 02) and third (T8M-3 Yellow Side No. 03) flying examples, modified by Sukhoi OKB engineers from the previously mentioned Su-25UB airframes, were introduced to the flight-test programme in 1985 and 1986 respectively. Both of these aircraft, unlike the first prototype, had the full normal fuel tank capacity intended for the type (4,890 litres/1,075 imp gal) and a full equipment specification. Additionally, T8M-3 was fitted with a special active infra-red jamming system mounted in a cylindrical pod under the rudder. Chaff and flare dispensers were also mounted in the forward section of this installation. Perhaps not widely known, but of great interest, is the fact that all three prototypes of the Su-25T were 'decorated' with a non-existent instructor's cockpit, painted on the raised fairing behind the real cockpit, to make them look like standard Su-25UBs, in order to deceive American 'spy satellites'! The aircraft were flown in this 'disinformative' style, both at Zhukovskiy and later, at the State Red Banner Scientific Research Centre of the Soviet Air Force (GK NII VVS) at Akhtubinsk.

The performance of the aircraft was comparatively quickly established during the factory flight-test stage, although the same cannot be said for the development

The second prototype Su-25T (T8M-2), painted in a more standard camouflage scheme than T8M-1, also had a false canopy painted on the raised fairing behind the cockpit. This aircraft was later lost in a flight-test accident. *(Yefim Gordon)*

and trials of the new I-251 round-the-clock automatic targeting complex with the integrated *Shkval* (Squall) electro-optical system. This proved to be highly complex and led to the factory tests being somewhat protracted, as a result of which the conduct of the I-251 trials, combined with the first stage of the State Joint Trials (GSI) of the Su-25T, were only completed at the end of 1990.

During the course of the test flight programme, both flight performance and maintenance characteristics were evaluated, and firings were carried out with all types of live weapons, which demonstrated the effectiveness of the new integrated weapons system, especially the *Shkval* and the *Vikhr* missile. The concluding document drawn up to consider the results of the first stage of the State trials noted the requirement to eliminate certain defects, but proposed that the new 'shturmovik' should be allowed to go on to the second stage of the State Joint Trials. Moreover, the State Commission also gave its preliminary approval for the new aircraft to be put into series production.

It was decided to initiate series production of the Su-25T at the Tbilisi plant, where it was to gradually replace the standard single-seat Su-25 on the production line from 1990. Working drawings of the Su-25T (T8-M) were transferred to the factory, where preparations had already been made for manufacture of the new variant. Assembly of a total of twelve aircraft of an initial trials batch had been completed during the course of 1990 and the first half of 1991, including the

static test example, T8M-0. This number also included T8M-4 and T8M-5, which were intended to be used in the continuation of the trials programme for the new aircraft. The first series production Su-25T was T8M-6, which was completed at Tbilisi towards the summer of 1990 and was test flown at the factory on 26 July by Sukhoi OKB test-pilot Korostiev. However, the general political situation in the country and the uncertainty of financing projects associated with the military-industrial complex of Russia, which began in the early days of 'perestroika', or social reform, slowed down the pace of further work on the aircraft.

The State trials of the Su-25T which had been operated by the Russian Air Force, were successfully completed in 1993. Several aircraft from the initial trials batch were then later used by the 4th Combat Application and Aircrew Conversion Centre at Lipetsk from 1996 onwards for operational field evaluation. The Su-25T was also used successfully in combat operations in Chechnya, about which more will be said in the next chapter.

By 2001, the first stage of the experimental field evaluation of the anti-tank Su-25T had been completed, which showed that the *Shkval* electro-optical sighting system and the *Vikhr* anti-tank missile fully justified the idea of priority development of precision-guided munitions and that the combat potential of the aircraft exceeded that of the basic Su-25 by an order of magnitude. As the field evaluation showed, the new 'shturmovik' variant was able to demonstrate highly accurate delivery of laser-guided anti-tank missiles, and the Su-25T, equipped with the *Shkval* system, is the only aircraft in the Russian Air Force capable of destroying small, mobile, armoured targets. During the field evaluation trials at Lipetsk, a group of pilots, plus ground engineering and support personnel, were trained to carry out any task involving the destruction of ground targets, and in particular, the destruction of mobile armour.

The Su-25T was first demonstrated in public in November 1991 at the Dubai International Air Show. This was not actually a series-production aircraft, but the third prototype, T8M-3, repainted, and wearing the generic Side No. 25 in yellow. Later, one of the series-production examples of the Su-25T (T8M-10 Blue Side No. 10) was exhibited at Mosearoshow-92 at Zhukovskiy in August 1992. In September 1993, the same aircraft was displayed again at Zhukovskiy during the renamed MAKS '93 (*Moskovskii Aviakosmicheskiy Salon*) Moscow Aviation and Space Salon.

The Russian press has in the past published certain information concerning the fact that following the declaration of independence by the Republic of Georgia, Tbilisi Aerospace Manufacturing (TAM) had received an order from the Georgian Air Force for fifty Su-25Ts, to be delivered over a period of seven years, but this order has never been realised. The possibility of acquiring the Su-25T, which would be manufactured by TAM, has also interested Ukraine, Kazakhstan and Uzbekistan. However, without the participation of Russia, the manufacture of the upgraded anti-tank 'shturmovik', in the form in which it was developed and tested, would be impossible because of the lack of essential equipment related to weapons systems.

In November 1992, in order to operate more effectively in Russia's emerging market economy, the Sukhoi OKB set up a special Scientific Production Concern, known as 'Shturmoviki Sukhovo', literally 'Sukhoi Shturmoviks', headed by Vladimir Petrovitch Babak, Chief Designer of the Su-25. Overall, 'Shturmoviki Sukhovo' embraced a total of forty-seven enterprises connected with the design, development and manufacture of the Su-25. The manufacture of the anti-tank Su-25T, and any future upgraded variants, was transferred to the plant in Ulan-Ude in Siberia, which was already involved in the manufacture of the Su-25UB and Su-25UBK twin-seat trainer variants. Currently, small numbers of Su-25T aircraft are being operated by the Russian Air Force.

The Su-25TK (T8-MK) Export Anti-tank Variant

An export variant of the Su-25T was projected at the same time as the development of the Su-25T (T8-M), known as the Su-25TK (T8-MK), which differed from the Russian version in certain items of electronic equipment, a traditional feature of Russian military aircraft exports. The suffix letter 'K' in the designation stands for *Kommercheskiy*, literally 'Commercial', a device mainly adopted by Sukhoi to designate the company's export products. Apart from avionics differences, it was also planned to install a different navigation system from that used on the Russian aircraft. No flying example of the export variant was ever built, although the third and tenth prototypes, T8M-3 and T8M-10, were exhibited at a number of airshows under the designation Su-25TK.

Design of the Su-25T (T8-M)

Fuselage. The fuselage of the Su-25T (T8-M) differs principally from the fuselage of the Su-25UB (T8-UB) by the presence of the No. 3 flexible fuel tank in the space occupied by the instructor in the trainer variant, above which is a new avionics compartment. The nose of the Su-25T is also slightly lengthened and widened to house the *Shkval* electro-optical system and its sighting windows. The cannon installation has been relocated under the No. 3 fuel tank, with the axis of the barrel offset to the right of the aircraft centreline by 273 mm (10.75 in). The space freed under the cockpit by relocation of the cannon is entirely taken up by elements of the *Shkval* system.

The central part of the fuselage and the air intakes share full commonality with the equivalent areas of the Su-25UB. An additional flexible fuel tank, No. 4, is mounted in the rear section of the fuselage, which also houses new avionics units and elements of the automatic flight control system (SAU), plus other aircraft and radio equipment. The engine nacelles have been modified to take the R-195 engine, although they remain compatible with the installation of the original R95Sh. Access to equipment, aircraft systems and engine components is via detachable and/or hinged panels on the fuselage and engine nacelles. The pilot's cockpit is pressurised, with a differential of 0.25 kg/cm^2 (3.55 lb/in^2), and offers protection against the ingress of nuclear, biological or chemical agents. However, the cockpit's design also provides for a more comfortable working environment for the pilot at higher altitudes, and the increased cabin pressure differential permits flight at altitudes up to 10,000 m (32,800 ft). This is particularly useful on ferry flights, where a higher cruising altitude offers a more efficient operating regime for the engines.

The cockpit is an all-welded armoured 'tub' of ABVT-20 aviation-grade titanium plate with a thickness of 17 mm (0.7 in), covered by a canopy. The cockpit canopy consists of a fixed framework with an armoured windscreen of mixed composition, consisting of several layers of silicon glass and one of plexiglass, having an overall thickness of 65 mm (2.56 in) and a hinged plexiglass opening section with a shaped armour-plated area above the pilot's head. The armour plating is made of KVK-37 aviation-grade thin sheet steel and has an overall thickness of 10 mm (0.4 in). The cockpit pressure differential is maintained automatically by means of a regulator system and an exhaust valve.

The brake parachute system serves to reduce the aircraft's landing run, augmenting the action of the main wheel brakes, and consists of the twin-canopy PTS-25 (*Posadochnaya Parashutno-Tormoznaya Sistema*) parachute assembly, working in conjunction with the *Fal* (Halyard) apparatus. The brake chute system of the Su-25T is installed in a cylindrical container in the tail section of the fuselage, as on the Su-25. Brake chute deployment and release after touchdown is achieved by means of a remotely controlled system (*sistema distantsionnovo upravlyeniya*).

Wing and empennage. The wing and empennage of the Su-25T shares full commonality with the wing and tail unit of the Su-25UB. The only major difference on the Su-25T concerns the airbrake housings, which are equipped with new antenna units for the *Irtysh* (one of Russia's longest rivers) electronic countermeasures system. Each wing semi-span is equipped with five underwing hardpoints, including up to four interchangeable BD3-25 (*Balochny Derzhatel'*) assemblies for the carriage and release of all types of bombs, unguided and guided ordnance cleared for use by the aircraft, or auxiliary fuel tanks. The outermost hardpoint is normally reserved for the installation of the APU-60-1 (*Aviatsionnaya Puskovaya Ustanovka*) launch pylon for a single R-60M (AA-8 *Aphid*) short-range self-defence air-to-air missile, the pylon's designation indicating association with the R-60 missile. All of the above-mentioned pylons are attached to the wing by single-pin connections. The BD3-25 weapons

pylons which are mounted nearest to the fuselage can be replaced by 'universal' pylons capable of carrying and releasing guided weapons and bombs with weights up to 1,000 kg (2,200 lb). Attachment of the pylon to the wing in this location is via a twin-pivot connection.

The tail unit of the Su-25T is also identical with that of the Su-25UB, in dimensions and design. The horizontal stabiliser has adjustable angle of incidence, with three main positions. These are 'flight', 'manoeuvring' and 'take-off and landing', and the positions are selectable by means of a hydraulic jack. Each of the two elevator sections has servo compensation and the deflection angles for the elevators are from +12° to −20°. The elevators do not have trimmers, since the elevator control circuit incorporates a BU-45A hydraulic booster. At the base of the rudder there are antennas for the *Irtysh* active jamming system and the cylindrical pod for the *Sukhogruz* (Cargo Vessel) active infra-red jamming system. Incorporated into the forebody of the *Sukhogruz* pod are dispenser units for infra-red decoy flares and radar-jamming chaff. The combined effect of the Su-25T's electronic warfare suite is to protect the aircraft from destruction by heat-seeking and radar-guided missiles.

Undercarriage. The undercarriage of the Su-25T is of standard tricycle layout. It comprises two main-wheel units, located under the central section of the fuselage, and a nosewheel mounted under the forward nose section of the aircraft, displaced 222 mm (8.74 in) to the left of the fuselage centreline. The nosewheel leg retracts backwards into the wheel well. The nose undercarriage leg is of the semi-levered type and is fitted with a single non-braked KN-27A wheel and tyre of 680 × 260 mm (26.75 × 10.25 in) diameter and a slotted mudguard. The displacement of the nosewheel unit to the left was necessary to facilitate housing of the NPPU-8M cannon installation. The mainwheel units are common with those of the Su-25 and Su-25UB and are equipped with braked KT136D wheels and tyres of 840 × 360 mm (33 × 14 in) diameter. The nose- and mainwheel wells are covered in flight and on the ground by the undercarriage doors, extension and retraction being performed with the aid of two hydraulic systems. The wheelbase of the Su-25T is 3.58 m (11.75 ft), and the track is 2.50 m (8.20 ft).

Powerplant. The powerplant of the Su-25T comprises two R-195 turbojet engines. The R-195 is an improved variant of the original R95Sh used by the Su-25, developed under the design leadership of S. Gavrilov and manufactured by the Ufa Engine Building

Production Association (UMPO) in the Republic of Bashkortostan. It is an unreheated engine, with a fixed nozzle, an accessories gearbox mounted underneath the main body of the engine and an autonomous electric start system. It develops a static thrust of 4,300 kgp (9,480 lb st) in so-called 'emergency mode' (*chrezvychainyy rezhim*, or '*ChR*') and a normal maximum thrust of 4,100 kgp (9,040 lb st). The R-195 differs from the R95Sh in having a nozzle that produces a lower infra-red signature. This is achieved by the installation of a conical centre-body mounted in the jet pipe, which is cooled by atmospheric airflow forced through an air intake mounted on top of the rear section of the engine nacelle. The gap between the outer surface of the nozzle and the inner wall of the nacelle forms a circular clearance ring, through which the air is expelled after being forced through the engine compartment. The R-195 is interchangeable with the earlier R95Sh engine.

The fuel system of the Su-25T provides fuel delivery from the fuel tanks to the engine in an established sequence which maintains the aircraft's centre of gravity within the acceptable range, in all flight regimes and regardless of the aircraft's attitude. Fuel is carried in four fuselage, two wing and one centre-section fuel tank on the Su-25T. The combined useable fuel capacity has been increased to 4,890 litres (1,076 imp gal), compared with 3,360 litres (805 imp gal) on the original Su-25. The fuel supply lines are on a 'ring main' system and guarantee fuel delivery to the engines from any feeder tank. The fuselage tanks are of flexible and protected construction in order to increase combat survivability. The protective measures adopted substantially reduce the likelihood of fire in the event of the tank being damaged. All the fuel tanks have 70% of their volume occupied by an open mesh polyurethane foam, which allows free flow of fuel within the tank, but prevents leakage if the tanks are pierced. The Su-25T can carry four PTB-800 or PTB-1150 auxiliary fuel tanks on long-range ferry flights, with 800-litre (176 imp gal) and 1,150-litre (253 imp gal) capacity respectively.

Armament. The armament options available on the Su-25T offer the choice of bombs, guided or unguided missiles and rockets, plus a built-in cannon and podded guns. A total of ten hardpoints are provided under the wings, of which the extreme outer stations are solely intended for the carriage of infra-red-guided R-60M (AA-8 *Aphid*) or R-73 (AA-11 *Archer*) short-range self-defensive air-to-air missiles. These are mounted on APU-60-1 launch pylons attached to PD-62-8 launch rail adapters.

Guided weapons cleared for use on the Su-25T comprise the following:

- sixteen **Vikhr** (Whirlwind) supersonic, semi-active laser-guided anti-tank (anti-armour) missiles mounted in two packs of eight on the second inboard pylon of each wing in multiple launcher units;
- four TV-guided Kh-25MT (AS-10 *Karen*) or two Kh-29T (AS-14 *Kedge*) air-to-surface missiles, four Kh-25ML (AS-10 *Karen*), four Kh-25LD (AS-10 *Karen*), laser-guided missiles or four S-25L 330mm laser-guided rockets, or two Kh-29L (AS-14 *Kedge*) laser-guided missiles, or two/four Kh-25MTP (AS-10 *Karen*) infra-red-guided air-to-surface missiles;
- one or two Kh-58Eh (AS-11 *Kilter*) anti-radiation missiles.

A variety of unguided rockets of calibres from 57 mm to 370 mm can be used by the Su-25T, including:

- up to eight pods of cumulative charge S-8KOM (**Kumulyativno-oskolochny**) or S-8T penetrating-charge unguided rockets (up to 160 rockets in total);
- up to eight pods of high-explosive fragmentation warhead S-13OF (**Oskolochno-fugasny**) or S-13OT penetrating fragmenting-charge unguided rockets (up to forty rockets in total);
- up to eight high-explosive fragmentation warhead S-24B or S-240 OFM (**Oskolochno-fugasny**) unguided rockets.

Bombs of between 100 and 500 kg (220–1,100 lb) calibre and of varying types can be carried, up to a maximum load of 4,360 kg (9,612 lb). This can comprise, for example, ten AB-100, ten AB-250 or eight AB-500 bombs, where the letters stand for 'aviation bomb' and the number refers to the weight of the bomb in kg. Special weapons can also be carried, such as the ZB-500 (**Zazhigatelnyy Bak**) incendiary (napalm) tank, of which eight can be mounted, or eight KMGU-2 universal (unified) containers for small bomblet charges. The latter can also be used by helicopters, hence the use of the word 'unified' in the designation, indicating unified application. Alternatively, up to eight RBK-250 or RBK-500 (**Razovaya Bombovaya Kasseta**) cluster bomb dispensers can also be carried. Apart from the above-named weapons, the Su-25T can also employ precision-guided munitions, such as the 500 kg

(1,100 lb) TV-guided KAB-500Kr (*Korrektiruye-maya Aviatsionnaya Bomba*) or the laser-guided KAB-500L bombs. The suffix designation of the TV-guided weapon refers to the fact that it uses image correlation (*Korrelatsiya*) in the targeting process, while the letter 'L' of the KAB-500L refers to its laser-guidance mode.

The cannon armament of the Su-25T comprises a single built-in fixed NPPU-8M installation, with a twin-barrelled Gryazov and Shipunov GSh-2-30 30 mm cannon and a total of 200 rounds. The aircraft can also carry two detachable SPPU-687 (*S'yomnaya Podvizhnaya Pushechnaya Ustanovka*) pods, with a single-barrelled GSh-301 30 mm cannon and 150 rounds of ammunition per pod, or two SPPU-22-1 pods with a twin-barrelled GSh-23 23 mm cannon and 260 rounds of ammunition.

Equipment. The avionics equipment of the Su-25T includes:

- a SUV-25T (8PM) *Voskhod* (Sunrise) weapons control system;
- flight navigation instrumentation;
- communications radios and ATC transponders;
- an *Irtysh* electronic countermeasures suite;
- a *Tester-ZU* flight data-recording system.

The *Voskhod* weapons-control system provides sighting and targeting information to enable the pilot to carry out effective daylight and night attacks using either single-type (i.e. all bombs, all rockets) or mixed-weapon loads. It also provides navigation data to enable the aircraft to fly out to the target area and return to base, or a designated alternate airfield. The SUV-25T (8PM) system comprises:

- the I-251 automatic targeting and sighting complex (*Kruglosutochnyy Avtomaticheskiy Pritselny Kompleks – KAPK*) providing round-the-clock operation, developed by the 'Zenit' Optical-Mechanical Plant in Krasnogorsk. The system is designed to provide automatic identification and tracking of small, moving targets (e.g. tanks, automobiles, patrol boats, etc.), target designation and missile guidance, as well as firing solutions for the cannon and unguided rockets;
- the IT-23M SOI (*Sistema Otobrazheniya Informatsii*) information display system (to be replaced in due course by the TV-109M system);
- a central computer;
- the IKV-1 inertial system;

- the DISS-7 Doppler ground-speed and drift indicator;
- the RV-15 radio altimeter;
- the RSBN-6S short-range navigation system and instrument landing system;
- the RSDN long-range navigation system.

The I-25I targeting and sighting complex supports the use of all types of guided and unguided weaponry cleared for use on the Su-25T, to attack ground and airborne targets. The information display sub-system projects navigation, aircraft-handling and target information on the head-up display (HUD) in all flight modes, while the central computer provides weapons-delivery solutions for the aircraft's standard weapons fit, as well as routine navigation of the aircraft.

The I-251 system comprises the *Shkval* daylight electro-optical sub-system, located in the nose of the aircraft, and includes a high-resolution TV camera with both wide (27° × 36°) and narrow (0.7° × 0.9°) fields of view and 23 times image magnification. The camera is linked to a target-tracking unit which has an accuracy of up to 0.6 m (2 ft) and a laser rangefinder and marked target seeker. The sensors are all mounted on a single platform which is stabilised in pitch, roll and yaw and can sustain angular displacements of up to +15° and -80° in the vertical and from +25° to -80° in azimuth, without losing sight of the target. The detection distance and lock-on to the target by the television system is 12 km (6.5 nm).

For night operations the I-251 system is augmented by the *Merkuriy* (Mercury) infra-red camera system, mounted in a pod under the central fuselage area, and has both wide and narrow fields of view, but is not stabilised in the three normal axes. Detection range and lock-on to the target is just a little less than 10 km (5.4 nm). Video information from the night-vision system's narrow field of view is presented on the monochrome TV screen used for the *Shkval* daylight camera, while that from the wide field of view channel is projected on the pilot's HUD.

The aircraft's radio equipment provides communication with ground command posts and control centres, as well as other aircraft, over its normal operational height and range limits, plus secondary surveillance radar responses and IFF responses when interrogated by other aircraft, ships and ground authorities. The aircraft's radio equipment consists of:

- the R-862 V/UHF communications radio;
- the R-828 VHF/FM radio for communication with ground forces units;

- the SO-69 aircraft transponder;
- the *Parol'* (Password) D-band IFF system;

The Su-25T is equipped with the *Irtysh* integrated electronic counter-measures suite, which comprises:

- the L-150 *Pastel'* (Crayon) advanced electronic surveillance measures and radar warning system;
- the *Sukhogruz* (Cargo Vessel) active infra-red jamming system, which provides effective protection in the rear hemisphere against a variety of infra-red homing missiles;
- chaff dispensers and chaff packages designed to jam radar-guided missiles;
- the UV-26 infra-red flare dispenser unit;
- the *Gardeniya-1FU* (Gardenia) active electronic countermeasures set.

The aircraft's flight-data-recording system includes:

- the *Tester-UZ* flight-data recorder;
- the *Ehkran* (Screen) built-in test, display and pilot-alerting system;
- an emergency visual warning system, informing the pilot about failures and malfunctions in the operation of the engines or major aircraft systems;
- an automatic female voice warning system, transmitting on the aircraft's normal V/UHF air-to-ground operating frequencies which informs the pilot and ground controllers of systems malfunctions and dangerous flight regimes;
- an 'objective control system' (*Sistema Obyektivnovo Kontrolya*) used in the post-flight analysis of the pilot's actions and systems performance when carrying out combat and routine training flights.

Electrical system. The Su-25T's electrical system provides both AC and DC power to the aircraft's systems. The DC supply system is identical with that on the Su-25UB. The AC system consists of two separate circuits, with each AC circuit being supplied by a 30 KvA PGL-40 generator providing 115 V at 400 Hz. A single PTS-800BM converter for each AC circuit acts as an emergency generator. The external lighting of the Su-25T is common to the corresponding systems on the Su-25 and Su-25UB.

Hydraulic system. The hydraulic system of the Su-25T is almost identical with that on the Su-25UB, with the minor difference that the new variant has a hydraulic booster in the elevator control circuit. Rudder control is achieved by means of two parallel autonomous hydraulic circuits. The main hydraulic system supplying the starboard aileron actuator and elevator is designated 2GS, with 1GS as the duplicate system. Similarly, the main system supplying the port aileron actuator is 1GS, with 2GS as the duplicate system. Each hydraulic system is of the closed-loop type and has an individual NP-34M pump mounted on the accessory drive unit of the appropriate engine, distribution pipes and control units. The hydraulic fluid used in the system is AMG-10 with a working pressure of 210 kg/cm^2 (3,000 lb/in^2).

Flight control system. The flight control system of the Su-25T is standard for this type of aircraft and employs ailerons, elevators and rudder. Control of the ailerons and rudder is identical to that of the elevators. The control circuits are of the irreversible type, with BU-45A hydraulic boosters, and allow for manual reversion in the event of the failure of both hydraulic systems. Artificial feel is provided in the pitch and roll channels by a spring-loaded mechanism. An MP-100M trim effect mechanism is installed in both control channels to relieve loads on the control column. The reduction of loads in the elevator-control channel in the event of the failure of both hydraulic systems is achieved by a 'kinematic' servo compensator mounted on each elevator. In order to increase the aircraft's combat survivability both elevator halves are interconnected by a universal shaft. Control of all aerodynamic surfaces is by the use of rods, designed for increased combat survivability.

The Su-25T has the SAU-8 automatic flight control system, which in conjunction with the SUV-25T (8PM) *Voskhod* weapons control system, provides:

- stabilisation of the aircraft in all axes;
- stabilisation of the barometric height of the aircraft;
- automatic return of the aircraft to normal horizontal flight from any attitude;
- damping of any short-period oscillations;
- automatic and flight-director-mode control of the aircraft at low level with inputs from the SUV-25T weapons control system;
- automatic and flight-director-mode control during guidance onto the target, route navigation, return to the designated airfield for landing and approach down to a height of 50 m (165 ft) using inputs from the SUV-25T weapons control system;
- automatic breakaway from the target and avoidance of weapons fragments, or pull-up from a dangerously low height, commanded by the SUV-25T weapons control system.

Emergency escape system. The emergency egress system of the Su-25T guarantees the pilot the ability to eject from the aircraft throughout its normal flight envelope, albeit requiring a forward speed of 75 km/h (40 kt) on the runway if an emergency occurs during take-off or landing. The main element of the emergency escape system is the Zvezda K-36L (*Lyogkovyesnyy*) lightweight ejection seat, which operates in conjunction with emergency separation of the hinged, opening section of the cockpit canopy. All ejection seat and canopy mechanisms are activated by a single pull of the ejection seat handle.

The All-weather Multi-role Anti-tank Su-25TM (T8-TM, Su-39)

In January 1986, a resolution was issued by the Military Industrial Commission of the Council of Ministers of the USSR requesting the construction of a new all-weather variant of the Su-25T under the designation Su-25TM, with a widened range of combat applications. A number of designers, under the leadership of Chief Designer Vladimir Babak, had already started work on the new project, but in 1989 another decree, directly from the Council of Ministers, now required the Sukhoi OKB to prepare the preliminary design of a new 'frontal strike aircraft'. This was to be a multi-role fighter-bomber under the designation S-37 (not to be confused with the much later *Berkut* [Golden Eagle]

experimental forward swept-wing [FSW] aircraft of the same designation). Leadership of this project was also given to Vladimir Babak, who thus now had two major projects to manage, although the S-37 strike aircraft programme was given the highest priority. (It is worth noting that when the strike aircraft project was first mooted, with the designation S-37, the FSW design had been given the provisional designation of S-32.)

In projecting the design of the S-37 the main idea was to achieve the maximum benefit from the most modern equipment and weapons in the Soviet Union at that time, but using a very non-traditional (for the USSR) aerodynamic layout for the aircraft. This was to have produced a design having a single, albeit very powerful, engine, which would permit not only an increase in combat payload, but also the number of hardpoints for weapons and other external stores, thanks to the use of a large wing and partial carriage of weapons under the wide integral fuselage/wing centre section. The S-37 was designed with a canard layout and a trapezoidal wing and was novel in Soviet aircraft design terms not only in having this layout, but also in the use of many non-traditional design solutions, such as, for example, additional control surfaces on the rear fuselage to compensate for the lack of a conventional tailplane.

In essence, the S-37 was a hybrid of the best ideas embodied not only in the more recent Soviet designs of the time, such as the Su-24, Su-25 and the Su-27, but also in a number of foreign designs as well. These ideas were

This striking head-on view of the prototype Su-25TM (T8TM-2) shows clearly the extent of nosewheel offset required by the relocated cannon installation. Also evident is the larger size and reshaping of the electro-optical sighting window in the nose. *(Yefim Gordon)*

This oblique frontal view of the Su-25TM (T8TM-2) accentuates the hump-backed appearance of this highly modified single-seat variant. *(Yefim Gordon)*

transformed into the design of a new, highly manoeuvrable strike aircraft of canard layout, as mentioned, capable of operating over a wide speed range and employing an extensive range of weapons types. In the opinion of the designers, the S-37 would be able to not only destroy any ground or seaborne target with its designated weapons, but also conduct manoeuvring air combat using medium- and short-range air-to-air missiles such as the R-27 (AA-10 *Alamo*) or R-60M (AA-8 *Aphid*). The preliminary design of the S-37 was studied in the various institutes attached to the Ministry of Aircraft Production (MAP) and the Ministry of

Defence and was given a positive reception. Moreover, it was actually planned to construct the aircraft in one of the MAP factories after carrying out the normal cycle of tests, but the impending collapse of the Soviet Union and the worsening political and economic situation in the country meant that these plans could not be realised.

Following cessation of work on the S-37 project, Chief Designer Vladimir Babak decided to incorporate some of the ideas developed for it in the new all-weather variant of the Su-25T, the Su-25TM, where the suffix 'M' indicated, as usual, a modified version of an existing type. The Su-25TM project could, in any case, be

The prototype Su-25T, representing the Su-25TM (T8TM-2) standard, was exhibited in the winter of 1992 at a specially organised air show and exhibition at Minsk-Machulishchi in Byelorussia (now the Republic of Belarus'), for the benefit of the Russian leadership. The aim of the exhibition was to demonstrate the achievements of the Russian aerospace industry and the range of new aircraft and weapons which were then expected to enter service with the Soviet Air Force. Within weeks, the Soviet Union was to disintegrate, and unfortunately, a decade later, very little of this great potential has been realised and most of the innovative aircraft programmes have stagnated. *(Sergey Skrynnikov)*

accomplished much more easily since the Su-25T baseline anti-tank variant had already entered production at that time.

It has already been noted that the distinguishing feature of the Su-25TM (T8-TM) compared with the Su-25T (T8-M) should be regarded as the all-weather capability of the former. In addition, the rapid development of enemy air-defence systems necessitated the use of new means of suppressing these systems, and it was decided that it would be useful to install a radar as part of the aircraft's navigation-attack system. Since it was also decided that it would be inexpedient to change the basic design structure of the aircraft, a podded location for the radar was chosen. Initially, the *Kinzhal* (Dagger) was selected for the new variant, a small, fighter-sized radar developed by the Leninets Scientific Production Association of St Petersburg. Eight units of the *Kinzhal* system were built for testing, which were used for airborne trials in various flying test-beds at Zhukovskiy and at Akhtubinsk. This radar, however, required substantial and costly modification and further tests, which in the difficult financial situation following the collapse of the Soviet Union was simply impossible to achieve. Therefore, it was decided to use the already developed *Kop'yo* (Spear) system, a radar developed by Fazotron of Moscow for small fighter types, and in particular for upgraded versions of the MiG-21bis *Fishbed-L/N*. The adoption of the *Kop'yo* radar for the MiG-21 was made

with export sales in mind, and this objective was to be realised when Russia and India signed a contract for the upgrade of 125 MiG-21bis fighters of the Indian Air Force, as the MiG-21-93. More recently, the designation MiG-21-93 has been dropped in favour of the more explanatory MiG21UPG, for 'Upgrade'. The use of the same radar on the Su-25T also promised evident benefits, since it would not only satisfy the requirements of the military in terms of expanding the operational capabilities of the aircraft, but also increase its export potential. Although the new 'shturmovik' was now more expensive, its combat effectiveness was even greater than before.

It should be noted that the *Kop'yo* radar works in the centimetric waveband and is therefore inferior to the *Kinzhal* (8 mm wavelength) in terms of resolution when working against ground targets, so it had to be modified for use on the Su-25T. The new variant of this radar for the Su-25T was, nevertheless, developed in a very short timescale and was given the designation *Kop'yo-25*. This radar and the upgraded *Shkval-M* electro-optical system form the basis of modifying the Su-25T into the Su-25TM.

At the beginning of the 1990s, the design team at 'Shturmoviki Sukhovo' were totally involved in the development of the upgraded systems of the new aircraft and bringing it up to the level of a true all-weather round-the-clock weapons system, capable of using

Regularly exhibited at the Moscow Aerospace Salons in recent years, the prototype Su-25TM (T8TM-2) is seen at MAKS '95 at Zhukovskiy with a typical 'air show' array of weapons. The most potent of these is the Kh-29T (AS-14 *Kedge*) TV-guided missile on the inboard station, flanked by eight **Vikhr-M** anti-armour missiles, a FAB-500 bomb, a B-13L five-tube launcher for 122 mm S-13 unguided rockets and an AA-11 *Archer* air-to-air missile outboard. *(Yefim Gordon)*

BELOW: Close-up detail of the large hexagonal window of the **Shkval** electro-optical system. Note the KAB-500L laser-guided bomb on the starboard inboard pylon, counterbalancing the AS-14 on the other side. Also evident in this head-on view is the offset nosewheel of this variant. *(Yefim Gordon)*

The full armoury of offensive weapons available for the Su-25TM is shown here, both on and off the aircraft. The underwing weapons pylons are loaded identically with Kh-29L (AS-14 *Kedge*) laser-guided air-to-surface missiles, two packs of eight **Vikhr-M** anti-armour missiles, two S-25L laser-guided rockets, two B-13L 122 mm rocket launchers and two AA-11 *Archer* self-defence missiles. In front of the aircraft are two large-calibre rockets, and six FAB-500 and four OFAB-250ShP iron bombs. *(Sergey Skrynnikov)*

BELOW: The first series-production Su-25TM (T8TM-3), which first flew on 15 August 1995, was displayed a few days later at MAKS '95 at Zhukovskiy, with the mock-up of the **Kop'yo**-25 radar on the fuselage centreline pylon. The large radar-guided weapon next to the drop tank is the Kh-35 (AS-20 *Kayak*) anti-shipping missile, and the red missile is a drill round of the AA-12 *Adder* AAM. An **Omul'** ECM pod is carried on the outer pylon. *(Yefim Gordon)*

ABOVE: Close-up of the hemispherical antenna covering the ARGS-35E seeker head of the radar-guided Kh-35 (AS-20 *Kayak*) anti-shipping missile mounted on an Su-25TM. Alongside it is a pack of eight 9M120M ***Vikhr-M*** laser-guided anti-armour missiles. *(Yefim Gordon)*

BELOW: This configuration represents a useful air-to-ground arsenal for the Su-25TM, with a Kh-29T (AS-14 *Kedge*) TV-guided missile inboard, eight ***Vikhr-M*** anti-armour missiles in the centre and a five-tube B-13L rocket launcher inboard of the AA-11 *Archer* AAM. *(Yefim Gordon)*

The cockpit of the Su-25TM is dominated by analogue instrumentation, the large TV display of the **Shkval** electro-optical system and the weapons status indicator (**mnemoskhema**) at the bottom of the main panel being the main concessions to modernity. Of interest, however, is the square panel below the yellow brake-chute selector on the centre left of the photo. The panel's three-position switch (with settings PK, MK and VPK) enables the pilot to control the parameters for the wing's high-lift devices. For normal flight, PK (**Polyotnoye Krylo** – literally 'Flight Wing') is selected, MK (**Manyevryennoye Krylo** – 'Manoeuvring Wing') is selected to enable the automatic flaps and slats to function in response to varying flight loads, and the 'Take-off and Landing' setting VPK (**Vzlyotno-posadovchnoye Krylo**) is used to allow the appropriate settings to be made for those phases of flight. *(Yefim Gordon)*

all types of precision-guided munitions. In 1995 this modernised version of the Su-25T was given a new designation, Su-39, and its export variant, having only minor differences from the domestic version, was also given the same designation.

As already mentioned, the main identification feature of the Su-25TM (Su-39) is the installation of the (3 cm wavelength) *Kop'yo-25* multi-function radar and

the *Shkval-M* upgraded electro-optical system. The radar has a flat-plate slotted antenna array of 500 mm (20 in) diameter. Although still superficially similar to the original Su-25 'shturmovik', the expansion of the range of combat applications of the Su-25TM made it possible to reclassify the aircraft as an all-weather, multi-role tactical combat aircraft. The *Kop'yo-25* enables the pilot to carry out all-weather detection and

This series-production Su-25T (T8M-6) was displayed at MAKS '97 to represent the definitive Su-25TM and was equipped with a mock-up of the **Kop'yo-25** radar in an under-fuselage pod. It also carried a typical 'air show arsenal' of offensive and defensive missiles, including Kh-31 (AS-17 *Krypton*) and Kh-29T (AS-14 *Kedge*) air-to-surface missiles. Additionally, it has **Vikhr-M** anti-armour missiles, plus AA-12 *Adder* and AA-11 *Archer* for self-defence. Of interest is that it is also decorated with both the Sukhoi winged archer emblem and the Ulan-Ude prancing bear. *(Yefim Gordon)*

The mock-up of the **Kop'yo-25** radar under Su-25T (T8M-6) on display during MAKS '97 at Zhukovskiy. *(Yefim Gordon)*

LEFT: The larger window of the **Shkval** and **Shkval-M** electro-optical targeting system of the Su-25T and Su-25TM is clearly apparent in this head-on underside view. *(Yefim Gordon)*

ABOVE: The electro-optical sensors of the **Merkuriy** (Mercury) LLTV/FLIR system are located in a very substantial pod carried on the fuselage centreline. A protective 'door', with powerful lever-action operation, covers the delicate sighting windows when not in use. *(Yefim Gordon)*

Detail view of the tail unit of the Su-25TM, showing the **Sukhogruz** jammer, the rudder and its upper yaw damper section, the handle-shaped antenna of the R828 radio and the blade antenna of the **Parol'** D-band IFF system. Note that the 'leading edge' of the delta-shaped blade is facing backwards, to optimise transmission and reception in the rear hemisphere. *(Yefim Gordon)*

preliminary target designation in a variety of attack modes, including ground mapping.

Apart from the standard air-to-ground armament of the Su-25T, incorporation of the **Kop'yo-25** radar into the weapons system of the improved Su-25TM (Su-39) permitted the use of the supersonic Kh-31A (AS-17 *Krypton*) tactical anti-shipping missile, with an active radar homing head and the subsonic Kh-35 (AS-20 *Kayak*). The latter weapon employs a combination of inertial mid-course guidance with an active radar seeker for the terminal phase of attack. The Su-25TM (Su-39) can carry from two to four anti-ship missiles. Thus, a flight of Su-25TM (Su-39) could represent a real threat to a tactical group of surface vessels and attack a destroyer (displacing around 8,000 tonnes) without entering the lethal zone of the ship's air-defence guns.

Installation of the **Kop'yo-25** radar on the Su-25TM (Su-39) permits it to undertake an active air combat role. The radar guarantees detection of fighter-sized airborne targets with a 5 m² (54 ft²) radar cross-sectional area at a distance of up to 57 km (31 nm) in the forward hemisphere. In the rear hemisphere this figure is up to 25 km (13.5 nm), with the capability of tracking up to ten targets and engaging two of them with missiles. The capability of carrying all-aspect R-77 (AA-12 *Adder*), with their combined guidance systems, permits the Su-25TM (Su-39) to conduct medium-range air combat on equal terms with fighters armed with Raytheon Sparrow or AMRAAM (Advanced Medium-Range Air-to-Air Missile) missiles.

In close-in air combat, the Su-25TM is also dangerous to any potential adversary. The R-73 (AA-11 *Archer*) which can be carried by the aircraft is considered to be one of the best short-range missiles in the world, while the **Sukhogruz** infra-red jammer, currently the only active built-in infra-red jammer on a fixed-wing aircraft, is an effective counter to the widely deployed AIM-9 Sidewinder missile. Moreover, to destroy the heavily armoured Russian aircraft using the 20 mm Vulcan cannon, for example, would require at least 30 hits – no easy task for the pilot, especially at low level, where the turning radius of the Su-25 is less than that of most foreign fighters.

The structure of the upgraded aircraft underwent practically no changes, compared with the Su-25T. The modernised and improved **Shkval-M** electro-optical (EO) system is mounted in a lengthened and widened nose, with the TV image displayed on the right-hand side of the pilot's instrument panel. During approach to the target, at a distance of around 10–12 km (5.5–6.5 nm), the

EO system is engaged in scanning mode. Depending upon the flight altitude, the **Shkval** camera observes a strip of terrain with a width of between 0.5 and 2 km (0.3–1 nm). Observing the results of a missile or rocket launch, or a burst of cannon fire, the pilot can, if necessary, carry out a second approach and then depart from the target area.

Shkval-M can, for example, identify a single isolated building at a distance of up to 15 km (8 nm), or a tank at a distance of up to 8–10 km (4.3–5.5 nm). A target selected by the pilot can be bracketed for automatic tracking, with the target image 'memorised' by a special function of the EO processing system. The EO system is able to maintain a 'lock' on the target, even when the aircraft is manoeuvring, and provide an accurate range read-out to it. This then makes it possible to achieve direct hits with guided munitions, while the accuracy of unguided ordnance, including free-fall bombs, is increased many times. The **Shkval-M** also permits detection of targets illuminated by a ground-based forward air controller (FAC) and attack them in automatic mode. This is particularly important when operating close to the FLOT (Forward Line of Own Troops), in order to avoid incidents of 'fratricide'.

A new electronic countermeasures system was also developed for the Su-25TM (Su-39), known as MPS-410 **Omul'** (a Lake Baikal salmon) and designed by the Central Scientific Research Radiotechnical Institute. The equipment is housed in two pods which are mounted on the outer pylons of each wing.

Two prototype Su-25T aircraft (T8M-1 and T8M-4) were selected for conversion to test the new on-board systems of the Su-25TM, these aircraft becoming T8TM-1 and T8TM-2 respectively. T8TM-1 achieved its first flight on 4 February 1991, and T8TM-2 flew for the first time six months later, on 19 August, the test-pilot on both occasions being A.A. Ivanov of the Sukhoi OKB. The first aircraft was used for trials of the electronic countermeasures (ECM) system and a new pod for the **Khod** (Pace, or Movement) forward-looking thermal imaging system, and the second aircraft was used to continue development work on the **Kinzhal** radar. Work on the **Khod** and **Kinzhal** systems was terminated in 1994 and a mock-up of the **Kop'yo-25** radar was mounted on T8TM-2 (Blue Side No. 09) to represent the Su-25TM configuration. In this guise the aircraft was displayed at MAKS '95 at Zhukovskiy, although prior to this it had also been shown to selected military personnel at special restricted military displays at Zhukovskiy and Minsk-Machulishche (in Belarus') in the winter of 1992.

A total of sixteen 9M-120M *Vikhr-M* supersonic anti-armour missiles give the Su-25TM devastatingly destructive firepower against tanks and armoured vehicles. *(Yefim Gordon)*

In 1993, work commenced at Ulan-Ude to prepare the jigs for series production of the Su-25TM, using the existing production experience of manufacturing the Su-25UB to speed up the process. The first series-production aircraft (actually the third prototype – T8TM-3 with White Side No. 20) took to the air on 15 August 1995, in the hands of Sukhoi OKB test-pilot Oleg Tsoi. A few days later, this aircraft was displayed at MAKS '95 at Zhukovskiy, equipped with a mock-up of the *Kop'yo-25* radar. Testing of the new aircraft began on 5 February 1997, at the State Flight-Test Centre (*Gosudarstvennyy Lyotno-ispytatel'nyy Tsentr – GLITs*, formerly known as *GNIKI VVS*) at Akhtubinsk, flown by Sukhoi test-pilot I.E. Soloviev. The fourth prototype (or second series-production aircraft), T8TM-4 (White Side No. 21), also assembled at Ulan-Ude, made its first flight on 25 March 1998, with Oleg Tsoi at the controls. Throughout the course of 1999–2000, all four aircraft took part in Joint State Trials.

A series-production Su-25T (T8M-6) with Black Side No. 21 was displayed at the MAKS '97 air show at Zhukovskiy, made to represent the Su-25TM, with a mock-up *Kop'yo-25*, although two years later, in August 1999, the real Su-25TM (T8TM-4, White Side No. 21) was shown at MAKS '99. It is of interest to note that many visitors to the show thought that the aircraft displayed at MAKS '99 was simply the repainted aircraft displayed two years earlier, since it had the same side number, albeit white instead of black. Currently, the Su-25TM is completing the final phase of State Joint Trials and is being prepared for series production.

In the late 1990s, the 'Shturmoviki Sukhovo' (Sukhoi Shturmoviks) organisation started to become very active in the international marketplace. In 1996, it submitted a proposal to Poland, which was planning to modernise its combat aircraft fleet, and 'Shturmoviki Sukhovo' officially offered to supply 100 Su-39 (Su-25TM) attack aircraft in exchange for foodstuffs. Similar offers were made to the Czech Republic and Hungary, although in both cases they were rejected. It is known, however, that in 1998 the Ulan-Ude Aviation Plant received a State order from the Russian Federation for the manufacture and delivery of several Su-25TMs for operational units of the Russian Air Force.

The Upgraded Su-25SM (T8-SM) 'Shturmovik'

The original Su-25, as conceived in the 1970s, was intended for direct (close) air support of ground forces over the battlefield up to 100 km (62 miles) behind the front line, in simple (daylight VFR) meteorological conditions and in an active ECM environment. This basic Su-25 was built to augment other strike aircraft in service with the Soviet Air Force at that time, including the Su-17M, Su-24, MiG-27 fighter-bombers and the Tu-22 bomber. In this way, by the middle of the 1980s, the Soviet Union had created a powerful military aviation 'system', in which each type of aircraft performed an assigned role which mirrored that of its potential adversaries. Significantly, these aircraft were available to the Soviet Union and the air forces of the Warsaw Pact in huge numbers.

The collapse of the Soviet Union (and the Warsaw Pact military organisation with it), the creation of new independent democratic states and the transition of many of these countries to a market-based economy, had a radical impact on the tasks set before the newly retitled Russian Air Force. Almost immediately a large number of strike aircraft were withdrawn from service, including Su-17M3/Su-17M4s and MiG-27s, plus MiG-21 and MiG-23 interceptors, as well as major reductions being made in the fleet of Su-24/Su-24Ms, MiG-29s, Su-27s and Su-25s. A little later, the Russian Air Force itself underwent reorganisation, which involved absorption of the previously autonomous Homeland Air Defence force (**Protivo-Vozdushnaya Oborona,** or **PVO**) into the main body and command structure of the air force. The tasks of the newly reorganised units were also changed, and now ranged from the ability to conduct global warfare, down to participation in 'localised conflicts' and involvement in international peacekeeping missions.

All of this led in turn to changes being made in the demands placed upon the Su-25, which had become virtually the main strike asset available to the Russian Air Force for use in 'localised conflicts'. Among its many applications in these combat situations were the following:

- the destruction of ground targets in VFR and IFR weather conditions, day or night;
- detection and suppression (neutralisation) of ground-based air-defence systems, plus destruction of enemy command and control elements, using standard weapons and armament;
- destruction of targets with increased accuracy using standard weapons, plus destruction of pinpoint targets with precision-guided munitions (PGM);
- destruction of targets exhibiting high radar contrast;
- escort and top cover for groups of other Su-25s performing ground-strike or anti-shipping missions;
- top cover of own airfield against air strikes by enemy groups;
- destruction of airborne targets, such as transport aircraft, tactical fighters and fighter-bombers and helicopters;
- air support for air landing of troops by transport aircraft and tactical paratroop drops over the dropping zone (DZ);

The first converted Su-25SM, seen at MAKS 2001, wearing Su-25SM titles and the badge of the 121st Aviation Repair Plant at Kubinka, where the conversion work was carried out. *(Yefim Gordon)*

- attacks on airborne and seaborne landing elements and units of enemy air-mobile forces;
- destruction of surface ships, up to the size of a destroyer, either operating singly or as part of a naval task group;
- training aircrew in weapons application, using special 'simulator' modes incorporated in the aircraft's on-board electronics package.

In order to carry out any, or all, of the above-listed tasks required a radical modernisation programme to be implemented, covering the entire fleet of Su-25s currently in service with the Russian Air Force, and in February 1998 the Sukhoi OKB started work on transforming this requirement into reality. The main thrust of modernising the original standard 'shturmovik' into the rejuvenated and upgraded Su-25SM largely focused on the complete replacement of the old avionics, the inclusion of PGMs into the weapons inventory of the aircraft and redesigning the cockpit layout. Since all of this work was to be carried out on ordinary squadron aircraft, withdrawn from service for the period of the modification, the upgraded aircraft were to be known as Su-25SM, where 'SM' stands for '*Stroyevoy Modernizirovanny*' – literally '(front) line (aircraft) modernised'.

The new equipment of the Su-25SM was to include:

- the *Pantera* (Panther) integrated navigation-attack and weapons-control system, incorporating a new high-speed digital computer;
- the RLPK-25SM (*Radiolokatsionnyy Pritselnyy Kompleks* for the Su-25SM) radar, based on the Fazotron *Kop'yo*;
- a pod-mounted ECM system, incorporating electronic surveillance measures (ESM) and a target designation facility, as well as an active jamming unit.

The *Pantera* system was intended to:

- increase navigation accuracy by a factor of ten, which would permit successful first-pass attacks on the target;
- maximise automation of search, identification and destruction of the target;
- facilitate the use of PGMs with both laser and TV guidance heads;
- offer the possibility of using new attack modes, which employed standard weapons types (for example, in-flight correction of preprogrammed target co-ordinates and bombing of targets as navigation

'waypoints' (navigational bombing);
- facilitate the use of several types of weapon on one attack;
- reduce pilot work-load by providing a modern cockpit information-management system, with colour multifunction displays and a wide-angle head-up display, as well as the automation of weapons selection and release.

The RLPK-25SM was designed for installation in the nose of the Su-25SM, in the compartment used for the *Klyon-PS* (Maple) laser rangefinder on the original aircraft. As previously mentioned, the *Kop'yo-25* radar, used in podded form on the Su-25TM, was intended for target detection and designation in the air-to-air, air-to-surface and air-to-sea modes, as well as for ground mapping. The new integrated electronic warfare (EW) system of the Su-25SM was designed to permit a more sophisticated level of radar warning than the earlier SPO-15 *Beryoza* (Birch) type of radar warning receiver (RWR) on the standard Su-25. The new system can warn the pilot of the level of threat from an enemy radar, target the illuminating radar with anti-radiation missiles, initiate deception, noise, blink and terrain-bounce jamming, as well as control the operation of infra-red flare dispensers. Equipping the Su-25 with a new weapons-control system will allow a wide range of precision-guided (with laser and TV homing) air-to-surface, air-to-sea and anti-radiation missiles to be added to its existing arsenal.

Airborne targets can be effectively engaged using the RLPK-25SM radar system, in concert with air-to-air missiles, such as the R-27R[Eh] (AA-10 *Alamo*), R-77 (AA-12 *Adder*) and R-73 (AA-11 *Archer*). The R-27R[Eh] designation indicates that it is a semi-active radar variant, the 'Eh' suffix meaning '*ehnergeticheskiy*', literally 'energetic', but in the sense of having longer range, rather than implying extra agility. This offers the possibility of providing top cover for a group of 'shturmoviks' carrying out ground strikes, not by the use of conventional fighter aircraft, as was previously the case, but by using modernised Su-25SM 'shturmoviks', themselves operating as fighters. Studies carried out by the designers of this new and cheaper version of the basic Su-25 have shown that the modified Su-25SM, armed with the above-mentioned air-to-air missiles, will be able to perform top-cover missions with no less success in air combat than even the formidable F-16 Fighting Falcon.

Installation of the new equipment has required a partial reworking of the forward fuselage, mainly in the nose section, in order to house the new radar, since the original Su-25 was not designed to have one. In the cockpit, the use of the new SIU-25 (*Sistema Indikatsii i Upravlyeniya*) control and indication system has required changes to be made in the layout of the instrument panel and side control panels. As far as the powerplant is concerned, no changes will be made to the standard R95Sh, since it has proved to be so reliable and resistant to combat damage, but the considerable amount of operational experience with the engine means that its time between overhauls (TBO) can be extended. Also unchanged will be the empty weight of the aircraft, retaining all of the uniquely effective combat survivability features in terms of armour plating and systems protection.

The main objective of upgrading the Su-25 to the Su-25SM standard is to increase its combat effectiveness at minimal cost. This also involved improving ease of maintenance and modernising its servicing procedures. Automated input of flight data (navigation waypoints and combat tasking data), plus automated ground-checking of equipment serviceability, with fault diagnosis down to line-replaceable unit (LRU) level using built-in test equipment (BITE), will permit reductions of 25–30% in labour costs in servicing the Su-25SM, compared with the basic Su-25. The modification will permit a more than two-fold increase in its combat effectiveness, and the relatively moderate price of the upgrade (around US$2.5–3 million) ought to interest the many countries which operate the Su-25K. More than 400 Su-25s are in service outside Russia (i.e. including CIS countries), so there are hopes for many customers for the upgrade among these operators.

There is another important argument in favour of the upgrade of the Su-25 to the Su-25SM standard – the economic argument. The baseline variant of the Su-25 was designed for a service life of 25 years and an airframe life of 3,000 hours, which equates to an average annual airframe usage of 110–120 hours. As a consequence of the changes in the military-political and general economic situation within Russia and the member countries of the CIS (Commonwealth of Independent States), the average annual flight time per aircraft does not even amount to 50% of the planned rate. So, by the time the calendar period of 25 years has expired, Russian Air Force Su-25s could possibly still have more than half their airframe life remaining. Since it would be too expensive to replace the aircraft with a new type, it

would be more rational instead to extend the period in service up to the time when its airframe life expires.

Unfortunately, in 2000, the Russian Air Force was compelled by ever-present financing difficulties to review the Su-25SM upgrade programme and a cheaper option was adopted for the initial modernisation of the Su-25 fleet. This has resulted in a reduction in the capabilities of the current Su-25SM. Technical documentation for a simplified Su-25SM was then issued to the 121st Aviation Repair Plant (*121 Aviaremontnyy Zavod*) at Kubinka, near Moscow, and the plant initiated work soon afterwards on the first batch of conversions. The first modernised Su-25SM 'shturmovik' (Red Side No. 33/c/n 255.081.09.033) was rolled out by 121 ARZ in time to take part in the static display at MAKS-2001 at Zhukovskiy in August 2001. The most significant difference between the 'new' Su-25SM and the original specification for the aircraft is the lack of the RLPK-25SM radar, which must be a huge disappointment for the Russian Air Force, since so much of the improved performance of the upgraded aircraft depended on it. Altogether, it is planned to upgrade around 40% of the Su-25 fleet still in service with the Russian Air Force, over the next three years. This total is believed to be *c.*250 aircraft, giving a total of *c.*100 Su-25s which could be upgraded to 'SM' standard.

Information made available at the end of 2002 confirms that the prototype Su-25SM had successfully completed its preliminary test programme of forty-one flights by the end of November and was due to commence State Joint Trials in December 2002. This phase of flight-testing is expected to last for one year and will involve several hundred hours of flying and a total of four aircraft (three Su-25s and one Su-25UBM). It was also reported that the Su-25SM will now be equipped with the *Bars* (Snow Leopard) integrated navigation and attack complex, based on a new high-speed digital computer and presumably a variant of the *Pantera* unit originally intended for the upgrade. The integrated EW/ESM system, or SRTR (*Sistema Radio-Tekhnicheskoi Razvedki*) has been confirmed as the *Pastel'* unit introduced on the Su-25T, which holds an extensive library of electronic intelligence (Elint) parameters for a large number of threat emitters, selectable by using 'soft keys' around the framework of the screen (*knopochnoye obramleniye*). This system is thought to be capable of analysing signals in the 2–18 GHz frequency spectrum, embracing a wide variety of ground-based, airborne and (if appropriate for a given theatre of operations) shipborne threat radars.

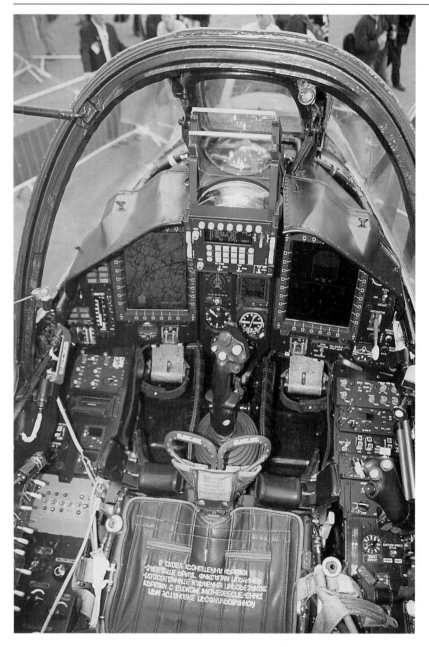

Elbit Systems has transformed the cockpit of the Su-25KM, giving it a very modern appearance, with clear presentation of flight and mission data on two large multifunction displays and virtually eliminating the cluttered look of the original aircraft. Noteworthy, however, is the retention of the SPO-15 radar warning display in the centre of the panel, identifiable by its MiG-21-like aircraft symbol. SPO-15 is a complex system to interpret, often criticised for this particular shortcoming, but its retention suggests that it is worth including in this radically improved *Frogfoot* variant. *(Yefim Gordon)*

The Su-25UBM (T8-UBM) Upgraded Combat Trainer

Along with upgrades of the basic Su-25 to the Su-25SM standard, it is proposed to modernise the twin-seat Su-25UB to an equivalent Su-25UBM (T8-UBM) standard. The single-seat Su-25SM and the twin-seat Su-25UBM will share systems commonality to the same degree as the Su-25 and Su-25UB. The first

Su-25UBM is scheduled to join the flight-test programme at Zhukovskiy in the third quarter of 2003.

Su-25KM

A somewhat unexpected Su-25 upgrade programme was announced early in 2001, involving a partnership between the original manufacturer, Tbilisi Aerospace

Manufacturing in Georgia, and Elbit Systems of Israel. Using a standard Su-25 airframe, the result of this collaborative venture has been named Scorpion and the aircraft's designation has been changed to Su-25KM (***Kommercheskiy Modernizirovannyy***), indicating that it is a modernised export variant. Making its maiden flight on 18 April 2001 at Tbilisi, the prototype Scorpion carries full Georgian Air Force markings, although the aircraft is primarily a systems demonstrator and no orders have yet been placed by either Georgia or any other air force. There has, however, been enormous interest in the Su-25KM from a number of quarters, including Africa and, allegedly, the Slovak Republic. Further interest is expected to be shown by countries of the Commonwealth of Independent States who are still operating the original Su-25 in significant numbers, such as Belarus', Turkmenistan, plus Ukraine. Israeli involvement in the project will undoubtedly also see a very proactive marketing campaign aimed at more recent operators of the Su-25, such as the Democratic Republic of Congo and Peru. Unfortunately, however, Russia is challenging the legality of such upgrades, which are being undertaken without the full authority of Sukhoi, even if they are being performed by the original authorised design authority for the aircraft, Tbilisi Aerospace Manufacturing (TAM), the former Tbilisi Aircraft State Association (TASA). At issue are the intellectual property rights of Sukhoi and the legacy

rights of the MiG fighter and Mil helicopter designs, which are the subject of planned upgrades by a number of specialist groups around the world. The worldwide upgrade market is a lucrative source of additional revenue for original equipment manufacturers (OEM), and it seems only natural that they should be the principal beneficiaries when a successful design is given a second lease of life by modernising it.

Like the recent, scaled-down Russian Su-25SM upgrade, the Scorpion does not involve airframe alterations, all of the improvements being in the cockpit, or in the weapons carried, although a weight saving of 315 kg (700 lb) has been achieved by replacing older Russian avionics with modern digital systems. Retaining all of the inherent ruggedness and practicality of the original Su-25, the modified Su-25KM Scorpion offers the pilot a wholly new cockpit information presentation system, with two Elbit Systems 15 × 20 cm (6 × 8 in) multifunction colour displays and an improved head-up display (HUD). In addition to the full nomenclature of Russian weapons of the Su-25, the Scorpion is also able to use Western ordnance, such as Elbit's infra-red-guided Opher and the new Lizard laser-guided bombs, plus the ubiquitous Mk 82. Elbit's well-known DASH (Display And Sight Helmet) helmet-mounted sighting and cueing system is also available as a customer option, further enhancing the pilot's situation awareness in the new cockpit. The overall cockpit layout has been rationalised

Seen landing at the Paris Air Show in 2001, the prototype Su-25KM Scorpion was presented jointly by TAM of Georgia and Elbit Systems of Israel, and was flown by Israeli test-pilot Yehudi Shafir. In addition to its Paris display number 316 and notional Georgian Air Force Bort number 01, the Su-25KM also wears the TAM/Elbit Systems' Scorpion badge under the cockpit. Shafir's pièce de résistance in his flight demonstration was to make his final landing approach off the top of a loop! *(Yefim Gordon)*

and gives this latest manifestation of the Su-25 a twenty-first-century appearance, considerably in advance of its original utility design. In fact, the Scorpion demonstrates in the most effective way possible the real value of an avionics and systems upgrade, by transforming a comparatively basic aircraft into an advanced weapons platform, the upgrade package being nothing less than a 'brain transplant' for this simple battlefield 'war-horse'.

The then President of Georgia, Eduard Shevardnadze, discusses the joint Georgian–Israeli Su-25KM upgrade with Israeli test-pilot Yehudi Shafir, who is seated in the Su-25KM at the Tbilisi Aerospace Manufacturing factory in Tbilisi. Shevardnadze was a keen supporter of the Georgian aerospace enterprise, recognising it to have the potential to serve as a model for the nation's post-Communist industrial regeneration, following the achievement of independence a decade ago. *(TAM)*

The airframe chosen to serve as the prototype of the Su-25KM (c/n 255.081.10629) seen inside a hangar at the Tbilisi Aerospace Manufacturing plant, being prepared for conversion. *(TAM)*

7

The Su-25 in Service and in Combat

Afghanistan

EARLY operational experience by Soviet Air Force Frontal Aviation aircraft in Afghanistan revealed their ineffectiveness in the mountainous conditions of the country when attempting to conduct what was, in essence, an anti-guerrilla war. Apart from this, Frontal Aviation aircrew were also insufficiently trained for this type of combat operation. The supersonic Su-17 and MiG-27 fighter-bombers, designed for use in the European theatre, were unsuited to manoeuvring flight in the mountains, and their navigation-attack systems were practically useless for pinpointing small ground targets. The functions which these aircraft had been designed to perform were not required in the Afghan theatre and combat results against ground targets were low. The most appropriate aircraft in these conditions turned out to be the well-armed and well-protected Su-25, easy to fly and highly manoeuvrable and which had received high marks from the military during its trial period in the country (*see* Operation *Rhombus* in Chapter 2).

Immediately after completion of the initial Afghan trials, in February 1981, the first Su-25 combat unit was formed – designated the 80th Independent Shturmovoi Aviation Regiment (*80-y Otdyelnyy Shturmovoy Aviatsionnyy Polk*). This regiment was based at Sital-Chai on the Caspian Sea coast, 65 km (40 miles) from Baku, the capital of Azerbaijan, at the time one of the component republics of the Union of Soviet Socialist Republics and now an independent member of the Commonwealth of Independent States (CIS). The choice of Sital-Chai was hardly accidental; series production of the Su-25 had been set up at Tbilisi in the neighbouring Republic of Georgia (also part of the former USSR and now independent), which meant that any unforeseen technical problems could be addressed quite quickly. Furthermore, there was a well-equipped bombing range nearby where pilots could hone their skills on the aircraft in mountain conditions, and more importantly perhaps, mastery of the new aircraft could be achieved not far from Afghanistan.

The first twelve series-produced Su-25s were handed over to the 80th Independent Shturmovoy Air Regiment (*80 OShAP*) in April 1981. The urgent need to get the

This pair of Su-25s reveals two different camouflage patterns for the aircraft. In operational use, the *Frogfoot* has worn a variety of camouflage patterns and colours, to a large extent, but not exclusively, determined by the theatre of operations. *(Yefim Gordon)*

new 'shturmovik' in service was emphasised when the Deputy Commander-in-Chief of the Soviet Air Force, Marshal A.N. Yefimov, flew in to Sital-Chai on 28 April 1981. He ordered that a squadron of Su-25s had to be formed as quickly as possible for service in Afghanistan, and commanded that the most experienced pilots on the type be assigned to it. The new squadron was designated the 200th Independent Shturmovaya Air Squadron (*200 Otdyel'naya Shturmovaya Aviaehskadrila*), and the Deputy Regimental Commander (Training) of 80 OShAP, Major A.M. Afanasyev, was appointed as its first Commanding Officer. Test-pilots from the Sukhoi OKB, Akhtubinsk and the 4th Centre for Combat Application and Aircrew Conversion at Lipetsk were also drafted in to the new unit, in order to accelerate the pace of training on the Su-25.

Initially, the entire command staff, pilots and technicians underwent training at Lipetsk. Here, the training was purely theoretical, but for more practical experience on the aircraft personnel were detached to the manufacturing plant in Tbilisi, where, after acquiring the first batch of aircraft, the pilots were also able to commence initial familiarisation flying. At this time there were no twin-seat Su-25s, and many pilots carried out the first stage of their conversion training on the Su-17UM *Fitter-E*, which was clearly a less than ideal aircraft on which to be taught the techniques of flying the new 'shturmovik'.

The 200th Independent 'Shturmovaya' Air Squadron arrived in Afghanistan on 19 July 1981 and was assigned to Shindand Air Base in the west of the country, whose personnel were already familiar with the operation of the Su-25 from Operation *Rhombus-1*. The squadron and its new aircraft were protected by detachments of Soviet Army motor-rifle and airborne forces, plus the 21st Infantry Brigade of the Afghan government forces. The Su-25s went into action only a few days after their arrival, and to evaluate their effectiveness a senior officer of the military combat inspectorate, Major-General V. Khakhalov, arrived soon after with a personal order from the Commander-in-Chief of the Soviet Air Force to assess the aircraft's strike results.

The 200th Independent 'Shturmovaya' Air Squadron (*200 OShAE*) was tasked with strikes not only against targets in the mountains, but also against a number of Afghan towns and villages. In the struggle to regain control of Herat, for example, which had become the centre of opposition in the west of the country and was situated around 120 km (75 miles) to the north of Shindand, Su-25s carried out strikes against buildings and houses controlled by Afghan rebels (*dushmany* – i.e. Dushman, or Afghan revolutionary). The buildings turned out to be rebel strongholds, containing weapons stashes and ammunition.

The Su-25 had to operate not only over very difficult geographical terrain, but also in very unforgiving weather conditions. Dust always hung in the air above the valleys, up to heights of around 1,500 m (5,000 ft), seriously hampering visibility, while summertime temperatures rose up to 50°C and sand which got into the engines damaged engine compressor blades. To add to

One of the earliest published photographs of the Su-25 was this view taken during operations over Afghanistan during the early period of Soviet occupation of the country. *(Yefim Gordon archive)*

the problems of aircraft handling in these conditions, the majority of flights were carried out with two PTB-800 underwing auxiliary fuel tanks, in order to extend the aircraft's endurance.

Combat activities in the south of Afghanistan commenced in September 1981, not far from the city of Kandahar, which also fell within the 'zone of responsibility' of the 200 OShAE. The main roads and caravan routes to the south passed through Kandahar, Afghanistan's second largest city, which also lies close to the border with Pakistan. Mountains surrounded Kandahar to the north, which provided strongholds for the mujahideen fighters, and even had fortresses dating from the time of British occupation of Afghanistan between 1838 and 1919.

Thanks to its large wing area and powerful high-lift devices, the Su-25 differed notably from other Soviet combat aircraft in its excellent take-off and landing performance. An Su-25 armed with eight FAB-500s required a take-off run of 1,200–1,300 m (3,900–4,260 ft), while the co-located Su-17M *Fitter-C* fighter-bombers could only manage to get airborne with two such bombs at the very end of the runway. The Su-25's excellent manoeuvring performance also turned out to be extremely useful in the mountainous terrain. Its low turning radius greatly helped the pilots when setting up an attack. After detecting a target, it was possible to bank steeply to turn back onto it, and during repeat attacks on the same target, to carry out orbits without losing sight of the enemy, dispensing ammunition

'economically' to finish it off. Pilots of other Soviet fighters and fighter-bombers turning back for another attack were often unable to find the target again. In October 1981, one of the 200 OShAE pilots managed to knock out a mujahideen fire position hidden in rocks at the end of a long winding ravine. Previous attempts to bomb the position from above had been unsuccessful, but the Su-25 had managed to fly into the dark 'funnel' of rocks, manoeuvring between the sides of the ravine, and after hitting the target it climbed out using a steep combat turn to escape.

Almost the entire arsenal of weapons available to the Su-25 was used in Afghanistan. Different weapons were used dependent upon given conditions and the disposition of the target. Thus, for example, 100 kg (220 lb) and 250 kg (550 lb) bombs were used most often over relatively flat terrain, along with 57 mm S-5M and S-MO rockets, carried in 32-shot UB-32-57 pods. Usually, two or three attacks were made on the target, with eight to twelve rockets released in salvo in a dive on each attack. However, it must be said that when operating with weapons on the pylons, the aircraft's performance naturally deteriorated, and when carrying four UB-32-57 pods, for example, the Su-25 did not handle well and had a tendency to 'sink' when coming out of a diving attack, losing height and speed. Smaller-calibre unguided rockets gradually replaced the more powerful S-8 rockets, for instance, which were widely used in various denominations, including the S-8M, S-8BM and S-8DM. Also used very effectively was the ODAB-500P

The first Su-25s to operate out of Afghan airfields during that ill-fated campaign wore a camouflage pattern which extended the pale blue-grey underside colours up the sides of the fuselage. Here, the aircraft is taxiing on pierced steel planking (PSP), an invaluable aid to mobility on the otherwise ill-equipped airfields when the Soviet Air Force first arrived in the country. *(Yefim Gordon Archive)*

fuel-air explosive (FAE), which in terms of blast damage effect was three times more powerful than a blast fragmentation warhead of the same calibre. DAB-500 (*Dymovaya Aviabomba*) smoke bombs were also used, and one of the most effective weapons combinations available to the Su-25 was two DAB-500 smoke bombs and six ODAB-500P FAE bombs. (ODAB stands for *Ob'yomno-Detoniruyushchaya Aviabomba* – literally Volume Detonating Bomb, from the fact that the given volume of fuel-air explosive is detonated after dispersal from the core of the bomb.)

Also used very successfully in Afghanistan was the heavy-calibre S-24 240 mm unguided rocket, which demonstrated great accuracy and an effective high-explosive fragmenting warhead, which proved useful against a wide range of targets. The accuracy of the rocket from a height of 2,000 m (6,500 ft) was, typically, being able to place a salvo in a circle of 7–8 m (23–26 ft) diameter. The aircraft's GSh-2-30 cannon was generally used against machine-gun 'nests' and vehicles, where its high rate of fire was devastating. The operations manual for the cannon recommended short bursts of around one second, loosing off around fifty armour-piercing or high-explosive fragmentation shells, although pilots very often ignored the manual and tried to obliterate the target 'decisively' with long bursts.

The aircraft's ASP-17BTs-8 automatic gunsight earned itself a good reputation against targets in flat terrain, and was used to aim the cannon and rockets and also for bombing. It gave very good results over flat terrain, but in the mountains its effectiveness deteriorated. This was because the abrupt changes of height and complex terrain features prevented the sight's computer from carrying out an accurate firing solution, and pilots had to use it more like a collimating gunsight when firing the gun and had to release bombs using the 'Mark 1 eyeball' technique.

The aircraft's combat survivability was also demonstrated to be highly effective, and the well-thought-out armoured protection of major systems, and the cockpit itself, frequently permitted the Su-25 to return to base with numerous significant hits from anti-aircraft artillery on its armour plating. The cockpit's titanium armour and the armoured glass of the windscreen prevented damage and penetration from small-arms fire. There are recorded incidents of shells and bullets severing rods for the flying controls and engines, putting the hydraulic system completely out of action, but the pilots were still able to nurse their aircraft back to base. A working party of specialist engineers from the factory in Tbilisi

were permanently stationed with the 200 OShAE at Shindand, along with engineers from the Sukhoi OKB, who were there to monitor the aircraft's initial operational debut. In the first fifteen months of operations in Afghanistan, the Su-25 'shturmoviks' of 200 OShAE carried out more than 2,000 sorties without losing a single aircraft in combat.

The first accidental loss of an Su-25 actually occurred in December 1981 as a result of the pilot, Captain A. Dyakov, exceeding the permitted diving speed during an attack on a target: Captain Dyakov was killed in the accident. According to some sources, the cause of this accident was acknowledged to be his exceeding the permitted diving speed, but other sources claim that as a result of non-symmetrical release of his bomb load the aircraft went into a steep banking turn from which the pilot was unable to bring the Su-25 under control. Evidently there was insufficient aileron control to straighten up the aircraft and it flew into a mountainside. Another Su-25 was lost as a result of the ground engineers failing to recharge the hydraulic accumulator, and during its take-off run the pilot was unable to retract the undercarriage. The heavily loaded aircraft, slowed down by the drag of the extended undercarriage, stalled soon after getting airborne, but the pilot managed to eject.

A considerable amount of damage to the Su-25 was caused by heavy landings which were themselves the result of having to employ an evasive technique, involving the aircraft landing 'fast' to avoid the threat of attack from shoulder-launched SAMs. The aircraft would land with minimum fuel remainders and without using flaps or airbrakes, sometimes bursting tyres or even losing an entire undercarriage leg if the landing was particularly heavy. For example, on 4 October 1988 an Su-25 landed at Bagram Airport, Kabul, touching down before the threshold, hit the concrete edge of the runway and sliced off all three undercarriage legs and slid down the runway on its belly. The pilot did not even receive a scratch.

Among some of the deficiencies of the Su-25, pilots had remarked on the ineffectiveness of the airbrakes, particularly during a dive. This resulted in the aircraft continuing to accelerate, losing stability and trying to 'turn on its back'. Other defects noted were the not particularly high reliability of the ARK-15 automatic radio compass and the RSBN-6S short-range tactical navigation system. Of even more concern on a combat aircraft in a war zone was the difficulty of arming the aircraft. For example, it took two men 40 minutes to

A pair of Su-25s head out from base on a routine training mission. *(Yefim Gordon)*

Air-to-ground rocketry is an important task for the *Frogfoot*, demonstrated here as two Su-25s dive onto their target at one of Russia's many live-firing ranges. *(via Yefim Gordon)*

reload the cannon, and they had to work on their knees during this time, feeding the heavy ammunition belt into the magazine above their heads. Also, as a result of not having powered trolleys, technicians and armourers preparing the Su-25 for flight had to push bombs and rockets to the aircraft on hand trolleys. A number of noted defects were eliminated on subsequent series of aircraft, and as a result of the type's initial operational combat baptism in Afghanistan the Sukhoi design team incorporated several minor improvements and modifications designed to simplify and speed up servicing and preparation for flight.

In the autumn of 1982, an operation code-named '*Ekzamen*' (Examination) was completed at Shindand with a very positive assessment by the evaluation team. The objective of '*Ekzamen*' was to test and evaluate the Su-25 in real combat conditions, using standard series-produced aircraft. In essence, the aircraft was subjected to a cycle of 'troop trials' which would allow an authentic assessment of its combat effectiveness, eliminate any obvious defects and shortcomings and apply any appropriate corrections to the way it was used in combat. From 19 July to the end of October 1982 200 OShAE pilots and groundcrew completed a total of 2,000 sorties in support of the Soviet Army, destroying major mujahideen targets and providing top cover for columns of motorised infantry troops and their escorting helicopters. At the end of '*Ekzamen*' there was a changeover of aircrew and ground personnel, with 200 OShAE being replaced by another squadron from Sital-Chai, the commander of the new contingent being Major V.N. Khanarin.

It was at this time that everyone connected with Su-25 operations in Afghanistan started to refer to the aircraft as the '*Grach*' (Rook), the name being derived from its usual radio callsign. Many of the Su-25s were later adorned with emblems showing a comic-style rook flapping its wings, painted on the side of the aircraft. The nickname and the decoration have stuck with the Su-25 until the present day, and Russian ground forces have great respect for the aircraft, without the support of

which it would have been impossible to conduct certain military operations in Afghanistan. Indeed, motor-rifle and airborne forces units would only conduct operations if there was air support from the '*Grach*'.

Even during the course of the early operations against the mujahideen in Afghanistan, the Soviet Army realised that it was unable to defeat the rebel units, and it became obvious that the Air Group supporting the limited contingent of Soviet Forces in Afghanistan would have to be reinforced. A year after the changeover of pilots and groundcrew, under the command of Major Khanarin, yet another squadron arrived to take over the task of combating the Afghan rebel forces. Thus, squadrons from the 80th Independent Shturmovoi Air Regiment (*80 OShAP*) at Sital-Chai, providing aircraft and personnel on a rotational basis, fought in Afghanistan up to September 1984. Then a new Su-25 regiment was formed, drawing personnel from 80 OShAP and another regiment, 90 OShAP, which had been set up at Artsyz (Artsiz) in the Ukraine. The new regiment became the 378th Independent Shturmovoi Air Regiment (*378 OShAP*), commanded by Lt.-Col. A. Bakushev, and was the first such regiment to be deployed in full strength outside the borders of the Soviet Union. Two of the regiment's squadrons were

Armed only with its 30 mm cannon, this Su-25 makes a sprightly departure from its base. *(Yefim Gordon)*

OPPOSITE PAGE: A *Frogfoot* pilot poses in front of his mount. The rather cumbersome-looking harness connects the pilot to the parachute of the Zvezda K-36L ejection seat. *(via Yefim Gordon)*

deployed at Bagram Airport, Kabul, and the third squadron was deployed to Kandahar.

The Soviet Air Group in Afghanistan was eventually reinforced with other types of aircraft, which periodically changed their operating locations in the country. When necessary, the Su-25s were redeployed close to their designated area of operations, and as well as operating out of Kabul Airport they also flew from packed-earth runways at Mazar-e-Sharif and Kunduz in the north of the country. The packed-earth airfields had to be brought up to a suitable operating standard by providing 'hard-standing' areas with corrugated iron sheeting, hundreds of tonnes of which was brought in to the bases by the truck-load. Over time, some of the assault tasks were taken over by Army Aviation Mi-8s and Mi-24s, and the Su-25 was assigned the task of providing air cover from 'standing air patrols', in case they were needed to assist the helicopters at any point. Forward air controllers (FAC) were used very effectively in Afghanistan, and they not only guided the Su-25s onto their targets, but also carried out bomb damage assessment (BDA) and evaluated the performance of given weapons used in the attacks. In the opinion of the FAC teams, a single Su-25 achieved greater success than several fighter-bombers assigned to similar targets.

Joint operations by helicopters and Su-25s turned out to be a particularly effective combat technique, where the helicopter crews were able to study the terrain from low altitude and at relatively low speed in the area of an intended strike. Initially, a pair of Mi-8s would circle over the target, carrying out a preliminary reconnaissance of the area and revealing the location of the enemy groups by firing off signal rockets or a burst of tracer fire, after which two to four Su-25s would come in to knock out any anti-aircraft artillery (AAA) positions. This would be followed by a pair of Mi-24s which would come in to 'clean up' the area for a strike group of one or two flights of Su-25s and attack helicopters. A typical example of joint helicopter/Su-25 operations took place on 2 February 1983, during an operation in the province of Mazar-e-Sharif, where Soviet civilian technical specialists working at a nitrogen fertiliser plant had been captured and murdered. Four Su-25s were assigned to attack the mujahideen group responsible, along with a flight of Mi-24s and six supporting Mi-8s. The Su-25s destroyed the main force of the enemy group, using ODAB-500P fuel-air explosives and ordinary high-explosive bombs, plus 80 mm S-8 rockets, while the helicopters were used to

ensure that none of the rebel group was able to escape the onslaught.

The Su-25 was also used in Afghanistan for aerial minelaying, carrying two or four KMG-U dispenser pods, each loaded with twenty-four POM anti-personnel mines or PFM fragmentation mines in BK cassettes. Aerial minelaying was carried out at a speed of 700–750 kph (378–405 kt) and a height of 900–1,000 m (2,950–3,280 ft), although for a more dense distribution of the mines the height was often reduced to 300–500 m (985–1,640 ft). In 1984, the Su-25 was responsible for 80% of all aerial minelaying sorties.

The Su-25 was also used on so-called 'free hunt' (*svobodnaya okhota*) combat missions. The actual area of operation would be briefed to the pilots from reconnaissance data analysed and prepared in the Headquarters of the 40th Army, the Soviet Army's operational authority in Afghanistan. When the Su-25 was assigned a 'free hunt' task it was usual to carry a pair of UB-32-57 57 mm rocket pods (or B-8M 80 mm rocket pods) and two 250 kg (550 lb) or 500 kg (1,100 lb) free-fall bombs. From the autumn of 1985, 'free hunt' operations were also carried out at night, even though the aircraft had no special equipment for night missions. Caravans of vehicles used by the mujahideen fighters gave themselves away at night by the beams of their headlights, and these lights served as targets for the Su-25. Pilots on 'free hunt' missions would often not actually hit the caravans of vehicles themselves, but would use high-explosive bombs dropped on the mountainsides, which would then cause a landslide. With the vehicles in the caravan halted in this way, it was then relatively easy to pick off the targets with greater accuracy. However, such missions also required particular concentration on the part of the pilots, in order not to fly into the mountainside itself, and there was at least one such incident in 1985. Snr Lt. A. Baranov was killed when he flew into high ground during a night 'free hunt' sortie.

From the spring of 1985 the Su-25 was used for standing patrols over Kabul Airport and the Headquarters of the 40th Army, in an attempt to counter artillery and rocket attacks on the city and the Soviet units in the area. A pair of Su-25s was held on permanent readiness at Bagram, mainly in order to strike at units of the forces of Ahmed Shah Masood, who was the most powerful and respected mujahideen leader at the time, held in high esteem by the Afghan population. So feared and hated by the occupying Soviet forces was Ahmed Shah Masood that any pilot confirmed to have killed the

A lone Su-25 seen during a simulated 'free hunt' sortie. Normally, for this type of operation, the aircraft would be armed with an appropriate mix of bombs and rockets. *(Yefim Gordon)*

Afghan leader had been promised an immediate award of the coveted Hero of the Soviet Union decoration. As the air defences of the mujahideen became more effective with the acquisition of better man-portable missile systems (MANPADS) and guns, the Su-25 began to suffer more frequent serious damage from such attacks. One aircraft established something of a record when it returned from a sortie with a total of 165 hits! Although the reliable defensive armour saved the pilot in many cases, AAA fire very often damaged the engines, fuel tanks and control rods, and disabled various vital aircraft systems, although the aircraft was usually able to limp back to base. Nevertheless, aircraft were soon returned to operational service thanks to the Su-25's excellent 'repairability' and the fact that many components and systems were interchangeable.

In order to counter the mujahideen's increasing air-defence capabilities, the Su-25 was compelled to use new types of weapon, combining high destructiveness with great aiming accuracy, capable of being used against the enemy without entering his own firing zone. One response was to start using B-13L heavy-calibre rocket pods loaded with 130 mm S-13-OF unguided rockets with high-explosive fragmentation warheads, a range of up to 4 km (2.16 nm) and capable of penetrating earth reinforcements, covered with rocks, to a depth of 3 m (10 ft). Even more powerful 330 mm S-25-OF and S-25-OFM unguided rockets also started to form part of the Su-25's arsenal, with a warhead weight of up to 200 kg (440 lb). Sometimes, in operations against concentrations of mujahideen personnel, SPPU-22-01

gun pods with GSh-23 depressible barrel cannons would be used by the Su-25. In one operation, in April 1986, four Su-25s supporting a helicopter assault landing (**vertolyotnyy desant**) at Dzhavar used SPPU gun pods to 'clean up' the area for the approaching helicopters, none of which was lost to enemy ground fire.

The first live combat use of guided air-to-surface missiles (ASM) by the Su-25 was also recorded in April 1986, when the Commanding Officer of 378 OShAP, Lt.-Col. Aleksandr V. Rutskoy, and one of his squadron commanders, Major Vysotsky, launched Kh-23 (AS-7 *Kerry*) ASMs against rebel targets. The use of the radio-command-guided AS-7 missile did not prove to be too successful against the mujahideen, since it was difficult for the pilot to find the target and then guide the missile onto it while simultaneously trying to carry out 'jinking' manoeuvres to avoid possible ground fire. The Kh-25ML (AS-10 *Karen*) and Kh-29L (AS-14 *Kedge*) laser-guided weapons were much more effective and could be 'illuminated' either by using the aircraft's own **Klyon-PS** laser rangefinder and marked target seeker (LRMTS), or a wingman's LRMTS. However, the best results were obtained by using a forward air controller on the ground. Initially, the ground-based laser target designators were mounted on vehicles in a rather improvised fashion, but later a specialised vehicle was designed for the job. This was based on the successful GAZ (**Gor'kovskiy Avtomobil'nyy Zavod**) BTR-80 (**Bronyetransportyor**) armoured personnel carrier and designated BOMAN (**Boyevaya Mashina Avia-Navodchika**), literally 'air controller combat vehicle'. The BOMAN has

This Su-25, parked alongside an Su-24 at the Ostrov aircraft disposal site in western Russia, is the last Su-25 to have been flown by Col. Alexander Rutskoi, former Deputy Commander of the 40th Air Army in Afghanistan and erstwhile Vice-President of Russia. It was originally believed that this time-expired aircraft would not be broken up, but instead be presented to Alexander Rutskoi to form the centrepiece of a monument in honour of Afghan veterans in the Kursk district, of which he was Governor until 2000. Having fallen from grace as a consequence of an alleged tax scandal, it is now unlikely that Rutskoi will receive this honour. *(Yefim Gordon)*

sophisticated land inertial navigation and communication systems, adding R-862 and other aircraft radios to facilitate communication between the FAC team and the aircraft, while retaining standard troop radios to communicate with reconnaissance platoons on the ground. The sighting optics and laser designator equipment is installed inside the vehicle and only exposed when required for use.

The accuracy of laser-guided missiles was very high, and the heavy Kh-29L (AS-14 *Kedge*), which had a warhead weight of 317 kg (700 lb) was particularly effective. Also used with great effect was the simpler S-25L 330 mm laser-guided rocket, which had a guidance unit identical to that of the laser-guided versions of the AS-10 *Karen* and AS-14 *Kedge*. Launch of the S-25L was normally carried out from a distance of 4–5 km (2.16–2.7 nm), from a shallow dive (25–30°), and the average dispersion from the centre of the target area usually did not exceed 1.5–2 m (5–6.5 ft). According to data collated by the Sukhoi OKB, a total of 139 air-to-surface missiles were fired from all types of Soviet

fighter-bombers during the Afghanistan campaign, of which 137 hit their targets.

Sometimes, the Su-25 was also used for reconnaissance missions, even though it did not have any relevant equipment and such operations were carried out on a purely visual basis. However, at the personal behest of one of the most famous Su-25 pilots of the Afghan campaign, Lt.-Col. Aleksandr Rutskoy, at least one Su-25 was adapted for photo-reconnaissance tasks, with an improvised pod carrying camera equipment for bomb damage assessment (BDA).

As a consequence of the aircraft's ability to undertake a wide variety of tasks, the Su-25 was used extremely intensively in Afghanistan, and Su-25 pilots often had considerably more flying hours on type than their colleagues on the Su-17, MiG-23 and MiG-27. On average, the '*Dvadtsat' pyahty*' (literally 'twenty-fifth' – a typical Russian military style of reference to numbered vehicles, weapons or aircraft, using the adjectival form) performed around 500 combat sorties per year, although some examples even recorded as many as 900–950 sorties annually. Aircraft with such high airframe usage were usually returned to Russia when their pilots underwent 'roulement' at the end of their designated period of duty in Afghanistan.

Reliable radio communications were among the most important aspects of military operations in Afghanistan, and specially equipped An-26RT (**Retranslayator**) *Curl* radio relay platforms maintained a continuous airborne watch in order to guarantee uninterrupted communications between ground controllers and aircraft from anywhere within the Afghan theatre of operations. Occasionally, Army-level Ilyushin Il-22 *Coot-B* airborne command posts would also operate over Afghanistan. These aircraft, based on the Il-18 airliner, were equipped with powerful command and control communications systems, capable of co-ordinating the military operations of an entire air army. The Su-25 itself had an R-828 **Ehkvalipt** (Eucalyptus) FM/VHF radio to enable the pilot to communicate directly with troops on the ground, albeit only in line-of-sight conditions over flat terrain.

When the mujahideen began to acquire more and better MANPADS missiles, the statistics for combat losses also began to worsen. The mujahideen mainly used the Soviet **Strela-2** (Arrow) SA-7 *Grail* shoulder-launched SAM, obtained from various Arab countries or from China (in its **Hongying 5** guise), the American General Dynamics FIM-43 Redeye, acquired via Pakistan, or less often, the ubiquitous British-made Shorts Blowpipe. The first Su-25 to be downed by a surface-to-air missile was the aircraft flown by Lt.-Col. P.V. Ruban, a squadron commander, who was shot down on 16 January 1984. His aircraft was initially damaged by missile fragments which damaged the engine and control rods and the aircraft started to lose height, leaving Ruban no choice but to eject, but with insufficient height his ejection was unsuccessful and he was killed.

There was one curious incident, where an Su-25 had been hit by a missile and returned to base with the unexploded weapon protruding from one of the engine nacelles. On another occasion, on 28 July 1987, an Su-25 returned to base from a sortie with a large hole in the fuselage side where a missile had destroyed one of the engines and almost completely burned through the elevator control rods. The fire continued to rage throughout the entire approach phase, but the pilot was able to land the aircraft successfully. An even more remarkable escape was recorded by Lt. P. Golubtsov, whose Su-25 had half its tail section blown off by a missile, although the engines continued to function normally. After touchdown, the aircraft rolled off the end of the runway with brake failure, directly into the defensive minefield designed to thwart mujahideen sabotage attacks on the airfield. There the pilot had to wait until a platoon of sappers could reach him and release him from the aircraft! One of the most amazing incidents involving an Su-25 pilot was that experienced by Lt.-Col. Aleksandr Rutskoy in April 1986 when he was shot down by a ground-launched missile which entered the left engine air intake, destroying the engine and causing the right engine to surge. Missile and aircraft fragments also damaged the flying control rods, making the aircraft barely controllable. The aircraft was finished off by a burst of AAA fire (or machine-gun fire?) and Rutskoy only just managed to eject in time, before the aircraft struck the ground. However, because the Su-25 was barely controllable and becoming inverted, the ejection angle took him towards the ground rather than up and away from the aircraft. In the subsequent hard landing he sustained serious spinal injuries, a broken leg and severe bruising to his head. By some miracle, Russian doctors were able to save his life after he had been repatriated to a Soviet Air Force hospital in Moscow. Later, following his recovery and in defiance of his doctors' wishes, Rutskoy returned to Afghanistan as the Deputy Commander of the 40th Air Army, to resume his flying career, once again flying the Su-25 and taking part in several more combat missions.

At this point it is perhaps appropriate to digress a little. Altogether, during his periods of service in Afghanistan, Colonel Aleksandr Rutskoy flew a total of 364 combat missions. On one mission, to attack a stronghold in the Charikar region, near Khost in eastern Afghanistan, Rutskoy was shot down for a second time, although this time his attacker was a Pakistan Air Force F-16. It took two missile hits to bring Rutskoy's Su-25 down; the explosion from the first missile did not do any damage and the aircraft remained flyable. Lt.-Col. Rutskoy was able to turn back towards Bagram, the large Soviet air base near the Afghan capital, Kabul. However, the Pakistani F-16 pilot launched another missile, a Raytheon Sparrow, with an expanding-rod warhead which literally tore the Su-25 to shreds. Fortunately, however, the cockpit remained intact, saving Rutskoy from serious injury, and he was able to eject from the stricken 'shturmovik'. He was taken prisoner by a band of **dushmany** after landing and was eventually handed over to the Pakistani authorities. The Pakistan Air Force treated him with respect, as a fellow military professional; he was introduced to the F-16 pilot who shot him down and even taken back to the place where his aircraft had landed on Pakistani territory. (The shootdown took place right on the Afghanistan–Pakistan border.) For his conspicuous gallantry in Afghanistan, Rutskoy was awarded the title of Hero of the Soviet Union in 1988 as a Colonel, later rising to the rank of Major-General and becoming head of the 4th Combat Application and Aircrew Conversion Centre at Lipetsk. On return to civilian life he became actively involved in politics at the time when the Soviet Union was beginning to disintegrate, and for a short time was Vice-President of Russia. While his political career may have been short lived and comparatively inauspicious, Maj.-Gen. Rutskoy must be regarded as one of the Soviet Air Force's most inspiring modern-day commanders.

Returning to the theme of combat operations by the Su-25 in Afghanistan, the aircraft were equipped with four cassettes of ASO-2V infra-red flare dispensers, loaded with 26 mm PPI-26 (*Piro-Patron Infra-krasnny*) pyrotechnic flare cartridges; the PPI-26 is sometimes also referred to as LO-56. However, the pilots rarely ever used the flares; the control panel for the ASO (*Avtomat Sbrosa Otrazhateley*) was on a side panel in the cockpit, and selection of the particular release sequence was too much of a distraction at the most crucial point in an attack. Apart from this, when a pilot detected the launch of a missile towards his aircraft it was already too late to release any flares, and after the missile's seeker head had locked onto the target it would simply continue undeflected towards its target anyway. Because the standard four-cassette pack of flares proved to be insufficient protection for the aircraft on a typical sortie, ground engineers produced a local modification which involved adding additional ASO-2V cassettes to the top of the engine nacelles, doubling the number of flares carried. The firing sequence of the flares was then made automatic, on depression of the firing button on the control column and continuing for a period of 30 seconds.

The American Raytheon Stinger missile began to appear in Afghanistan at the end of 1986, an important feature of this weapon being its highly sensitive selective seeker head. This had the ability to distinguish between the characteristic range of temperatures of a jet engine and the heat from a decoy flare. In the first week of the Stinger's appearance, in November 1986, four Su-25s

An Su-25 from the regiment (899 OShAP) based at Buturlinovka, near Borisoglebsk in western Russia, seen preparing for flight during a brief deployment to Kubinka air base in March 1998. Note the laser-guided AS-10 *Karen* missile on the pylon adjacent to the drop tank. (*Yefim Gordon*)

were shot down, killing two of the pilots. Later, on 21 January 1987, an Su-25 piloted by Snr Lt. Konstantin Pavlyuk was shot down by a Stinger just after getting airborne out of Bagram airfield. Lt. Pavlyuk was able to eject successfully from the aircraft, albeit sustaining slight injuries when he landed in a tree, but search and rescue helicopters were unable to locate him immediately. The injured Pavlyuk was then surrounded by mujahideen, and he started to fight them off with his personal weapons. When all his ammunition ran out he enticed the band of mujahideen closer, and when surrounded by a group of six of them he detonated a hand grenade, blowing himself up and killing all six mujahideen in an act of selfless and exemplary heroism. By September 1987, 'shturmovik' losses amounted to a whole squadron's worth of aircraft.

In order to combat the Stinger it was originally proposed to install the *Sukhogruz* (Cargo Vessel) active infra-red jammer on the Su-25. This was already widely used on helicopters, as the *Ispanka* (Spanish Lady), or L-166V-11E, and had given a good account of itself in combat. However, the suggestion was not taken up because of the very high electrical power requirements of *Sukhogruz*, as result of which it was decided instead to increase the aircraft's survivability by means of additional protection of the most vulnerable equipment assemblies.

The Chief Designer of the Su-25, Vladimir Babak, visited Afghanistan several times to observe the aircraft in its combat environment. After one visit, an engine from an Su-25 which had been damaged by a missile and still showed signs of fire damage was returned to the Sukhoi OKB for study. After detailed examination of the engine, the engineers were able to come up with a range of measures to enable a damaged engine to be isolated from the other and at the same time prevent the spread of fire inside the compartment. Starting with aircraft Construction Number (c/n) [255.081].09077, 5 mm (0.2 in) steel plates and glass-fibre mats were installed along the sides of the engine compartment between Frames 18 and 21, and between Frames 21 and 25. The titanium flying-control rods were replaced by fire-resistant steel rods, isolation of the fuel lines was changed, placing them under protective screening panels, and the fuel shut-off system was made to automatically trigger when the fire-suppression system was switched on. The latter measure would prevent an explosion in the event of a fuel leak, by avoiding fuel continuing to be pumped through the fuel lines at the same time as the fire retardant was

being activated. Additional air intakes were installed on top of the rear part of the engine nacelles to provide cooling airflow through the engine compartment itself and for cooling the engine exhaust nozzle. These measures would reduce the engine's thermal signature. Also included in the package of defensive improvements was the addition of armoured 'blinds' for the cockpit canopy. The overall weight of these additional measures, designed to protect vitally important elements of the aircraft, was 1,100 kg (2,425 lb), or around 11.5% of the total structural weight of the Su-25. The first deliveries of Su-25s with 'increased combat survivability' (*povyshennaya boyevaya zhivuchest'*) were made to 378 OShAP in August 1987, although an order was issued at the end of 1986, forbidding pilots to descend below 4,500 m (14,800 ft), in order to avoid being hit by man-portable SAMs.

Towards the end of the Soviet campaign in Afghanistan, the Su-25 began to be used more for night operations, in an attempt to reduce losses due to missile attacks. The Su-25s were assisted in finding their targets by Su-17 fighter-bombers, which illuminated the area with SAB (*Svetyaschayasya Avia-Bomba*) flare bombs. However, the Su-25 often bombed not only the enemy, but also the positions of their 'own' Afghan government forces.

As the Soviet withdrawal from Afghanistan got under way, and troops were withdrawn from the garrison at Kandahar, in the south of the country, the Su-25s were relocated to Shindand and Bagram. Another Su-25 squadron was based at Kabul. An additional task was added to the range of missions performed by the Su-25 in Afghanistan – that of escorting and covering columns of troops and performing regular precautionary strikes along the routes leading out of Afghanistan. From 23 January 1989, the Su-25 also took part in Operation '*Taifun*' ('Typhoon'), which concluded with a series of massive strikes, with the objective of inflicting the largest possible losses on the mujahideen forces in the central and northern regions of Afghanistan before the Soviet Army's final withdrawal. The Su-25 departed from their Afghan bases in the final days of January 1989.

Summing up the combat operations by the Su-25 during the Soviet campaign in Afghanistan, it should be noted that a total of 118 'shturmoviks' were assigned to the theatre during the almost ten-year period of combat. Of this total, twenty-three aircraft were lost for a variety of different reasons. The aircraft flew a total of 60,000 combat sorties throughout the campaign, giving an average of 2,800 combat sorties for every Su-25

A pair of Su-25UB trainers performing a 'high-speed' fly-by over Kubinka air base. *(Yefim Gordon)*

BELOW: A Russian Navy Su-25UTG takes the wire on board the *Admiral Kuznetsov*, maintaining the characteristically flat attitude of this aircraft during an arrested landing. *(via Yefim Gordon)*

This view of the Su-25UTG clearly shows the blanking panel fitted over the laser rangefinder window, which is not required for naval training operations. *(Ulan-Ude Plant)*

lost, and each downed aircraft sustained an average of eighty to ninety hits. By this index of combat surviv-ability, the Su-25 considerably exceeded that of other Soviet combat aircraft in the theatre (the Su-17 sustain-ing an average of fifteen to twenty hits before suc-cumbing to the damage), as well as that of American types during the Vietnam War.

At the same time as the war in Afghanistan was rag-ing, several new regiments of Su-25s were being formed as aircraft rolled off the production line. These regi-ments were based both on Soviet territory as well as in the neighbouring republics. Two independent regiments were also assigned to the Western Group of Forces (for-merly entitled Group of Soviet Forces Germany) in the former East Germany. These were the 357th Indepen-dent Assault Regiment (***357-oy Otdyelnyy Shturmovoy Aviatsionnyy Polk***) at Brandis and the 368th Indepen-dent Assault Regiment (***368-oy Otdyelnyy Shturmovoy Aviatsionnyy Polk***) at Demmin-Tutow. Initial opera-tional experience with the Su-25 in ordinary front-line squadrons showed the type's high reliability, and the new 'shturmovik' earned the reputation among pilots as the most reliable and safe combat aircraft then in service with the Soviet Air Force. During the first twelve years of operation (from 1981 to 1993) not a single aircraft was lost as a result of technical failure. However, a

number of aircraft were lost because of servicing errors and incidents related to 'human factors'. For example, there was a case of a technician who forgot to lock the brake parachute housing doors and rear fuselage hatch-es after installing a repacked chute assembly. After take-off, the pilot could not level off the aircraft because the elevator had been jammed by a hatch cover and he had to eject. There were also many cases of radio equipment failure and other minor systems failures, although these were of a lesser magnitude and did not lead to in-flight emergencies.

Apart from series production of the Su-25 and Su-25UB, as noted elsewhere in this book, a small batch of navalised Su-25UTG twin-seat trainers also entered service with Russian Naval Aviation. These are used primarily as land-based procedural trainers for the Su-33 *Flanker-D* at Severomorsk, in Northern Russia. When required, they are also flown out to the Russian Navy's sole aircraft-carrier, RNS *Admiral of the Fleet Kuznetsov*, although because they do not have wing-folding mechanisms they must remain parked on the deck during such deployments. A small number of standard Su-25s also served for a while with the Russ-ian Navy's Pacific Fleet at Khorol, although later these aircraft were put into open storage at the Russian Naval Air Station at Severomorsk.

A standard series-production Su-25UTG positioning for take-off at Saki naval air station in the Crimea. *(Yefim Gordon)*

Iran–Iraq War

The Su-25 also saw combat during the Iran–Iraq War, which started in 1980 and ended in 1989. When the conflict began to assume a more serious character and it was evident that it would be a long-drawn-out affair, Iraq realised that it would need a more appropriate attack aircraft for battlefield close air support of the troops. In May 1986, Iraqi defence officials visited Moscow to negotiate the purchase of such aircraft. After watching a demonstration of the aircraft at Kubinka (put on by the base's 237th Aircraft Demonstration Centre) and inspecting the Su-25 at close quarters on the ground, the Iraqi officials declared that it was just what they were looking for. They decided immediately to purchase a regiment of Su-25s, and between 1987 and 1989 these aircraft were to participate in the major regional conflict between the two Islamic states. There are reports of the Iraqi Air Force frequently achieving up to 1,200 combat sorties per day during the Iran–Iraq War, of which *c.*900 were performed by the Su-25 carrying out the bulk of the offensive strikes. In the most intensive periods of fighting each Su-25 was performing up to fifteen sorties per day. Although this might sound somewhat improbable, these are actually official Sukhoi

OKB statistics and not from the Iraqi Air Force. Saddam Hussein decorated all of the Iraqi Air Force's Su-25 pilots with the country's highest military decoration at the end of the Iran–Iraq War. There was one recorded incident where an Iraqi Air Force Su-25 was shot down by an Iranian Hawk surface-to-air missile, but the pilot managed to eject.

The Gulf War (Operation *Desert Storm*)

The air superiority of the coalition forces in Operation *Desert Storm* was so great that the majority of Iraqi Air Force Su-25s did not manage to get airborne from their own bases. In fact, the Iraqi basing philosophy for all of its combat aircraft meant that the Su-25s were deployed to various locations throughout the country's vast complex of airfields and reserve landing strips, some in shelters, but many parked out in the open.

On 25 January 1991, seven Iraqi Air Force combat aircraft fled from Iraq and landed on the territory of their former enemy, Iran. Initially, these flights were conducted individually, as can be judged from the fact that the fleeing aircraft were made up of differing types of aircraft, arriving at different Iranian airfields. Later, the process of ostensible 'refuge seeking' became more organised, and most probably 'managed' by the Iraqi Air Force itself. It seems that the Iraqi military command authorities hoped that by sending its military aircraft to Iran for safe keeping it might be possible to preserve some of its assets intact. With the bitter experience of the Iran–Iraq War still fresh in their collective memories, this can only be seen as an act of the utmost naïvety, and none of the combat aircraft has ever been returned. Over the course of several weeks of the war a total of 115 Iraqi combat aircraft fled to Iran and other neighbouring countries. The total included 44 Su-22 *Fitter-K*s, twelve MiG-23 *Flogger*s, seven MiG-25 *Foxbat*s, four MiG-29 *Fulcrum*s, twenty-four Su-24 *Fencer-D*s and twenty-four Dassault Mirage F-1EQ fighters of various sub-designations. The twenty-four Su-24s probably represented the entire Iraqi Air Force fleet of this type. An additional fifteen Il-76 *Candid* heavy transports, plus seventeen civil airliners, were also flown to Iran for 'safe keeping', along with possibly two Iraqi-modified Adnan-1 airborne early warning derivatives of the Il-76. Another two airborne early warning Il-76s are reported to have been destroyed on the ground by coalition forces.

On the evening of 6 February 1991, two USAF F-15C Eagle fighters of the 53rd Tactical Fighter Squadron, 36th Tactical Fighter Wing at Bitburg, Germany (79-0078 and 84-0019), operating out of Al Kharj Air Base in Saudi Arabia, intercepted a pair of Iraqi MiG-21s and a pair of Su-25s. All four Iraqi aircraft were shot down, both Su-25s coming down in the desert not far from the border with Iran.

Africa

As already noted in the chapter covering Su-25 operators around the world, the aircraft has also been involved in combat activities in Angola, the Democratic Republic of Congo and Ethiopia. The Su-25's 'baptism of fire' in Angola is described in some detail there (Chapter 5).

Nagorno-Karabakh

After the downfall of the Soviet Union in 1992, the conflict in Nagorno-Karabakh eventually developed into a long-drawn-out war between the former neighbouring republics of Armenia and Azerbaijan, during the course of which the small air forces of the two countries became involved. At this time, the 80th Independent Shturmovoi Regiment (**80-y OShAP**) was

located on the territory of Azerbaijan at Sital-Chai, and all of the regiment's personnel and aircraft were evacuated from the country. Before 1992, Su-25s flown by Azeri pilots had been involved in combat operations against Armenia, bombing Armenian military formations and mining the areas where combat was likely to take place. Rumours began to circulate in the press that Azerbaijan was using Su-25s acquired either from Georgia, Iraq or even Iran, the latter being a distinct possibility because of the ethnic links between 'Soviet' Azerbaijan and 'Iranian' Azerbaijan. The first proved acquisition of an Su-25 occurred in April 1992, when an Azeri pilot of the Soviet Air Force defected from Sital-Chai around the time of the Soviet withdrawal from the base. Later, this republic, along with Armenia, acquired around five Su-25s through 'secret channels', plus a single example which was flown out of Georgia by its defecting pilot. Four of the Azerbaijani Su-25s were reported to have been shot down during combat with Armenian forces. Armenia had acquired four Su-25s, which were used in action against Azerbaijan, and at least one aircraft is known to have been lost during combat operations.

Georgia–Abkhazia

The Su-25 was much more actively involved in the armed conflict between the independent Republic of Georgia and the breakaway Republic of Abkhazia, an ethnically separate region of Georgia, between the Black Sea and the Caucasus mountains, bordering the Russian Federation and Georgia itself. Decades of ill feeling since 1931 between the two entities erupted into military conflict in 1992, a conflict which lasted for 412 days and 'ended' with a UN-brokered ceasefire in 1994, although the dispute is far from settled even today. Georgia was able to call upon Su-25s which were still in final assembly at Tbilisi, and the former Russian Defence Minister Pavel Grachyov claimed that by mid-February 1993 the Georgian Air Force had seven Su-25s at its disposal. The aircraft wore standard Soviet-style camouflage, but retained the traditional Soviet red star and operated mainly from the military airfield at Kopitnari, a former Soviet Air Force Su-24 *Fencer* tactical bomber base. The 'shturmoviks' carried out attacks on Abkhazian military objectives and troop concentrations, as well as on the cities of Sukhumi and Gagra and the settlement of Nizhniye Ehshery, where Abkhazian artillery pieces were often deployed close to the Russian Armed Forces' Seismological Laboratory No. 24.

The Russian Su-25s which took part in the early stage of this conflict belonged to 'shturmovoi' regiments of the North Caucasus Military District and the Group of Russian Forces in the Transcaucasus. In order to distinguish the Russian aircraft from the Georgian Air Force Su-25s, the Russian red, white and blue tricolour was painted on the fins of all the Russian Su-25s. The Russian Air Force Su-25s were mainly involved in attacks on Georgian artillery positions which had been shelling Nizhniye Ehshery, as well as escorting Russian attack-helicopter groups supplying the blockaded town of Tkvarcheli. It is highly probable that Abkhazian pilots flew some of the Russian Su-25s, and on 20 February and 16 March 1993, an unidentified Su-25 carried out a strike on some apartment blocks in Sukhumi, the capital of Abkhazia, which had been captured by Georgian forces at that time. Georgia blamed Russia for the attack, but the Abkhazian side eventually accepted full responsibility.

Throughout the period of conflict between Georgia and Abkhazia, a total of nine Su-25s were reported shot down, of which seven belonged to the Georgian Air Force. The first Georgian Su-25 was shot down on 6 February 1993, over the Russian Seismological Laboratory at Nizhniye Ehshery, the Georgian pilot, Major Nodareishvili ejecting from his aircraft. Another Su-25 was shot down on 1 May by an Abkhazian MANPADS missile, while on 6 July the Georgians shot down one of their own Su-25s by mistake. Subsequently, on 13 July and 23 and 24 September another four Georgian Air Force Su-25s were shot down, killing three of the pilots. Earlier, on 6 January of the same year, the Georgians shot down an 'enemy' Su-25, although the Russian side asserted that none of its aircraft was airborne in the region on that day. The Abkhazian side reported that a Major O. Chamba, presumably of the Abkhazian 'air force', had not returned from his mission, confirming that the Abkhazian side also had access to the Su-25. A Russian Su-25 crashed on 17 September, albeit for unknown reasons. Later, after the end of the conflict in Abkhazia, Georgian Air Force Su-25s were used in the struggle against armed bands of supporters of one Colonel L. Kobaliya, an ally of the ex-President of Georgia, Zviad Gamsakhurdia. On 10 October 1994, a pair of Georgian Su-25s, presumed to have been attempting to carry out an attack on Kobaliya's forces, mistakenly hit a Russian border post. Georgia immediately issued an apology to Russia for this incident.

Tajikistan

Sukhoi's latter-day 'shturmovik' also saw action in Tajikistan. At first, Uzbekistan Air Force Su-25s operated in the newly independent republic, supporting Tajik government forces. After the overrunning of the 12th Border Post by Tajik opposition forces and Afghan mujahideen, Russia decided to reinforce its own military contingent in the region. On 24 July 1993, the 186th Instructor 'Shturmovoi' Air Regiment (*186-oy Instruktorsko-Shturmovoy Aviapolk – 186 IShAP*) was relocated from Abkhazia to Kokaidy, in Uzbekistan, and commenced combat operations almost immediately. The Su-25s carried out strikes against armed opposition groups, river crossings over the Pyandzh River and enemy artillery positions on both banks of the river. In the first days of their operations out of Kokaidy, 186 IShAP were dropping up to 80 tonnes of bombs daily. The Su-25s were always flown with two R-60 (AA-8 *Aphid*) short-range air-to-air missiles for self-protection, since the possibility could not be excluded that Afghan Air Force fighters would attack from just across the Tajik–Afghan border. In the summer of 1994, when the Tajik opposition intensified their military action, aircraft again played a significant part in the campaign. There are no data suggesting that the Russians lost any Su-25s in Tajikistan, most probably a consequence of the fact that the Tajik opposition did not have any viable air defence weapons. It is known, however, that on 11 April 1998 a Russian Su-25UB experienced a technical malfunction and crashed some 150 km (95 miles) to the south of the city of Dushanbe, killing both pilots.

Chechnya

The First Chechen War

The most recent combat experience with the Russian Air Force's Su-25s concerns the aircraft's intensive use in the two recent so-called Chechen Wars, which are usually referred to simply as 'the war in Chechnya'.

Towards evening on November 29 1994, on several airfields of the North Caucasus Military District (*Severniy Kavkazskiy Voyennyy Okrug – SKVO*), a hastily assembled group of around 140 combat aircraft had been brought together, albeit not without some organisational problems. The group included Su-17M4 *Fitter-K* fighter-bombers, Su-24M *Fencer-D* tactical bombers and Su-25 *Frogfoot* 'shturmoviks'. The core of the group was made up of elements of the 4th Air Army (today the 4th Air Army of the Russian Air Force and Air Defence). Later the combat air group was reinforced by reconnaissance, tactical bomber and long-range bomber units from the neighbouring military districts.

Up to this particular time, because of 'cash starvation', a considerable number of Russian Air Force aircrew had experienced a significant decline in their flying skills in instrument meteorological conditions (IMC), as well as regular practice in weapons usage. They were now suddenly confronted with the need to undertake combat sorties in the extremely complex weather conditions which characterise the meteorology of the North Caucasus, particularly in the autumn–winter period. Although the Chechen 'air force' was only able to deploy unguided weapons against the Russians, it did nevertheless represent a threat to air bases, military HQ and Federal forces as they were moving into their assigned operating areas. The decision was taken to carry out a pre-emptive strike on Chechen airfields, with the objective of destroying the air assets of Chechen President Dudayev, on the ground.

The first strike was carried by Russian Air Force Su-25s early in the morning of 1 December 1994, attacking the airfields at Kalinovskaya and Khankala, where the Chechen 'air force' L-39s were based. The Su-25s used unguided rockets and iron bombs, which totally destroyed the entire air assets of the Dudayev regime in a single sortie. The air defences of the two airfields were taken completely by surprise, because of the blinding suddenness of the attacks, and not a single Russian aircraft was lost during the raids.

During the afternoon of the same day, Grozny-North Airport came under attack, where the remaining Chechen aircraft were destroyed, including the personal Tu-154 *Careless* airliner of President Dudayev, along with several helicopters. It was later confirmed that the attacks were carried out with such precision by the 'shturmoviks' that the runways and taxiways, airport buildings and equipment received only minimal damage. During the attack on Grozny Airport the attacking aircraft came under heavy AAA fire, although once again no aircraft were lost.

Also at the beginning of December, the rebel stronghold of Katayama in the north-west suburbs of Grozny and a tank regiment base at Shali were subjected to air attacks. The Su-25 and the Su-24M tactical bomber began to be employed on a limited scale in attacks on targets in the city from 3 January 1995, when called in by ground troops to suppress defensive pockets of Chechen fighters and to block the approach routes for reinforcements coming into the city. In a number of cases, the close proximity of the positions of Russian troops and 'Dudayev rebels' demanded of the pilots and forward air controllers extreme accuracy in their flying and target designation. There were unfortunate cases when, because of errors in target designation, or because of the rapidly evolving and changing nature of the combat, buildings were destroyed which were still occupied by Russian troops.

From the military viewpoint, the most spectacular success from the use of air power in Chechnya occurred at the beginning of 1995. This was the destruction of the main headquarters of Dudayev's forces, located in the building formerly used by the Grozny District Committee of the Communist Party of the Soviet Union, which was also used as the 'official' residence of President Dzhokar Dudayev. For reasons which were not entirely clear, this building had not previously been subjected to air attacks, and perhaps lulled into a false sense of security as a result, the rebels had set up their main HQ here. Moreover, the building had been constructed to a higher level of structural integrity than normal and the Dudayev separatists had turned it into a powerful 'fortress', with an underground passageway linking one of the main blocks of the building with the underground bunker of Dudayev. Attacking the building with mortars did not have the desired effect.

On 17–18 January, as soon as the local weather conditions permitted, a group of Su-25s carried out several air raids on the rebel HQ, with heavy S-24B 240 mm unguided rockets and concrete-piercing BETAB-500 500 kg (1,100 lb) bombs. The unguided rockets, which are actually more accurate than their designation suggests, easily destroyed the main above-ground structure of the building, while the BETAB-500 (*Betonoboinaya Aviabomba*) destroyed the bunker and the underground passageway. In the underground part of the building alone some 130 rebels were killed.

After the destruction of Dudayev's residence and HQ, the rebels moved out of the town beyond the River Sunzha and later began a general withdrawal of their forces from Grozny itself. Frontal Aviation aircraft and Army Aviation helicopters started to conduct armed patrols to disrupt the rebels' lines of communication and isolate their fighting zones, with the aim of preventing the dispersal of large groups of rebel forces into the surrounding countryside. During the course of this operation, two BTR-type armoured personnel transporters and more than fifty smaller vehicles were destroyed and many rebels killed.

The Su-25 did not only conduct operations over Grozny and its suburbs, and 25 January 1995 was a particularly busy day for the '***Grach***' away from the capital. On that day, a force of eighteen Su-25s was used to destroy underground storage depots for weapons and military equipment used by the rebels, to the north-west of the town of Bamut. The rebels had set up the storage depots in four R-12U (SS-4 *Sandal*) launch silos previously used by the medium-range missile unit based there. The base was once a part of the Soviet Strategic Missile Force. On the same day, the Su-25s also destroyed another large weapons store near the village of Arshty, as well as attacking an assembly point for the rebel forces and their vehicles.

Up to February 1995, the Russian Air Force had not lost a single aircraft during combat operations, although twelve Su-25s had suffered damage from AAA fire. All the aircraft returned to their bases – one of the aircraft limping back to the airfield with a badly damaged tailplane and another making it back on one engine. Then, on 4 February 1995, an Su-25 was shot down in an ambush of three ZSU-23-4 23 mm self-propelled cannon, during an attack on a rebel stronghold to the south of Chechen-Aul. The pilot managed to eject, but was presumed to have been murdered by the rebels when he landed by parachute.

In three and a half months of combat operations (from 1 December 1994 to 17 March 1995), the Russian Air Force had destroyed, in addition to Dudayev's entire air force, twenty tanks, twenty-five armoured personnel carriers, six self-propelled AAA pieces, as many as ten fixed artillery pieces and more than 130 military vehicles of various types. More than seven bridges had also been destroyed, as well as several petrol, oil and lubricant stores (POL), weapons storage areas and other militarily significant targets. In this

A *Frogfoot* pilot gives a confident thumbs-up sign to his crew chief before setting off on a combat mission. *(Ulan-Ude Plant)*

period, two aircraft had been lost (one Su-25 and one Su-24M), the latter probably not as a result of ground fire from the enemy. A total of fourteen aircraft had suffered combat damage, as mentioned above.

On 21 March the Russian forces went onto the offensive. On 22 March, the Dudayev rebels, supported by tanks, attempted to break the blockade on Argun from the direction of Shali and Gudermes, but Su-25s and Mi-24D *Hind-D* and Mi-24V *Hind-E* attack helicopters, called up by forward air controllers, forced them to retreat from the town, suffering serious losses. The *Hind*s, using AT-6 *Spiral* anti-armour missiles, destroyed nine tanks and armoured personnel carriers, while the Su-25s attacked the rebel force with 80 mm S-8 rockets equipped with cumulative fragmentation warheads. On 23 March, Argun fell to the Russian onslaught, and a week later, on 30 March, Chechnya's second-largest city, Gudermes, was also taken by the Russians.

From the beginning of April 1995, the weather in Chechnya improved noticeably, permitting the wider use of Su-25 assault aircraft and the combat helicopter force. A particular characteristic of the application of air power (as exemplified by the battles to regain Shali, and in mid-April to regain the mountain township of Bamut) was for the Army to conduct its attacks without preliminary 'softening' of the target by aircraft and helicopters. Russian commanders justify this action (in contrast to classic military practice) as the desire to minimise collateral damage to property and the civilian population. Only after meeting stiff resistance from the rebels and, perhaps, suffering significant losses, would Russian troops call up fire support from the Su-25s and Mi-24s. This tactic was only abandoned in May, when combat moved into the more mountainous regions, with significantly less population density and the enemy could be targeted with less risk of involving innocent civilians in attacks.

The tempo of combat operations was once again slowed by the moratorium on the use of the armed forces in Chechnya from 28 April to 12 May, declared by President Yeltsin before the traditional May Day holiday and Victory Day on 9 May. Federal forces were compelled to cease all combat operations, conducting only routine patrol and reconnaissance flights over Chechen territory during this period. The Dudayev camp, on the other hand, were able to take advantage of this breathing space to build up their forces and reinforce their positions, while not missing the opportunity to fire on watchtowers and convoys of federal troops.

In this period of 'peace', on 5 May, an Su-25 was shot down while conducting a patrol flight in accordance with the Presidential directive. The aircraft was one of a pair flying at low level in the vicinity of Venoi. While following the contours of a mountain ridge, the leading aircraft of the pair was suddenly hit by a hail of gunfire from a DShK (*Degtyaryov Shpagin Krupnokalibernyy*) heavy-calibre machine-gun situated on the side of the mountain. The aircraft went out of control, struck the ground and exploded after its pilot had been killed instantly in the cockpit, the heavy-calibre bullets of the DShK smashing through the more vulnerable sides of the cockpit canopy.

As the federal troops advanced, so the resistance of the Dudayev rebels increased, and the attacking Russian forces were given increased fire support by Frontal and Army Aviation units. The main targets were on open ground, with heavy but widespread concentrations of personnel, as well as more isolated individual targets, such as strongholds, ammunition dumps, rebel command posts and armoured vehicles. Groups of Su-24M and Su-25 aircraft, plus Mi-8MT and Mi-24 helicopters were widely engaged in these combat operations.

After Dudayev's rebels had retreated into the mountains, the town of Vedeno became the centre of his command and control structure and was turned into a major fortification. The Russian Air Force was then assigned the task of neutralising the command and control infrastructure of Dudayev's forces. On 28 May, Su-25s bombed Chechen positions in the choke points of the Vedeno and Argun gorges.

In the period from March to July 1995, the Russian Air Force lost two Su-25s and one Su-24M, the two Su-25s falling victim to ground fire from ZSU-23-4 self-propelled AAA and DShK machine-guns set up in ambush. A total of 24 aircraft suffered damage in combat, but the greatest losses were suffered by the 'shturmovoi' regiment based at Budyonnovsk, located around 140 km (87 miles) north of the Russian–Chechen border, in the Russian Federation.

The main weapons used by the Russian Air Force in the first Chechen campaign of 1994–6 were 57 mm S-5, 80 mm S-8 and 240 mm S-24B unguided rockets, high-explosive FAB-250 and FAB-500 bombs, fragmentation and high-explosive fragmentation bombs, plus BETAB-500 concrete-piercing bombs. The use of precision-guided munitions was often limited by weather conditions, which affected the guidance accuracy of Kh-25ML (AS-10 *Karen*) laser-guided air-to-surface missiles, or KAB-500L and KAB-500Kr laser-guided and TV-guided bombs respectively. For certain missions (for example, the destruction of bridges), the Su-24M would use the KAB-1500L 1,500 kg (3,300 lb) heavy laser-guided bomb. Fuel-air explosive (FAE), or thermobaric weapons (bombs and unguided rockets with FAE warheads), were not used. During the entire period of the first Chechen campaign, only 3% of the total quantity of weapons expended were precision-guided munitions.

Almost all of the Chechen rebels' AAA systems were mobile, including 23 mm ZSU-23-4 *Shilka* (a Siberian river) self-propelled anti-aircraft artillery guns, the simpler 23 mm ZU-23 AAA system mounted on the chassis of KamAZ trucks and 12.7 mm DShK machine-guns on Jeep Cherokee four-wheel-drive vehicles. The latter weapon was also mounted on Toyota and UAZ-469 jeeps, and grenade launchers and rifles were carried in cars and light commercial vehicles. At the start of the Chechen rebels' anti-Russian offensive, they had around forty mobile ZU-23 guns, more than eighty DShK installations on a variety of vehicles and twenty ZSU-23-4 systems, some of which had fully functioning *Gun Dish* fire-control radars. Apart from this, the rebels also had access to Strela-3 (SA-14 *Gremlin*), Igla-1 (SA-16 *Gimlet*) and the General Dynamics/Raytheon FIM-92A Stinger shoulder-launched SAMs.

Low-flying aircraft, and particularly helicopters, were engaged to a considerably greater extent by a much simpler type of weapon, the ubiquitous Russian-designed RPG-5 and RPG-7 rocket-propelled grenade. In general, the rebels' weak air defences (at least in terms of their technical characteristics and equipment) was compensated by precise organisation and well-thought-out tactics. All of the mobile air defence assets were very precisely controlled and co-ordinated with the aid of a well-organised radio communications plan, which, unaccountably, the Russian federal forces did not bother to jam and only occasionally bothered to monitor. They employed very cunning camouflage techniques and constantly changed their firing positions, which made it difficult for the Russian troops to locate and destroy them. One of the special tactics employed by the rebels was the use of ambush. Chechen gun crews and missile men would lie in wait until an aircraft or helicopter entered their firing zone and then open fire with a massive hail of bullets, shells and missiles from a number of different directions, concentrated on the target. Another tactic was to set up the air defence systems along the anticipated overflight route of Su-25s heading outbound to their targets, placing the weapons near the presumed target area and at the opportune moment opening fire on the luckless aircraft.

The Second Chechen War

Russian Air Force Su-25s were used equally intensively in the so-called Second Chechen War, which commenced in 1999, and some of their operations are highlighted here:

21 October 1999 – Russian Air Force aircraft carried out eight sorties on this day and a group of Su-25s destroyed two rebel BMP (***Boyevaya Mashina Pekhoty***) tracked armoured fighting vehicles in the region of Dabrankhi.

22 October – Frontal Aviation crews, including groups of Su-25s, carried out strikes on rebel troop concentrations in the regions of Achkhoi-Martan, Bamut, Raduzhnoye and Dolinskii.

24 October – Frontal Aviation aircraft carried out eighteen combat sorties. Russian Army artillery and the Russian Air Force struck at rebel positions located in the vicinity of several Chechen towns. These included Dabrankhi, Ilinskoye, Gudermes, Petropavlovskoye, Azamat-Yurt, Sovetskoye, Kurgan-Bolotnoye, Nagornoye, Bartkhoi, Dolinskii, Vinogradnoye, Goryacheistochnikskoye, Argun and Tsa-Vedeno. Warehouses in the vicinity of Vedeno, Ehlistanzhi and Komsomolskoye were also hit.

25 October – Frontal Aviation crews carried out a total of thirty sorties. Army artillery and Air Force aircraft hit rebel targets near several towns and villages including Kadi-Yurt, Ehngel-Yurt, Gudermes, Tsa-Vedeno, Dyshnye-Vedeno and the mountain areas of Charmoilam and Yastrebinaya, destroying the rebel base at Kharachoi. Su-25s destroyed an AAA position and two rebel vehicles on the southern edge of the Chechen capital, Grozny.

28 October – The Russian Air Force sortie rate rose to 100 combat missions. The houses of Chechen rebel leaders Shamil Basayev and Zelimkhan Yandarbiyev, plus those of several Chechen rebel field commanders, were destroyed during bombing raids.

29 October – An Su-25 carried out an attack on a vehicle convoy transporting rebel fighters and weapons. Two trucks were destroyed. Representatives of the International Committee of the Red Cross (ICRC) declared later that the attack had been carried out on their vehicles, which were clearly marked with the universally recognised Red Cross symbol. Two members of the ICRC working in Chechnya were killed in this bombing raid.

3 November – Su-25s and Su-24s carried out twenty combat missions. The main objectives of the strikes

Warfare is rarely conducted under ideal working conditions, as exemplified by these armourers preparing a FAB-500ShN 500 kg (1,100 lb) bomb for loading onto one of the Su-25s in the background, on the snow-covered airfield at Mozdok during the recent Chechen campaigns. The bomb's 'ShN' designation (***Shturmovaya Nizkovysotnaya***) denotes that it is intended for low-level-attack applications. *(via Yefim Gordon)*

were in areas near Samashek, Petropavlovskoye, Bamut, Chechen-Aul, Achkhoi-Martan and in the southern suburbs of Grozny. According to preliminary data at the time, up to 100 Chechen rebels were alleged to have been killed, about ten rebel strongholds destroyed, along with fifteen heavy lorries and four bridges.

10 November – The Russian Air Force struck at rebel troop concentrations and vehicle parks in the suburbs of Grozny, Gudermes and Samashek.

16 November – The Russian Air Force continued to provide close air support for the Russian Army. In the 24-hour period, Frontal Aviation Su-24s and Su-25s carried out fifty combat missions directed against Chechen rebel positions. These air attacks resulted in the destruction of ammunition depots and food supply warehouses, with eight camps used by the separatists destroyed in combined rocket and bombing raids.

22 November – A total of around fifty sorties were carried out. Strikes were mainly concentrated on Shatoi, Urus-Martan, Shali and the southern suburbs of Grozny.

24 November – The Russian Air Force carried out eighty-six sorties. A total of six rebel strongholds were

destroyed, along with a communications centre, a headquarters building, an AAA position and ten heavy trucks. Two bridges were also damaged. A factory which was used for the repair and maintenance of armoured vehicles was hit and put out of action in Grozny.

23 March 2000 – Su-25 'shturmoviks' and Su-24M tactical bombers carried out a total of fifteen sorties. Air Force aircraft and Army artillery hit rebel groups near the towns of Agishta, Koshkelda, Masi-Khutor, Dzhugurta and Leshkoraya.

24 March – The Russian Air Force carried out more than fifty sorties. Its aircraft struck at rebel targets near Orekhovo and Selmentauzen.

2 April – Frontal Aviation Su-24M tactical bombers flew two sorties, while the Su-25 carried out nine sorties.

3 April – Frontal Aviation Su-24Ms completed four sorties, while the Su-25 achieved fourteen. The Air Force and Army artillery units hit rebel troop concentrations in the vicinity of Benoi-Vedeno, Serzhen-Yurt and Roshin-Chu.

4 April – Su-24M tactical bombers carried out four combat missions; Su-25s achieved a total of twenty-two sorties. The missions were flown against troop concentrations near the towns of Tsentoroi and Zhani-Vedeno.

6 April – Su-25s carried out twenty-seven combat missions. The Russian Air Force, aided by Army artillery, struck at rebel troop concentrations near Shatoi, Belagatoi and Dyshnye-Vedeno.

7 April – Su-25 and Su-24M bombers carried out a total of thirty combat missions.

Between 9 April and 24 April 2000 – Su-25s completed a total of 170 combat sorties.

Thus, in only the first two months of the 'Second Chechen War', the Russian Air Force and Army Aviation carried out approximately 2,000 combat missions of various types over Chechnya. Of this total, *c*.1,000 sorties were flown by the Su-25. This aircraft also flew aerial reconnaissance missions, weather reconnaissance and also carried out other tasks. Such a comparatively large number of sorties resulted from the need to provide continuous air support for the Russian Army units on the ground, in an effort to minimalise their potential losses. Su-25s attacking targets in Chechnya carried out all missions releasing a virtually continuous stream of infra-red flares in order to thwart attacks by heat-seeking SAMs. Aircraft flying at ultra-low level during the attack phase also released flares as they commenced their climb-out from the area, when they were most vulnerable.

Initially, the Su-25 was used in Chechnya only for attacks on visually located targets; as a result sorties by the 'shturmoviks' depended heavily on weather conditions and on the cloud base in particular. In the second Chechen campaign, the upgraded Su-25T variant was also flown on a trial basis, with a variety of precision-guided weapons, alongside the standard Su-25. The new and more up-to-date Su-25T, or '*Super Grach*', was assigned to a small independent combat group. Retaining all the best characteristics of the original Su-25, the new attack variant possessed true all-weather capabilities and could also carry out combat operations at night. The Su-25T was equipped with the *Shkval* automatic nav-attack system, which was designed for operation with the supersonic AT-12 *Swinger* semi-active laser-guided anti-armour missile. The Su-25T was used to destroy a rebel An-2 *Colt* biplane, suspected of clandestine anti-Russian operations from Grozny Airport, scoring a direct hit on its parking location on the airfield with a Kh-25ML (AS-10 *Karen*) laser-guided ASM. The new variant was also used to knock out a communications centre, a radio relay station and other relatively high-value targets.

The President of Russia, Vladimir Putin, during a visit to one of the participating 'shturmovoi' regiments in Chechnya, while he was still only Prime Minister, stated that heavy losses of ground forces personnel had been avoided thanks to the accuracy of Russian Air Force combat missions. In gratitude, the pilots suggested that perhaps Prime Minister Putin would like to take a 'ride' in a combat aircraft while he was there! He accepted their invitation and made a twenty-minute flight over Chechnya in an Su-25UB, to some extent raising his own profile 'at home' by this gesture, but also boosting the morale of his pilots in this agonisingly protracted campaign. By placing himself at risk in a flight over hostile territory, albeit briefly, he was able to share with his pilots some of their daily fears and concerns and showed himself to be prepared to lead from the front in this highly contentious conflict.

Summing up the combat use of the Su-25 in the various wars and conflicts in which it has taken part, it deserves unanimous and positive recognition as a true latter-day 'shturmovik', fully justifying the accolade 'inherited' from its World War Two predecessor. The functionality of the Su-25 as a weapons system has been fully realised in operational service and its combat effectiveness has far exceeded the expectations of its designers. In truth, there are not many aircraft manufacturers around the world who can boast a similar achievement for their aircraft.

In bringing the description of the operational history of the of the Su-25 to a close, it is perhaps fitting to end by mentioning a much less bellicose role performed by this archetypal combat aircraft, albeit one which nevertheless maintained a link with Russia's earlier military traditions. This was its regrettably brief use as the mount for the Celestial Hussars (**Nebesniye Gusary**) aerobatic team, one of three such teams formed in 1991 under the auspices of the 237th Proskurov Guards Aircraft Demonstration Regiment, based at Kubinka. (The other two teams were, of course, the Russian Knights, on the Su-27 and the Swifts on the MiG-29). The Celestial Hussars (also frequently translated as Sky Hussars) were formed on four Su-25s from the Regiment's 3rd Squadron, with one spare aircraft, and the pilots themselves devised the aircraft's colour scheme, based on Russia's red, white and blue national colours. This was revised and improved by the then Commander of the Russian Air Force's Moscow Military District, Lt.-Gen. Nikolai T. Antoshkin, an enthusiastic advocate of the value of aerobatic teams in promoting the professionalism of

TOP: The four Su-25s and the spare aircraft of the now defunct Celestial Hussars aerobatic team in formation over Zhukovskiy. Although the team disbanded on the Su-25, they have re-formed on the L-39 Albatros. *(Yefim Gordon)*

ABOVE: One of the Celestial Hussars' Su-25s undergoing maintenance on a sun-soaked parking area at its Kubinka base. Noteworthy is the concertina-design transportable hangar in the background. *(Yefim Gordon)*

Detail of the former Soviet Air Force ensign which decorated the fin of the Celestial Hussars' Su-25s. A similar design is used today for the Russian Air Force ensign, with a modified central motif, incorporating the State Arms of the Russian Federation. *(Yefim Gordon)*

The Su-25 in Service and in Combat

both his pilots and the Russian Air Force in general. The underside of each Su-25 was painted to represent the silver-braided scarlet tunic of a nineteenth-century Russian hussar, hence the team's name. The first leader of the Celestial Hussars was Lt.-Col. A.A. Gornov. The team took part in several Russian military and civilian

air shows in the early years of its formation, but fell victim to the ever-present cash shortages affecting Russia's military air activities, and it was disbanded in 1995. However, the team was re-formed in 2001 on the Aero L-39 Albatros, also wearing the same colour scheme as the Su-25s.

Two time-expired Su-25s await their fate on a wet dispersal at the Ostrov aircraft disposal site. It is likely that the majority of such aircraft will be broken up, but they do form part of the large reserve of Su-25s which could eventually be upgraded to Su-25SM standard, if funding is available. *(Yefim Gordon)*

A large number of Su-25s withdrawn from service have been dumped on various airfields around Russia, in this case at Severomorsk in the north. Note the scrapped Yak-38 *Forger* V/STOL fighter in the background. *(Yefim Gordon)*

8

A Comparison Between the Su-25 and the Fairchild Republic A-10A

THE only Western aircraft which is truly analogous to the Su-25 is the Fairchild Republic A-10A Thunderbolt II (affectionately referred to as the Warthog, or simply 'Hog'), which was conceived and designed to a nearly identical set of performance criteria within an almost coincident timescale. There are, of course, other aircraft which perform the close-air-support and light strike role, such as the Douglas A-4 Skyhawk, the Vought A-7 Corsair II and the Brazilian/Italian AMX, the first two appreciably predating the Su-25, and the latter being designed shortly after the Su-25 entered service. (The Vought A-7, in its A-7D guise, was selected to fulfil the interim role of close air support for the US Army until the introduction of the Fairchild A-10, and flew almost 13,000 sorties in the South-East Asia theatre during the Vietnam War, with only four aircraft lost.) In spite of being intended as comparatively simple attack aircraft, they all differ from the Sukhoi and Fairchild Republic designs in being single-engined aircraft and did not have any of the combat survivability features that were designed into the Su-25 and the A-10. Other aircraft, like the Sepecat Jaguar and the BAE/Boeing Harrier, although operated in the close-air-support and attack roles, were not designed to quite the same austere standards as the Su-25 and A-10, and are not, therefore, truly comparable.

The A-10 was designed around the General Electric GAU-8/A Avenger seven-barrelled 30 mm rotary cannon, a fearsome weapon weighing 1,856 kg (4,100 lb), with an overall length of 6.71 m (22 ft), which effectively defined the large size of the aircraft and its high maximum take-off weight of 23,130 kg (51,000 lb). The GAU-8 is the most powerful gun ever to have been installed on a tactical combat aircraft, and is fed from a magazine of 1,175–1,350 rounds of ammunition, which can be expended in less than one minute at the high rate-of-fire setting of 4,200 rounds per minute.

Unlike the Su-25, the prototype of the Fairchild Republic A-10 did not differ substantially from the production version. The main external difference involved reshaping the leading-edge of the fins and the reprofiling of the nose to accommodate the GAU-8 Avenger rotary cannon, not fitted on the prototype. *(Fairchild Republic)*

One of the ammunition options is a depleted uranium round, capable of penetrating the hull of the most modern tanks, including the Russian T-80. Employment of this radioactive ammunition has been contentious, with much criticism from environmentalists following its use in the Gulf War and in Kosovo. By comparison, the Su-25 was designed as a much smaller and lighter aircraft, with a twin-barrelled GSh-2-30 30 mm cannon, giving a maximum take-off weight of 17,500 kg (38,600 lb). Both aircraft have practically identical engine thrust, the two R-95Sh turbojets of the Su-25 each delivering 4,100 kgp (9,040 lb st), while the two General Electric TF-34-GE-100 turbofans of the A-10 are rated at 4,112 kgp (9,065 lb st). However, the different all-up weights of the two aircraft result in quite different thrust-to-weight ratios, that of the A-10 being 0.37:1 against 0.47:1 for the Su-25.

As a result of its higher thrust-to-weight ratio, the Su-25 has a more sprightly rate of climb and faster acceleration time, essential characteristics for a battlefield close-air-support aircraft.

It would appear from these criteria that the Su-25 should have a manoeuvring advantage over the A-10, although the Russian aircraft has a much higher wing loading than the A-10, being 520 kg/m² (107 lb/ft²) against 454 kg/m² (93 lb/ft²) for the A-10. This affects other aspects of flight performance, to the advantage of the American aircraft. Nevertheless, many experts, observing the Su-25 performing aerobatics or advanced combat manoeuvres, have noted its unusually high agility, considerably greater, in fact, than the A-10, with,

for example, the latter exhibiting loss of speed during greater than 45° banked turns, whereas the Su-25 achieves this with no loss of speed at all.

The A-10 demonstrates clear superiority over the Su-25 in terms of radius of action, with the American aircraft having a radius of between 460 and 1,000 km (250–540 nm), dependent upon the type of mission, while the Su-25 has a narrower spectrum of range performance, from 250–300 km (135–160 nm). The A-10 is equipped with an in-flight refuelling system as standard and has more economical bypass turbofan engines, giving a cruising specific fuel consumption (sfc) of 0.37 kg/kg hr (0.82 lb/lb hr), compared with 1.28 kg/kg hr (2.82 lb/lb hr) for the more thirsty R-95Sh turbojets of the Su-25. The A-10's ability to be refuelled in flight was exploited to the full in both the Gulf War and during the Kosovo crisis, with flights of up to five hours' duration being commonplace, with a couple of fuel uplifts. Such operations clearly demonstrate the 'force multiplying' nature of in-flight refuelling, achieving with one aircraft what could ordinarily only be achieved by two or possibly more.

Another important index of comparison is the combat payload of the two aircraft, with the A-10 being able to carry a total of 7,250 kg (15,985 lb), against the Su-25's lesser payload of 4,400 kg (9,700 lb). However, Russian military analysts consider that there is no real sense in increasing the warload of a ground-attack aircraft beyond a certain level, since it is scarcely ever fully utilised. When operating against an adversary with an advanced air defence protection system for its ground forces, a 'shturmovik' or strike aircraft can only carry

Seen parked in front of one of Kubinka's transportable concertina-style hangars, White (outline) 85 is one of a number of Su-25s operated by the base's 237th Aircraft Demonstration Centre, used to show off the aircraft's capabilities to potential foreign clients. *(Yefim Gordon)*

The extent of nosewheel offset on the A-10, required to accommodate the huge GAU-8 cannon, is substantially greater than on the Su-25, the nose leg being mounted on the starboard edge of the forward fuselage. Note that on the prototype the cannon had not yet been installed. *(Fairchild Republic)*

out a maximum of two attacks on the same target, after which the likelihood of being shot down by those air defences increases significantly. Also, the Russian concept of the 'free hunt' (*svobodnaya okhota*) loses some of its rationale if a heavy warload is carried, since during a long 'hunt' there is an increasingly high chance of being engaged by enemy air defences, which would be difficult to outmanoeuvre if heavily laden. The airframe of the A-10, it has to be said, is also more robust than that of the Su-25 in this respect, being stressed for 7.33 *g* against the 6.5 *g* of the Russian aircraft.

Neither aircraft, as originally designed, was equipped with sophisticated avionics, although the Su-25T and Su-25TM do now have an advanced nav-attack system, which permits the use of precision-guided munitions in addition to the standard weapons for the aircraft's designated role (*see* Chapter 6). The main electronic aid on the A-10 when it was initially deployed was the pylon-mounted AN/AAS 35 *Pave Penny* laser-marked target seeker on the forward fuselage, capable of receiving reflected energy from a target illuminated by a ground Forward Air Controller or another aircraft. This can be used to cue its Hughes AGM-65A/B Maverick TV-guided air-to-surface missiles to 'look' in the appropriate direction. A total of six Mavericks can be carried on triple

launch racks, the video image from their nose-mounted TV cameras being projected on a cockpit screen in the upper right quadrant of the instrument panel, the pilot then moving a cursor on the screen to lock the missile onto the target. Once lock-on is achieved, the missile can be fired and then homes onto the target automatically, retaining the image of the target 'in memory' until the point of impact. *Pave Penny* can also be used to cue the A-10's laser-guided AGM-65E variant of the Maverick.

An important feature of aircraft such as the A-10 and the Su-25 is combat survivability. Both have extensive armour protection of vital systems: the weight of armour protection on the A-10 comprises 8.5% of the aircraft's normal take-off mass, while that of the Su-25 makes up 7.5% of the aircraft's take-off weight. Both aircraft have an armoured cockpit fabricated out of titanium (so-called titanium 'bath tubs'), foam-protected fuel tanks and fuel lines and hydraulic systems protected by armour plating. The cockpit of the Su-25 is of all-welded construction, while that of the A-10 is assembled from titanium sheets, which are bolted together. The A-10A and the Su-25 both have freon-gas-based fire-suppression systems, and many other systems are duplicated. The A-10 has a twin-fin layout, which increases its survivability in the event of one of the surfaces being damaged or destroyed, but

A Comparison Between the Su-25 and the Fairchild Republic A-10A

The American decision to build a twin-seat version of the A-10 was based on quite different thinking from that of the Sukhoi engineers, and it was intended not as a trainer, but rather as a specialised night-/adverse-weather-attack variant. Indeed, the two-seat 'evaluator' was designated A-10A N/AW to reflect this, although a basic trainer version of the A-10 was considered later. This plan was eventually shelved in 1983 when USAF officials deemed the A-10 simple enough to fly anyway and did not require a dedicated trainer version. The A-10A N/AW was evaluated by the USAF at Edwards Air Force Base in California in 1979, but conflicting philosophies concerning the function of the evaluator led to abandonment of the programme later that year. The A-10A N/AW is currently displayed in the Edwards Air Force Base museum. *(Fairchild Republic)*

has also resulted in the aircraft being heavier. Structurally the A-10 can survive direct hits from armour-piercing and high-explosive shells up to 23 mm calibre, but the smaller and lighter Su-25 has also demonstrated its ability to withstand severe structural damage in combat and still return to base.

On both aircraft, the flight-control system incorporates hydraulic boosters and has a back-up system. The A-10 employs control cables, whereas the Su-25 is equipped with titanium control rods which are 40 mm (1.57 in) in diameter, capable of sustaining a hit from a heavy-calibre bullet without causing loss of control of the aircraft. The control rods in the rear of the fuselage are made out of heat-resistant steel. The cable system of the A-10 is less damage resistant and not capable of sustaining direct hits by bullets, but is less vulnerable in the first instance because of the small diameter of the cable and the fact that cable runs are protected by the aircraft's structure.

The American and Russian designers of these two dedicated battlefield support aircraft used a twin-engined layout intended to offer maximum combat survivability and permit a return to base on one engine in the event that the other was disabled in combat. The R-95Sh engines of the Su-25 are located on the sides of the fuselage in such a way that they protect the fuselage-mounted fuel tanks, while the fuselage itself protects each engine from damage by the other. The designers of the A-10, while employing a similar philosophy, adopted a different approach, by mounting each engine on lateral pylons high on the rear fuselage, each nacelle being partially screened and protected by the fuselage. The self-sealing fuel tanks are protected by internal and external foam, as on the Su-25, and the hydraulic flying controls have a manual back-up, enabling the pilot to continue to fly the aircraft if hydraulic power is lost. The engine's infra-red signature is reduced by angling the jet pipes to produce a slightly upwards vectored exhaust efflux.

A Comparison Between the Su-25 and the Fairchild Republic A-10A

This view of an A-10A (BELOW) shows the cruciform plan view which it shares with the Su-25 (INSET), as well as revealing the substantial design differences between the two aircraft. Although the differences are appreciable, the objective in both cases was to maximise combat survivability. (BELOW: *USAF;* INSET *Yefim Gordon)*

The engine location on the A-10 offers the possibility of easily mounting a newer, more modern power-plant, to upgrade the aircraft, if required, as well as simplifying access for maintenance and repair of combat damage. In practice, the General Electric TF-34 engine is now proving to be increasingly difficult to maintain, and plans were revealed in 2001 to install the more powerful General Electric CF34-8, developing around 6,350 kgp (14,000 lb st) of thrust at sea level. This would provide better acceleration, quicker climb rates and a reduction in the fully loaded take-off run, but no firm decision has yet been taken on this upgrade. The engine layout of the Su-25, on the other hand, only permits interchangeability between the R-95Sh and the slightly more powerful R-195, and a radical redesign would be required to install new, significantly more powerful engines.

The R-95Sh (and R-195) engine of the Su-25 is more reliable and retains its full working capacity in all flight modes, right up to high altitude (when the operational profile requires it) and at any ambient temperature. By comparison, the TF-34-GE-100 bypass turbofans of the A-10 exhibit a reduction in performance as a function of altitude, characteristic of turbofans, although it must be said that the aircraft was optimised for extremely low-level operation, over the battlefield, where the turbofan cycle is at its most efficient. Unlike the A-10, the Su-25 can utilise other types of fuel, including the same diesel fuel as used in the Army's tanks and armoured fighting vehicles, a considerable advantage in logistics terms, although one which has not been well documented thus far in Russia's use of the Su-25 in actual combat.

Successful as the A-10 has been in USAF service, it came into being in an atmosphere of scepticism echoing that experienced by the designers of the Su-25, both aircraft being perceived as 'unglamorous' by air force leaders more used to fast aircraft with pointed noses and swept wings. As with many military aircraft, both were designed in response to a requirement which has undergone radical and unforeseen changes during their service life. Designed as 'tank busters' for an anticipated, and mutually feared, armoured confrontation between the armies of Eastern and Western Europe, led by Russia and the United States, both aircraft have ended up instead being used in 'low-intensity conflicts' (American definition) and so-called 'local wars' (Russian definition). By US criteria, the Gulf War was a 'low-intensity conflict', lasting only seven months, with very little opposing air activity and only forty-two days of aerial bombardment, although the A-10's contribution to the destruction of the Iraqi Army was quite phenomenal. This was no mean

baptism of fire for an aircraft which had waited almost twenty years to go into combat! The United States Army estimates that between 25 and 50% of the Iraqi Army's 4,000 tanks were destroyed by the A-10, along with more than 50% of its 4,000 artillery pieces and more than 30% of Iraqi armoured personnel carriers. The Su-25's involvement in Afghanistan and Chechnya, theatres which Russia describes as 'local wars', was, perhaps, less spectacular, and without the decisive military result of the A-10 in Iraq, but nevertheless a vital adjunct to the Russian Army's attempt to achieve victory in both campaigns. Without the Su-25's involvement in Afghanistan, Russian Army losses would have been significantly higher than the 9,511 killed in action in the nine-year war, out of a total of 14,453 Soviet personnel who died in that conflict. It has played, and continues to play, no less a part in the much more painful conflict in Chechnya, but has not been invincible in this theatre, against cunning and often unseen adversaries, and losses have been comparatively high in a war for which the aircraft was not designed.

After a long period of time in which the United States Air Force has consistently maintained a somewhat ambivalent position with regard to the A-10, the service has finally decided to inject money into upgrading the aircraft. This is in no small part due to the aircraft's outstanding performance in the Gulf War and further confirmed by operations over Kosovo in the airborne forward air-control role, and consolidated more recently by its use in Afghanistan during Operation *Enduring Freedom*. The decision came with the announcement in February 2001 that Lockheed Martin would institute a comprehensive modification programme for the aircraft. The objective is to add a precision attack capability to the entire fleet of A-10A and OA-10 aircraft, the OA-10 being a dedicated airborne forward air-control (AFAC) version developed in the late 1980s. Under the Lockheed Martin programme, the A-10 will receive a digital weapons-management system, 'smart' wiring to enable six of its eleven weapons stations to handle a new generation of bombs and a situational awareness data link (SADL) to keep the pilot in touch with everything happening around him on the battlefield. Although differing in scale and complexity, the A-10 upgrade has a similar objective to the Su-25T and Su-25TM upgrades in that it will enhance the aircraft's combat capability by adding a suite of advanced electronics and weapons which were not available when the aircraft first entered service.

The programme is referred to by the USAF as Precision Engagement (PE), and incorporates the greatest number of improvements to the A-10 since the introduction of the Low-Altitude Safety and Targeting Enhancement (LASTE) programme of 1990. This introduced a ground-collision avoidance system (GCAS), an enhanced attitude-control (EAC) function for aircraft stabilisation during gunfire and a low-altitude autopilot system. Commencing in 1999, the A/O-10 fleet was further upgraded with the installation of an Embedded Global Positioning System/Inertial Navigation System (EGI) as a precision aid to navigation, and this programme is ongoing. An important element of the PE improvements will be a TERPROM (Terrain Profile Matching) Digital Terrain System (DTS), designed to provide state-of-the-art ground-proximity and obstacle warnings, to avoid the possibility of controlled flight into terrain (CFIT), TERPROM being a computer-generated representation of the terrain ahead of the aircraft. The DTS will also provide vertical steering cues for low-level flight in hilly terrain and passive target-ranging information, by matching known target locations against the TERPROM image of the area. The PE upgrade will also include an infra-red threat detector working on the same principle as current missile-approach warning systems.

The upgraded A-10's offensive capability will be augmented by the inclusion of JDAM (Joint Direct Attack Munition) and WCMD (Wind Corrected Munition Dispenser) in the aircraft's weapons inventory. Both of the latter add a precision guidance tail kit module to otherwise 'dumb' iron bombs and munitions dispensers, considerably enhancing the already formidable firepower of the aircraft. With all of the elements of the Precision Engagement programme integrated as planned, the United States Air Force intends to keep its 360-plus A-10As and OA-10s flying until 2028.

In conclusion, it can be said that both aircraft, although differing in many aspects of design and operation, have followed almost parallel paths in terms of how they have adapted to the developing tactical doctrines of their respective air forces. Indeed, the parallel nature of their operations has continued right up to the present day, with the A-10 carrying out close-air-support operations from Bagram airfield near Kabul, less than two decades after Soviet Air Force Su-25s were performing similar missions out of the same base against a no less intractable adversary. The planned upgrades for the Su-25 and the A-10 should guarantee that these two very untraditional representatives of twentieth-century jet-powered aviation will be able to continue to play an important part in the unconventional conflicts which are likely to characterise warfare in the twenty-first century.

A fine study of an Su-25 taking off from a sun-bathed airfield armed with a pair of B-8M1 rocket pods and underwing drop tanks, suggesting that it is departing on a mission to a fairly distant air–ground firing range. *(Vyacheslav Martynyuk)*

A Comparison Between the Su-25 and the Fairchild Republic A-10A

Fairchild Republic A-10A/Sukhoi Su-25 Comparative Specifications

	A-10A	Su-25
Span	17.53 m (57 ft 6 in)	14.36 m (47 ft 1½ in)
Length	16.26 m (53 ft 4 in)	15.53 m (50 ft 11½ in)
Height	4.47 m (14 ft 8 in)	4.80 m (15 ft 9 in)
Wing area	47.01 m² (506 ft²)	33.7 m² (362.7 ft²)
Empty weight	9,730 kg (21,451 lb)	9,185 kg (20,235 lb)
Typical TO weight	N/A	N/A
Typical combat weight	13,850 kg (30,534 lb)	N/A
Max TO weight	23,133 kg (51,000 lb)	17,530 kg (38,647 lb)
Engines	Two General Electric TF-34-GE-100 turbofans	Two Tumanski R-95Sh/R-195 turbojets
Max TO thrust	4,112 kgp (9,065 lb st)	4,100 kgp (9,040 lb st)
Max internal fuel	6,231 litres (1,370 imp gal)	3,660 litres (805 imp gal)
Max external fuel	3 × 2,270 litres (500 imp gal)	4 × 1,150 litres (253 imp gal)
Max wing loading	454 kg/m² (93 lb st)	520 kg/m² (107 lb/ft²)
Max power loading	265 kg/kN (2.6 lb/lb st)	218 kg/kN (2.1 lb/lb st)
Max speed at sea level	720 kph (390 kt)	975 kph (526 kt)
Combat speed at sea level	610 kph (330 kt)	690 kph (373 kt)
Service ceiling	10,600 m (34,775 ft)	7,000 m (22,965 ft)
HI-LO-HI combat radius/ ordnance load	465 km/4,325 kg (250 nm/9,535 lb)	400 km/4,360 kg (215 nm/9,610 lb)
In-flight refuelling	Boom receptacle in front of cockpit	No provision
Laser ranger and marked target seeker	AAS-35 Pave Penny laser seeker in external front fuselage pod	Klyon-PS laser-ranger and seeker in nose
Radar warning receiver	AN/ALR-69(V)-5	SPO-15 *Beryoza*
IFF	AIMS	SRO-2M or *Parol'*
External ECM pod	AN/ALQ-119(V), AN/ALQ-131, or AN/ALQ-184(V)	SPS-141MVG *Gvozdika*
Chaff/IR flares cartridges	480	256
Internal gun	Seven-barrel 30 mm GAU-8A	Twin-barrel 30 mm GSh-30-2
Rounds for internal gun	1,350	250
External gun pods	Two 20 mm GAU-4	Two 23mm SPPU-22
Rounds for external gun	N/A	260rpg
No. of external store stations	11	10
Max external load	7,258 kg (16,596 lb)	4,340kg (9,570lb)
Laser-guided missile	AGM-65G Maverick	Kh-25ML (AS-10 *Karen*) Kh-29L (AS-14 *Kedge*)
Television-guided missile	AGM-65A/B Maverick	Kh-29T (AS-14 *Kedge*)
Imaging infra-red missile	AGM-65D Maverick	N/A
HUD or gunsight	HUD	Gunsight on Su-25, HUD on Su-25T/TM
Self-defence missile	AIM-9L/M Sidewinder	R-60 (AA-8 *Aphid*) R-73 (AA-11 *Archer*), R-27 (AA-10 *Alamo*) and R-77 (AA-12 *Adder*) on upgraded variants

Appendix I

Consolidated production list of known Su-25/Su-25K and Su-25UBK aircraft. This is clearly only a fraction of the total number of Su-25s known to have been produced at Tbilisi and Ulan-Ude.

Construction Number	Serial No.	Bort Number	Variant	Notes
		81 Yellow	T8-1 T8-1D	Sukhoi Design Bureau
		82 Blue 10 Red	T8-2D T8-2	Sukhoi Design Bureau
		83 Red	T8-3	Sukhoi Design Bureau
		84 Red	T8-4	Sukhoi Design Bureau
	0105	105 Blue–Soviet AF	Su-25	
255.081.01.006		? Soviet Air Force	Su-25	
		89 Blue	T8-9	Sukhoi Design Bureau
255.081.01.014		10 Blue	Su-25 (T8-10)	
255.081.01.02*			Su-25	
255.081.01.035		71 Blue-Soviet Air Force	Su-25	
255.081.01.038		? Soviet Air Force	Su-25	
255.081.01.044		? Soviet Air Force	Su-25	
255.081.01.045		? Soviet Air Force	Su-25	
255.081.01.056		66 Blue '66 Red'	Su-25 (T8-11)	Monino Air Force Museum
255.081.01.077		20 Red–Russian Air Force	Su-25	357 OShAP Brandis
255.081.01.079		36 Red–Russian Air Force	Su-25	357 OShAP Brandis
255.081.02.054		44 Red	Su-25	
255.081.03.012		12 Red	Su-25	Park of Victory Moscow
255.081.04.012		16 Red	Su-25	
255.081.05.003		5003 Czech Air Force	Su-25K	
255.081.05.006		5006 Czech Air Force	Su-25K	
255.081.05.007		5007 Czech Air Force	Su-25K	
255.081.05.008		5008 Czech Air Force	Su-25K	
255.081.05.020		? Soviet Air Force	Su-25	
255.081.05.033		5033 Czech Air Force	Su-25K	
255.081.05.034		12 Red	Su-25	
255.081.05.036		5036 Czech Air Force	Su-25K	
255.081.05.039		5039 Czech Air Force	Su-25K	
255.081.05.040		5040 Czech Air Force	Su-25K	
255.081.06.003		? Soviet Air Force	Su-25	
255.081.06.004		? Soviet Air Force	Su-25	
255.081.06.017		6017 Czech/Slovak AF	Su-25K	
255.081.06.018		6018 Czech Air Force	Su-25K	

Construction Number	Serial No.	Bort Number	Variant	Notes
255.081.06.019		6019 Czech Air Force	Su-25K	
255.081.06.020		6020 Czech Air Force	Su-25K	
255.081.06.861		22 Red–Russian Air Force	Su-25	357 OShAP Brandis
255.081.07.001		32 Red–Russian Air Force	Su-25	357 OShAP Brandis
255.081.07.002		33 Red–Russian Air Force	Su-25	357 OShAP Brandis
255.081.07.012		? Soviet Air Force	Su-25	
255.081.07.023		34 Red–Russian Air Force	Su-25	357 OShAP Brandis
255.081.07.024		35 Red–Russian Air Force	Su-25	357 OShAP Brandis
255.081.07.030?		29 Blue–Russian Air Force	Su-25	
255.081.07.032		37 Red–Russian Air Force	Su-25	357 OShAP Brandis
255.081.07.033		38 Red–Russian Air Force	Su-25	357 OShAP Brandis
255.081.07.037		39 Red–Russian Air Force	Su-25	357 OShAP Brandis
255.081.07.039		? Soviet Air Force	Su-25	
255.081.07.048		? Soviet Air Force	Su-25	
255.081.07.054		? Soviet Air Force	Su-25	
255.081.08.006		? Soviet Air Force	Su-25	
255.081.08.033		23 (Red?) Soviet AF	Su-25	
255.081.08.072		8072 Czech Air Force	Su-25K	W/o Sliač 27.5.1993
255.081.08.073		8073 Czech/Slovak AF	Su-25K	
255.081.08.074		8074 Czech/Slovak AF	Su-25K	
255.081.08.075		8075 Czech/Slovak AF	Su-25K	
255.081.08.076		8076 Czech Air Force	Su-25K	
255.081.08.077		8077 Czech Air Force	Su-25K	
255.081.08.078		8078 Czech Air Force	Su-25K	
255.081.08.079		8079 Czech Air Force	Su-25K	
255.081.08.080		8080 Czech Air Force	Su-25K	
255.081.08.081		8081 Czech Air Force	Su-25K	
255.081.09.013		9013 Czech Air Force	Su-25K	
255.081.09.014		9014 Czech Air Force	Su-25K	
255.081.09.033		33 Red–Russian Air Force	Su-25 Su-25SM	Prototype
255.081.09.093		9093 Czech Air Force	Su-25	
255.081.09.094		9094 Czech Air Force	Su-25K	
255.081.09.098		9098 Czech Air Force	Su-25K	
255.081.09.099		9099 Czech Air Force	Su-25K	
255.081.10.002		1002 Czech Air Force	Su-25K	
255.081.10.003		1003 Czech Air Force	Su-25K	
255.081.10.004		1004 Czech Air Force	Su-25K	
255.081.10.005		1005 Czech Air Force	Su-25K	
255.081.10.006		1006 Czech/Slovak AF	Su-25K	
255.081.10.007		1007 Czech/Slovak AF	Su-25K	
255.081.10.008		1008 Czech/Slovak AF	Su-25K	
255.081.10.015		1015 Czech Air Force	Su-25K	
255.081.10.027		1027 Czech/Slovak AF	Su-25K	
255.081.10.030		230 White–Bulgarian AF	Su-25K	

Construction Number	Serial No.	Bort Number	Variant	Notes
255.081.10.040		240 White–Bulgarian AF	Su-25K	
255.081.10.041?		241 White–Bulgarian AF	Su-25K	
255.081.10.046?		246 White–Bulgarian AF	Su-25K	
255.081.10.049?		249 White–Bulgarian AF	Su-25K	
255.081.10.050		73 Red	Su-25	
255.081.10.052		252 White–Bulgarian AF	Su-25K	
255.081.10.053		253 White–Bulgarian AF	Su-25K	
255.081.10.054		254 White–Bulgarian AF	Su-25K	
255.081.10.055		255 White–Bulgarian AF	Su-25K	
255.081.10.070		72 Red	Su-25	
255.081.10.076		26 Red–Russian Air Force	Su-25	357 OShAP Brandis
255.081.10.083		01 Red–Russian Air Force	Su-25	357 OShAP Brandis 368 OShAP Demmin-Tutow
255.081.10.085		02 Red–Russian Air Force	Su-25	357 OShAP Brandis
255.081.10.086		03 Red–Russian Air Force 73 Red–Russian Air Force	Su-25	357 OShAP Brandis 368 OShAP Demmin-Tutow
255.081.10.087		04 Red–Russian Air Force	Su-25	357 OShAP Brandis
255.081.10.088		05 Red–Russian Air Force	Su-25	357 OShAP Brandis
255.081.10.132		06 Red–Russian Air Force	Su-25	357 OShAP Brandis
255.081.10.134		08 Red–Russian Air Force	Su-25	357 OShAP Brandis
255.081.10.137		10 Red–Russian Air Force	Su-25	357 OShAP Brandis 368 OShAP Demmin-Tutow
255.081.10.138		11 Red–Russian Air Force	Su-25	357 OShAP Brandis
255.081.10.139		12 Red–Russian Air Force	Su-25	357 OShAP Brandis 368 OShAP Demmin-Tutow
255.081.10.140		14 Red–Russian Air Force	Su-25	357 OShAP Brandis
255.081.10.142		15 Red–Russian Air Force	Su-25	357 OShAP Brandis
255.081.10.143		21 Red–Russian Air Force	Su-25	357 OShAP Brandis 368 OShAP Demmin-Tutow
255.081.10.144		22 Red–Russian Air Force	Su-25	368 OShAP Demmin-Tutow
255.081.10.145		23 Red–Russian Air Force	Su-25	368 OShAP Demmin-Tutow
255.081.10.146		24 Red–Russian Air Force	Su-25	
255.081.10.147		24 Red–Russian Air Force	Su-25	368 OShAP Demmin-Tutow 357 OShAP Brandis 368 OShAP Demmin-Tutow
255.081.10.170		25 Red–Russian Air Force	Su-25	368 OShAP Demmin-Tutow
255.081.10.172		26 Red–Russian Air Force	Su-25	368 OShAP Demmin-Tutow
255.081.10.173		27 Red–Russian Air Force	Su-25	368 OShAP Demmin-Tutow
255.081.10.174		28 Red–Russian Air Force	Su-25	368 OShAP Demmin-Tutow 357 OShAP Brandis 368 OShAP Demmin-Tutow
255.081.10.175		29 Red–Russian Air Force	Su-25	368 OShAP Demmin-Tutow
255.081.10.176		30 Red–Russian Air Force	Su-25	368 OShAP Demmin-Tutow
255.081.10.179		31 Red–Russian Air Force	Su-25	368 OShAP Demmin-Tutow

Construction Number	Serial No.	Bort Number	Variant	Notes
255.081.10.180		34 Red–Russian Air Force	Su-25	
255.081.10.181		25 Red–Russian Air Force	Su-25	368 OShAP Demmin-Tutow 357 OShAP Brandis
255.081.10.182		33 Red–Russian Air Force	Su-25	368 OShAP Demmin-Tutow
255.081.10.192		15 Red, 301 Blue	Su-25 (T8-15)	First Su-25 with R-195 engines Khodynka Museum
255.081.10.231		?	Su-25	
255.081.10.262		17 Red–Ukrainian AF 17, Blue–Ukrainian AF	Su-25	
255.081.10.318		?? Ukrainian Air Force	Su-25	
255.081.10.355		04 Red, 17 Red	Su-25	
255.081.10.357		12 White	Su-25	
255.081.10.359		35 Red, 03 Red	Su-25	368 OShAP Demmin-Tutow 357 OShAP Brandis 368 OShAP Demmin-Tutow
255.081.10.360		36 Red	Su-25	368 OShAP Demmin-Tutow
255.081.10.361		37 Red	Su-25	368 OShAP Demmin-Tutow
255.081.10.362		38 Red–Russian Air Force	Su-25	368 OShAP Demmin-Tutow
255.081.10.363		?? Red–Russian Air Force	Su-25	
255.081.10.395		90 Red	Su-25	
255.081.10.408		45 Red	Su-25	
255.081.10.469		32 Red–Russian Air Force 47 Red–Russian Air Force	Su-25	
255.081.10.474?		25 Red–Russian Air Force	Su-25	
255.081.10.489		89 Red 12 Red	Su-25 Su-25BM	Prototype
255.081.10.503		11 Red–Russian Air Force	Su-25BM	368 OShAP Demmin-Tutow
255.081.10.505		02 Red–Russian Air Force	Su-25BM	368 OShAP Demmin-Tutow
255.081.10.506		14 Red–Russian Air Force	Su-25BM	368 OShAP Demmin-Tutow
255.081.10.507		04 Red–Russian Air Force	Su-25BM	368 OShAP Demmin-Tutow
255.081.10.509		15 Red–Russian Air Force	Su-25BM	368 OShAP Demmin-Tutow
255.081.10.510		18 Red–Russian Air Force	Su-25BM	368 OShAP Demmin-Tutow
255.081.10.512		16 Red–Russian Air Force	Su-25BM	368 OShAP Demmin-Tutow
255.081.10.513		17 Red–Russian Air Force	Su-25BM	368 OShAP Demmin-Tutow
255.081.10.518		06 Red–Russian Air Force	Su-25BM	368 OShAP Demmin-Tutow
255.081.10.519		07 Red–Russian Air Force	Su-25BM	368 OShAP Demmin-Tutow
255.081.10.520		08 Red–Russian Air Force	Su-25BM	368 OShAP Demmin-Tutow
255.081.10.521		09 Red–Russian Air Force	Su-25BM	368 OShAP Demmin-Tutow
255.081.10.529		18 White	Su-25BM	Con ?772.313.10.529?
255.081.10.568?			Su-25	
255.081.10.629		01 Black–Georgian Air Force	Su-25KM	Prototype/Demonstrator
255.081.11.005?		63 Yellow–Ukrainian AF	Su-25	
255.081.25.590?		25590 Iraqi Air Force	Su-25K	
255.081.25.591?		25591 Iraqi Air Force	Su-25K	
		01 Blue, 01 White contour	Su-25T	T8M-1
		03 Yellow, 25 Yellow	Su-25T	T8M-3

Construction Number	Serial No.	Bort Number	Variant	Notes
382.***.01.005		21 Blue–Russian Air Force	Su-25T	
382.***.01.014		10 Blue	Su-25TM	T8M-10
382.***.01.016		16 Red	Su-25T	T8M-16?
382.***.03.007		20 White	Su-25TM	
	01-01	201 Red–Soviet Air Force	Su-25UB	T8UB-1, Sukhoi Design Bureau
	01-02	202 Red–Soviet Air Force	Su-25UB	T8UB-2, Sukhoi Design Bureau
382.201.05.002	03-02?	07 Blue 302 Blue	Su-28	Sukhoi Design Bureau
382.201.10.050		71 Red–Russian Air Force	Su-25UB	357 OShAP Brandis 368 OShAP Demmin-Tutow
382.201.10.070		73 Red–Russian Air Force	Su-25UB	357 OShAP Brandis 368 OShAP Demmin-Tutow
382.201.11.463		14 Yellow (Demo)	Su-25UBK	
382.201.13.002		002 White–Bulgarian AF	Su-25UBK	
382.201.13.017?		017 White–Bulgarian AF	Su-25UBK	
382.201.13.147		147 White–Bulgarian AF	Su-25UBK	
382.201.26.147		50 Red–Russian Air Force	Su-25UB	368 OShAP Demmin-Tutow
382.201.26.411		? Soviet Air Force		
382.201.36.188		72 White	Su-25UB	
382.201.36.237?		3237 Czech/Slovak AF	Su-25UBK	
382.201.36.348?		3348 Czech Air Force	Su-25UBK	
382.201.41.172		08 Red	Su-25UTG	Sukhoi Design Bureau
382.201.41.254		11 Red–Russian Naval Air Force	Su-25UTG	
382.201.**.***	09-05	33 Yellow–Russian Air Force	Su-25UB	
382.201.**.***	11-09	36 Yellow–Russian Air Force	Su-25UB	

Armed Forces Museum in Moscow – Su-25 Bort No. 22 Red – Serial No. 0708

Appendix II

Three-view drawing of the Su-25.

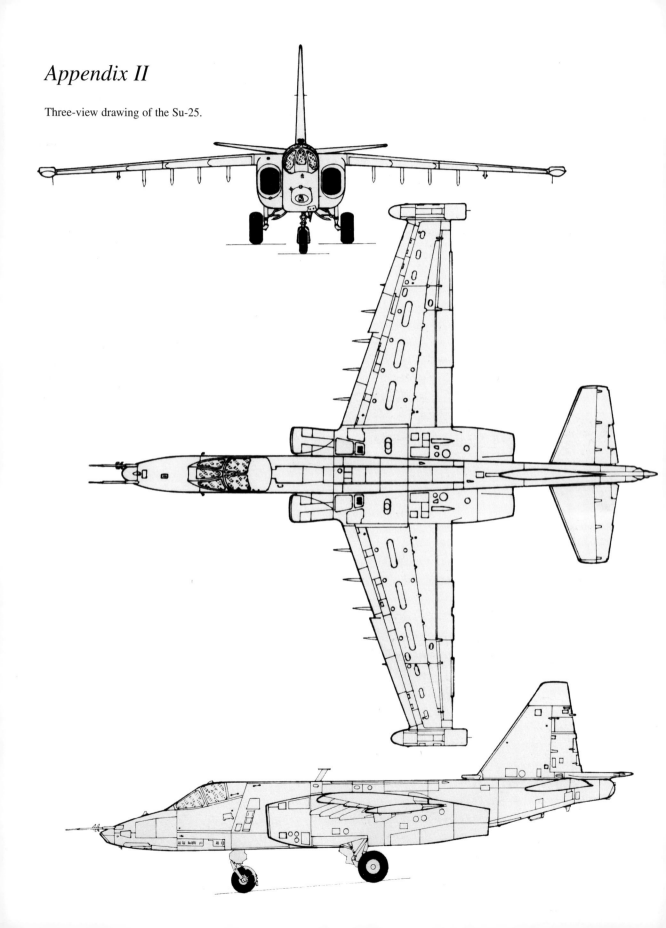

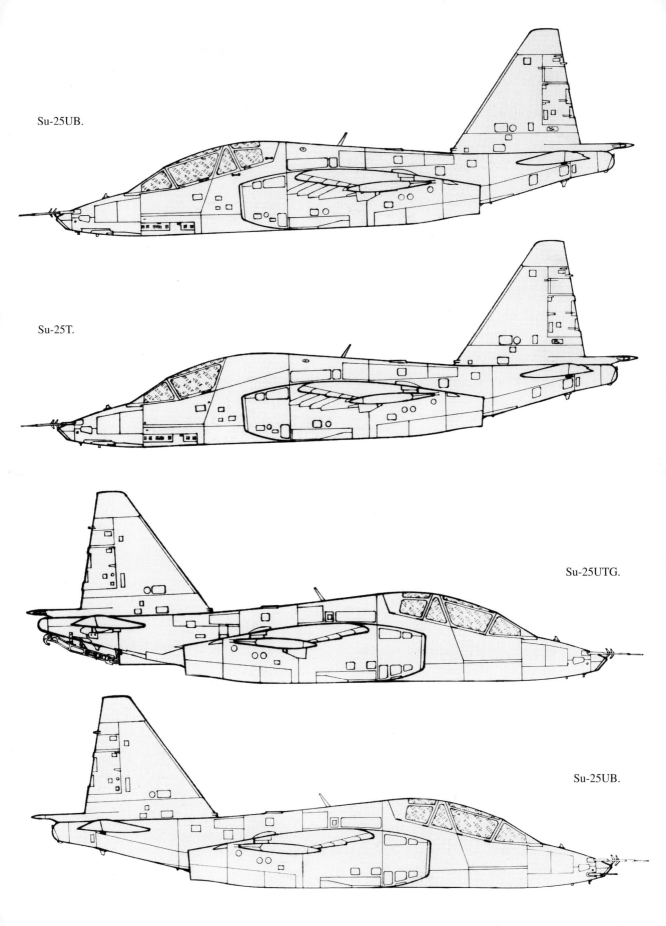

Su-25UB.

Su-25T.

Su-25UTG.

Su-25UB.

Index

Index